CAKES and CAKE DECORATING

CAKES and CAKE DECORATING

A COMPLETE GUIDE TO CAKE DECORATING TECHNIQUES, WITH OVER 100 PROJECTS, FROM TRADITIONAL CLASSICS TO THE LATEST IN CONTEMPORARY DESIGNS

angela nilsen and **sarah maxwell**

southwater

This edition is published by Southwater, an imprint of Anness Publishing Ltd,
108 Great Russell Street, London WC1B 3NA; info@anness.com

www.southwaterbooks.com; www.annesspublishing.com

If you like the images in this book and would like to investigate using them for publishing,
promotions or advertising, please visit our website www.practicalpictures.com for more information.

© Anness Publishing Ltd 2014

A CIP catalogue record for this book is available from the British Library.

Publisher: Joanna Lorenz
Project Editors: Judith Simons and Clare Nicholson
Photographer: Tim Hill
Home Economists: Sarah Maxwell and Angela Nilsen
Assistant Home Economist: Teresa Goldfinch
Stylist: Sarah Maxwell   **Assistant Stylist:** Timna Rose
Design: Axis Design

NOTES

For all recipes, quantities are given in both metric and imperial measures and, where appropriate, in standard
cups and spoons. Follow one set of measures, but not a mixture, because they are not interchangeable.
Standard spoon and cup measures are level. 1 tsp = 5ml, 1 tbsp = 15ml, 1 cup = 250ml/8fl oz.
Australian standard tablespoons are 20ml. Australian readers should use 3 tsp in place of 1 tbsp
for measuring small quantities.
American pints are 16fl oz/2 cups. American readers should use 20fl oz/2.5 cups in place of 1 pint
when measuring liquids.
Electric oven temperatures in this book are for conventional ovens. When using a fan oven, the temperature
will probably need to be reduced by about 10–20°C/20–40°F. Since ovens vary, you should check with your
manufacturer's instruction book for guidance.
Medium (US large) eggs are used unless otherwise stated.

PUBLISHER'S NOTE

ontents

$\mathcal{I}$ntroduction

This book is not only an invaluable foundation course in cake decorating techniques, but also a wonderful reference book for a host of tried-and-tested recipes for classic cake bases and icings, as well as inspirational cake projects, which you will use again and again.

Clearly structured, the decorating course leads you through all the different decorating techniques which can be applied to royal icing, sugarpaste, marzipan, chocolate and other icings. There are step-by-step instructions and photographs for piping, crimping, embossing, frills, plaques, colouring, run-outs, modelling, stencilling, flowers, using purchased decorations, such as sweet confections, ribbons and fresh flowers, and much more.

The wonderful decorated cakes featured in the project sections on Classic Cakes, Special Occasion Cakes, Novelty Cakes and Children's Party Cakes are a feast for the eye as well as the palate. Moreover, they provide wonderful working examples which you can follow step-by-step, giving you the opportunity to practise and develop the techniques described in the first section of the book with professional results.

Within each recipe, three sets of equivalent measurements have been provided in the following order: metric, imperial and cups. To avoid disappointing results, never mix the different types of measurement within a recipe. For best results, use eggs which are at room temperature. If you sift flour from a fair height, it will have more chance to aerate and lighten.

No two ovens are alike. If possible, buy a reliable oven thermometer and test the temperature of your oven. Always bake in the centre of the oven where the heat is more likely to be constant. If using a fan assisted oven, follow the manufacturer's guidelines for baking. Good quality cake tins will also improve results, as they conduct heat more efficiently.

Finally, there are some current health concerns about the use of raw egg in uncooked recipes. Home-made royal icing, marzipan and sugarpaste icing do include raw egg. An alternative recipe for royal icing, using pure albumen powder, has been provided in light of this. If you prefer to avoid raw egg, do buy ready-made marzipan and sugarpaste. Shop-bought versions are usually good quality products and, of course, very quick and easy to use.

Basic Cake Recipes

Cakes are the highlight of many celebrations. What birthday would be complete without a cake with candles to blow out, or a wedding without a beautiful cake to cut? Some of the most traditional cake recipes provide the best bases for decorating. Recipes can be found in this chapter, and are used as bases for the decorated cakes later in the book. None of the cakes involve complicated techniques, and several are as simple as putting the ingredients into a bowl, and mixing them together.

Fruit cake is one of our most popular special occasion cakes. Among its advantages is that it keeps really well and in fact improves with storage, so it can be baked well ahead of time and decorated in easy stages. It also provides a wonderfully firm base for all sorts of elegant or novelty decorations. There are other ideas, too, for those who prefer a less rich tasting cake, such as the Madeira or a light fruit cake, as well as a quick-mix sponge for those last-minute, spontaneous celebrations.

Baking Equipment

A selection of basic equipment is needed for cake making. Here are a few of the more necessary items:

Scales For good, consistent results, ingredients for cake making require precise measuring. An accurate set of scales is therefore essential.

Bowls Various sizes of glass or china heatproof bowls with rounded sides make mixing easier and are useful when baking.

Measuring Jug Whether you are working in imperial, metric or cup measurements, a glass measuring jug is easy to read and means liquids are calculated accurately.

Measuring Spoons These are available in a standard size, making the measuring of small amounts more accurate.

Sieves These are used to aerate flour, making cakes lighter, and to remove lumps from icing sugar.

Electric Whisks These whisks are particularly useful for beating egg whites for Swiss rolls.

Balloon Whisks Useful for beating smaller amounts of either egg or cream mixtures.

Greaseproof Paper Used to line cake tins to prevent cakes from sticking.

Wooden and Metal Spoons Wooden spoons in various sizes are essential

for beating mixtures together when not using an electric mixer, while metal spoons are necessary for folding in ingredients and for smoothing over mixtures to give a flat surface before baking.

Spatulas Because they are so pliable, plastic spatulas are particularly useful for scraping all the cake mixture from a bowl.

Cake Tins These are available in all shapes and sizes, and the thicker the metal the less likely the cake will be to overcook. Most cake icing specialists hire out cake tins, useful when very large or unusual shaped tins are required.

Oven Gloves Essential when removing anything hot from the oven. It is worth choosing a good quality, well lined pair of gloves.

Wire Racks Made from wire mesh, these are available in different sizes and shapes and allow cakes to 'breathe' as they cool.

Cake Boards Choose the shape and size to fit the cake. Thick boards are for large, heavy cakes, royal iced cakes and any other fruit cake coated in icing. The board should be 5 cm/2 inches larger than the size of the cake. Thinner boards are for small Madeira cakes and other lighter cakes covered with icings such as butter, glacé or fudge. These can be about 2.5 cm/1 inch larger than the cake size.

1   *glass mixing bowls*
2   *balloon whisk*
3   *large round cake tin*
4   *electric hand mixer*
5   *small round cake tin*
6   *scales*
7   *large square cake tin*
8   *measuring jug*
9   *measuring spoons*
10 *cake boards*
11 *pastry brush*
12 *pre-cut greaseproof paper*
    tin liners
13 *scissors*
14 *wooden mixing spoons*
15 *wire rack*
16 *sieve*
17 *oven gloves*
18 *plastic spatula*
19 *metal spoon*

Quick-mix Sponge Cake

Here's a no-fuss, foolproof all-in-one cake, where the ingredients are quickly mixed together. The following quantities and baking instructions are for a deep 20cm/8 inch round cake tin or a 20 cm/ 8 inch ring mould. For other quantities and tin sizes, follow the baking instructions given in the decorated cake recipes.

INGREDIENTS
115 g/4oz/1 cup self-raising flour
1 tsp baking powder
115 g/4 oz/½ cup soft margarine
115 g/4 oz/½ cup caster sugar
2 size 3 eggs

STORING AND FREEZING
The cake can be made up to two days in advance, wrapped in clear film or foil and stored in an airtight container. The cake can be frozen for up to three months.

FLAVOURINGS
The following amounts are for a 2-egg, single quantity cake, as above. Increase the amounts proportionally for larger cakes.
Chocolate *Fold 1 tbsp cocoa powder blended with 1 tbsp boiling water into the cake mixture.*
Citrus *Fold 2 tsp of finely grated lemon, orange or lime zest into the cake mixture.*

1 Preheat the oven to 160°C/325°F/ Gas 3. Grease the round cake tin, line the base with greaseproof paper and grease the paper, or grease and flour the ring mould.

2 ▲ Sift the flour and baking powder into a bowl. Add the margarine, sugar and eggs.

3 ▲ Beat with a wooden spoon for 2–3 minutes. The mixture should be pale in colour and slightly glossy.

4 Spoon the cake mixture into the prepared tin and then smooth the surface. Bake for 20–30 minutes. To test if cooked, press the cake lightly in the centre. If firm, the cake is done, if soft, cook for a little longer. Alternatively, insert a skewer into the centre of the cake. If it comes out clean the cake is ready. Turn out on to a wire rack, remove the lining paper and leave to cool completely.

This quick-mix sponge cake can be filled and simply decorated with icing for a special occasion.

$\mathscr{S}$wiss Roll

Swiss rolls are traditionally made without fat, so they don't keep as long as most other cakes. However, they have a deliciously light texture and provide the cook with the potential for all sorts of luscious fillings and tasty toppings.

INGREDIENTS
4 size 3 eggs, separated
115 g/4 oz/½ cup caster sugar
115 g/4 oz/1 cup plain flour
1 tsp baking powder

STORING AND FREEZING
Swiss rolls and other fat-free sponges do not keep well, so if possible bake on the day of eating. Otherwise, wrap in clear film or foil and store in an airtight container overnight or freeze for up to three months.

1 Preheat the oven to 180°C/350°F/ Gas 4. Grease a 33 × 23 cm/ 13 × 9 inch Swiss roll tin, line with greaseproof paper and grease the paper.

2 Whisk the egg whites in a clean, dry bowl until stiff. Beat in 2 tbsp of the sugar.

3 ▲ Place the egg yolks, remaining sugar and 1 tbsp water in a bowl and beat for about 2 minutes until the mixture is pale and leaves a thick trail when the beaters are lifted.

4 ▼ Carefully fold the beaten egg yolks into the egg white mixture with a metal spoon.

5 Sift together the flour and baking powder. Carefully fold the flour mixture into the egg mixture with a metal spoon.

6 ▲ Pour the cake mixture into the prepared tin and then smooth the surface, being careful not to press out any air.

7 Bake in the centre of the oven for 12–15 minutes. To test if cooked, press lightly in the centre. If the cake springs back it is done. It will also start to come away from the edges of the tin.

8 Turn the cake out on to a piece of greaseproof paper lightly sprinkled with caster sugar. Peel off the lining paper and cut off any crisp edges of the cake with a sharp knife. Spread with jam, if wished, and roll up, using the greaseproof paper as a guide. Leave to cool on a wire rack.

Vary the flavour of a traditional Swiss roll by adding a little grated orange, lime or lemon rind to the basic mixture.

$\mathcal{M}$adeira Cake

This fine-textured cake makes a good base for decorating and is therefore a useful alternative to fruit cake, although it will not keep as long. It provides a firmer, longer-lasting base than a Victoria sponge, and can be covered with butter icing, fudge frosting, a thin layer of marzipan or sugarpaste icing. For the ingredients, decide what size and shape of cake you wish to make and then follow the chart shown opposite.

STORING AND FREEZING
The cake can be made up to a week in advance, wrapped in clear film or foil and stored in an airtight container. The cake can be frozen for up to three months.

Madeira cake provides a firmer base for icing than a Victoria sponge. It can be covered with a thin layer of sugarpaste, as here, or marzipan, and is a great alternative for anyone who does not like fruit cake.

1 Preheat the oven to 160°C/325°F/ Gas 3. Grease a deep cake tin, line the base and sides with a double thickness of greaseproof paper and grease the paper.

2 ▲ Sift together the flour and baking powder into a mixing bowl. Add the margarine, sugar, eggs and lemon juice.

3 ▲ Stir the ingredients together with a wooden spoon until they are all well combined.

4 ▲ Beat the mixture for about 2 minutes until smooth and glossy.

5 Spoon the mixture into the prepared tin and smooth the top. Bake in the centre of the oven, following the chart opposite as a guide for baking times. If the cake browns too quickly, cover the top loosely with foil. To test if baked, press lightly in the centre. If the cake springs back it is done. Alternatively, test by inserting a skewer into the centre of the cake. If it comes out clean the cake is done. Leave the cake to cool in the tin for 5 minutes and then turn out on to a wire rack. Remove the lining paper and leave to cool.

MADEIRA CAKE CHART

Cake tin sizes	18 cm/7 in round	20 cm/8 in round	23 cm/9 in round	25 cm/10 in round	30 cm/12 in round
	15 cm/6 in square	18 cm/7 in square	20 cm/8 in square	23 cm/9 in square	28 cm/11 in square
Plain flour	225 g/ 8 oz/ 2 cups	350 g/ 12 oz/ 3 cups	450 g/ 1 lb/ 4 cups	500 g/ 1 lb 2 oz/ 4½ cups	625g/ 1½ lb/ 6 cups
Baking powder	1½ tsp	2 tsp	2½ tsp	1 tbsp	4 tsp
Soft margarine	175 g/ 6 oz/ ¾ cup	250 g/ 9 oz/ 1¼ cups	350 g/ 12 oz/ 1½ cups	400 g/ 14 oz/ 1¾ cups	550g/ 1 lb 3 oz 2¼ cups
Caster Sugar	175 g/ 6 oz/ ¾ cup	250 g/ 9 oz/ 1¼ cups	350 g/ 12 oz/ 1½ cups	400 g/ 14 oz/ 1¾ cups	550g/ 1 lb 3 oz/ 2½ cups
Eggs, size 3, beaten	3	4	6	7	10
Lemon juice	1 tbsp	1½ tbsp	2 tbsp	2½ tbsp	4 tbsp
Approx. baking time	1¼–1½ hours	1½–1¾ hours	1¾–2 hours	1¾–2 hours	2¼–2¼ hours

A traditional Madeira cake peaks and cracks slightly on the top. For a flat surface on which to ice, simply level the top with a sharp knife.

Rich Fruit Cake

This is the traditional cake mixture for many cakes made for special occasions such as weddings, Christmas, anniversaries and christenings. Make the cake a few weeks before icing, keep it well wrapped and stored in an airtight container and it should mature beautifully. Because of all its rich ingredients, this fruit cake will keep moist and fresh for several months. Follow the ingredients guide in the chart opposite for the size of cake you wish to make.

STORING

When the cake is cold, wrap in a double thickness of greaseproof paper or foil. Store in an airtight container in a cool dry place where it will keep for several months. During storage, the cake can be unwrapped and the bottom brushed with brandy (about half the amount used in the recipe). Re-wrap before storing again. As the cake keeps so well, there is no need to freeze.

A long-lasting cake which is full of rich flavours.

1 Preheat the oven to 140°C/275°F Gas 1. Grease a deep cake tin, line the base and sides with a double thickness of greaseproof paper and grease the paper.

2 ▲ Place all the ingredients in a large mixing bowl.

3 ▲ Stir to combine, then beat throughly with a wooden spoon for 3–6 minutes (depending on size), until well mixed.

4 ▲ Spoon the mixture into the prepared tin and smooth the surface with the back of a wet metal spoon. Make a slight impression in the centre to help prevent the cake from doming.

5 Bake in the centre of the oven. Use the chart opposite as a guide for timing the cake you are baking. Test the cake about 30 minutes before the end of the baking time. If the cake browns too quickly, cover the top loosely with foil. To test if baked, press lightly in the centre. If the cake feels firm and when a skewer inserted in the centre comes out clean, it is done. Test again at intervals if necessary.

6 Leave the cake to cool in the tin. When completely cool, turn out of the tin. The lining paper can be left on to help keep the cake moist.

Rich Fruit Cake Chart

Cake tin sizes	15 cm/6 in round 13 cm/5 in square	18 cm/7 in round 15 cm/6 in square	20 cm/8 in round 18 cm/7 in square	23 cm/9 in round 20 cm/8 in square	25 cm/10 in round 23 cm/9 in square	28 cm/11 in round 25 cm/10 in square	30 cm/12 in round 28 cm/11 in square	33 cm/13 in round 30 cm/12 in square
Currants	200 g/ 7 oz/ 1¼ cups	275 g/ 10 oz/ 1¾ cups	375 g/ 13 oz/ 2¼ cups	450 g/ 1 lb/ 3 cups	575 g/ 1¼ lb/ 3½ cups	675 g/ 1½ lb/ 4½ cups	800 g/ 1¾ lb/ 5 ¼ cups	900 g/ 2 lb/ 6 cups
Sultanas	115 g/ 4 oz/ ⅔ cup	200 g/ 7 oz/ 1 cup	250 g/ 9 oz/ 1½ cups	300 g/ 11 oz/ 1¾ cups	375 g/ 13 oz/ 2 cups	450 g/ 1 lb/ 2½ cups	550 g/ 1 lb 3 oz/ 3 cups	625 g/ 1 lb 6 oz/ 3½ cups
Raisins	65 g/ 2½ oz/ ⅓ cup	115 g/ 4 oz/ ⅔ cup	150 g/ 5 oz/ ¾ cup	175 g/ 6 oz/ 1 cup	200 g/ 7 oz/ 1 cup	225 g/ 8 oz/ 1¼ cups	250 g/ 9 oz/ 1½ cups	275 g/ 10 oz/ 1½ cups
Glacé cherries, halved	40 g/ 1½ oz/ ¼ cup	65 g/ 2½ oz/ ⅓ cup	90 g/ 3½ oz/ ½ cup	115 g/ 4 oz/ ½ cup	150 g/ 5 oz/ ⅔ cup	175 g/ 6 oz/ ¾ cup	200 g/ 7 oz/ 1 cup	225 g/ 8 oz/ 1¼ cups
Almonds, chopped	40 g/ 1½ oz/ ⅓ cup	65 g/ 2½ oz/ ½ cup	90 g/ 3½ oz/ ¾ cup	115 g/ 4 oz/ 1 cup	150 g/ 5 oz/ 1¼ cups	175 g/ 6 oz/ 1½ cups	200 g/ 7 oz/ 1⅔ cups	225 g/ 8 oz/ 2 cups
Mixed peel	40 g/ 1½ oz/ ¼ cup	65 g/ 2½ oz/ ½ cup	65 g/ 2½ oz/ ½ cup	90 g/ 3½ oz/ ⅔ cup	115 g/ 4 oz/ ¾ cup	150 g/ 5 oz/ 1 cup	175 g/ 6 oz/ 1 cup	200 g/ 7 oz/ 1⅓ cups
Lemon, grated rind	½	1	1	2	2	2	3	3
Brandy	1½ tbsp	2 tbsp	2½ tbsp	3 tbsp	3½ tbsp	4 tbsp	4½ tbsp	5 tbsp
Plain flour	150 g/ 5 oz/ 1⅓ cups	200 g/ 7 oz/ 1¾ cups	250 g/ 9 oz/ 2 cups	300 g/ 11 oz/ 2¾ cups	400 g/ 14 oz/ 3½ cups	450 g/ 1 lb/ 4 cups	550 g/ 1 lb 3 oz/ 4½ cups	625 g/ 1 lb 6 oz/ 5½ cups
Ground mixed spice	1 tsp	1 tsp	1¼ tsp	1½ tsp	1½ tsp	2 tsp	2½ tsp	1 tbsp
Ground nutmeg	¼ tsp	½ tsp	½ tsp	1 tsp	1 tsp	1 tsp	1½ tsp	2 tsp
Ground almonds	40 g/ 1½ oz/ ½ cup	50 g/ 2 oz/ ⅔ cup	65 g/ 2½ oz/ ¾ cup	75 g/ 3 oz/ 1 cup	90 g/ 3½ oz/ 1¼ cups	115 g/ 4 oz/ 1⅓ cups	130 g/ 4½ oz/ 1½ cups	150 g/ 5 oz/ 1⅔ cups
Soft margarine or butter	115 g/ 4 oz/ ½ cup	150 g/ 5 oz/ ⅔ cup	200 g/ 7 oz/ scant 1 cup	250 g/ 9 oz/ scant 1¼ cups	300 g/ 11 oz/ scant 1½ cups	375 g/ 13 oz/ scant 1¾ cups	425 g/ 15 oz/ scant 2 cups	500 g/ 1 lb 2 oz/ 2¼ cups
Soft brown sugar	130 g/ 4½ oz/ ⅔ cup	175 g/ 6 oz/ ¾ cup	225 g/ 8 oz/ 1 cup	275 g/ 10 oz/ 1⅓ cups	350 g/ 12 oz 1½ cups	400 g/ 14 oz/ scant 2 cups	450 g/ 1 lb/ 2 cups	500 g/ 1 lb 2 oz/ 2¼ cups
Black treacle or molasses	1 tbsp	1 tbsp	1 tbsp	1½ tbsp	2 tbsp	2 tbsp	2 tbsp	2½ tbsp
Eggs, size 3, beaten	3	4	5	6	7	8	9	10
Approx. baking time	2¼–2½ hours	2½–2¾ hours	3–3½ hours	3¼–3¾ hours	3¾–4¼ hours	4–4½ hours	4½–5¼ hours	5¼–5¾ hours

Light Fruit Cake

For those who prefer a lighter fruit cake, here is a less rich version, still ideal for marzipanning and covering with sugarpaste or royal icing. Follow the ingredients guide in the chart opposite according to the size of cake you wish to make.

STORING AND FREEZING
When the cake is cold, wrap well in greaseproof paper, clear film or foil. It will keep for several weeks, stored in an airtight container. As the cake keeps so well, there is no need to freeze, but, if wished, freeze for up to three months.

1 Preheat the oven to 150°C/300°F/ Gas 2. Grease a deep cake tin, line the sides and base with a double thickness of greaseproof paper and grease the paper.

2 ▲ Measure and prepare all the ingredients, then place them all together in a large mixing bowl.

3 ▲ Stir to combine, then beat thoroughly with a wooden spoon for 3–4 minutes, depending on the size, until well mixed.

4 ▲ Spoon the mixture into the prepared tin and smooth the surface with the back of a wet metal spoon. Make a slight impression in the centre to help prevent the cake from doming.

5 Bake in the centre of the oven. Use the chart opposite as a guide according to the size of cake you are baking. Test the cake about 15 minutes before the end of the baking time. If the cake browns too quickly, cover the top loosely with foil. To test if baked, press lightly in the centre. If the cake feels firm, and when a skewer inserted in the centre comes out clean, it is done. Test again at intervals if necessary.

6 Leave the cake to cool in the tin. When completely cool, turn out of the tin. The lining paper can be left on to help keep the cake moist.

Round, square, ring or heart-shaped – the shape of this light fruit cake can be varied to suit the occasion.

Light Fruit Cake Chart

Cake tin sizes	15 cm/6 in round 13 cm/5 in square	18 cm/7 in round 15 cm/6 in square	20 cm/8 in round 18 cm/7 in square	23 cm/9 in round 20 cm/8 in square
Soft margarine or butter	115 g/ 4 oz/ ½ cup	175 g/ 6 oz/ ¾ cup	225 g/ 8 oz/ 1 cup	275 g/ 10 oz/ 1⅓ cups
Caster sugar	115 g/ 4 oz/ ½ cup	175 g/ 6 oz/ ¾ cup	225 g/ 8 oz/ 1 cup	275 g/ 10 oz/ 1⅓ cups
Orange, grated rind	½	½	1	1
Eggs, size 3, beaten	3	4	5	6
Plain flour	165 g 5½ oz/ 1½ cups	200 g/ 7 oz/ 1¾ cups	300 g/ 11 oz/ 2¾ cups	400 g/ 14 oz/ 3½ cups
Baking powder	¼ tsp	½ tsp	½ tsp	1 tsp
Ground mixed spice	1 tsp	1½ tsp	2 tsp	2½ tsp
Currants	50 g/ 2 oz/ ⅓ cup	115 g/ 4 oz/ ⅔ cup	175 g/ 6 oz/ 1 cup	225 g/ 8 oz/ 1½ cups
Sultanas	50 g/ 2 oz/ ⅓ cup	115 g/ 4 oz/ ⅔ cup	175 g/ 6 oz/ 1 cup	225 g/ 8 oz/ 1⅓ cups
Raisins	50 g/ 2 oz/ ⅓ cup	115 g/ 4 oz/ ⅔ cup	175 g/ 6 oz/ 1 cup	225 g/ 8 oz/ 1⅓ cups
Dried apricots, chopped	25 g/ 1 oz/ 7	50 g/ 2 oz/ 14	50 g/ 2 oz/ 14	75 g/ 3 oz/ 21
Mixed cut peel	50 g/ 2 oz/ scant ½ cup	75 g/ 3 oz/ good ½ cup	115 g/ 4 oz/ ¾ cup	150 g/ 5 oz/ 1 cup
Approx. baking time	2¼–2½ hours	2½–2¾ hours	2¾–3¼ hours	3¼–3¾ hours

*T*ruffle Cake Mix

This is a no-cook recipe, using leftover pieces of sponge cake or plain shop-bought sponge to make a moist, rich cake mixture, which is used in several of the novelty cakes.

INGREDIENTS
175 g/6 oz plain sponge cake pieces
175 g/6 oz/2 cups ground almonds
75g/3 oz/scant ⅓ cup dark brown muscovado sugar
1 tsp ground mixed spice
pinch of ground cinnamon
finely grated zest of 1 orange
3 tbsp freshly squeezed orange juice
5 tbsp clear honey

STORING AND FREEZING
The mixture can be made up to two days in advance, wrapped in clear film and stored in an airtight container. Not suitable for freezing.

1 Place the sponge cake pieces into the bowl of a food processor or blender and process for a few seconds to form fine crumbs.

2 Place the cake crumbs, ground almonds, sugar, spices, orange zest, orange juice and honey in a large mixing bowl. Stir well to combine into a thick, smooth mixture.

3 ▲ Use the mixture as directed in the novelty cake recipes. The truffle mixture can be made and moulded into any simple shape, such as a log or round balls. The moulded mixture can be covered with marzipan or sugarpaste icing.

*T*ip
Dampen your hands slightly before handling the truffle mixture, as it is very sticky.

Here the truffle mixture has been rolled into a log shape to form the sausage in this sweet-tasting novelty Hot Dog cake.

LINING CAKE TINS

Greaseproof paper is normally used for lining cake tins. The paper lining prevents the cakes from sticking to the tins and makes them easier to turn out. Different cake recipes require slightly different techniques of lining, depending on the shape of the tin, the type of cake mixture, and how long the cake needs to cook. Quick-mix sponge cakes require only one layer of paper to line the base, for example, whereas rich fruit cakes that often bake for several hours if they are large in size need to be lined with a double layer of paper on the base and sides. This extra protection also helps cakes to cook evenly.

Lining a shallow round tin

This technique is used for a quick-mix sponge cake.

1 Put the tin on a piece of greaseproof paper and draw around the base of the tin. Cut out the circle just inside the marked line.

2 ▲ Lightly brush the inside of the tin with a little vegetable oil and position the paper circle in the base of the tin. Brush the paper with a little more vegetable oil.

Tip

Softened butter or margarine can be used as a greasing agent in place of vegetable oil, if wished.

Lining a Swiss roll tin

1 Put the tin on a piece of greaseproof paper and draw around the base. Increase the rectangle by 2.5 cm/1 inch on all sides. Cut out this rectangle and snip each corner diagonally down to the original rectangle.

2 ▲ Lightly brush the inside of the tin with a little vegetable oil and fit the paper into the tin, overlapping the corners slightly so that they fit neatly. Brush the paper with a little more vegetable oil.

Lining a deep round cake tin

This technique should be used for all rich or light fruit cakes and Madeira cakes. Use this method for a square tin, but cut out the sides separately.

1 Put the tin on a double thickness of greaseproof paper and draw around the base. Cut out just inside the line.

2 For the sides of the tin, cut out a double thickness strip of greaseproof paper that will wrap around the outside of the tin, allowing a slight overlap, and which is 2.5 cm/1 inch taller than the depth of the tin.

3 Fold over 2.5 cm/1 inch along the length of the side lining. Snip the paper along its length, inside the fold, at short intervals.

4 Brush the inside of the tin with vegetable oil. Slip the side lining into the tin so the snipped edge fits into the curve of the base and sits flat.

5 ▲ Position the base lining in the tin and brush the paper with a little more vegetable oil.

Basic Icing Recipes

Cakes can take on many guises, and nothing enhances their appearance more for that extra special occasion than a little icing. This chapter offers a range of simple classic icing recipes to suit the type of cake you have made and which can be adapted according to the occasion. Ideas range from quick-mix icings, such as butter icing and satin chocolate icing, which may be instantly poured, spread, swirled or piped on to sponge and Madeira cakes or Swiss rolls, to the more regal icings, such as royal icing and sugarpaste icing. These are ideal for covering and decorating fruit cakes intended for more formal occasions, such as anniversaries, christenings and weddings.

The icings in this section are all fairly traditional. However, if you want to substitute any of them with a favourite icing recipe when decorating, make sure that it suits the cake on which you are working.

Decorating Equipment

With a few simple tools, it is possible to create the most stunning of cake decorations. Thick swirls of butter icing formed with a palette knife, or stark white icing sugar dusted over a contrastingly dark chocolate icing, instantly provide an impressive effect. As your skills develop, however, you will probably want to invest in some specialized pieces of icing equipment, such as those listed here.

Icing Turntable This is one of the most expensive but useful items for either the novice or more advanced cake decorator. Because it revolves, it is particularly handy for piping, or for icing the sides of a round cake with royal icing.
Straight-edge Ruler Choose one made of stainless steel so that it will not bend as you pull it across a layer of royal icing, to give a smooth, flat surface to a cake.
Plastic Scrapers These can have straight or serrated edges for giving a smooth or patterned surface to the sides or tops of cakes coated with royal, butter or fudge icing.
Small Rolling Pin Made in a handy size for rolling out small amounts of marzipan or sugarpaste icing for decorations.

Nozzles There are numerous shapes and sizes to choose from, but it is best to start off with some of the basic shapes. Small straight-sided nozzles fit home-made greaseproof paper piping bags. Larger ones are more suitable for the commercially-made material bags when piping large amounts of icing.
Nozzle Brush A small wire brush which makes the job of cleaning out nozzles a lot easier.
Flower Nail Used as a support when piping flowers.
Crimping Tools These are available with different end-shapes which produce varied patterns and offer a quick way of giving a professional finish to a cake.
Paintbrushes Brushes for painting designs on to cakes, adding highlights to flowers or modelled shapes, or for making run-outs are available at cake icing specialists, stationers or art supply shops.
Florist's Wire, Tape and Stamens All available from cake icing specialists, the wire, available in different gauges, is handy for wiring small sugarpaste flowers together to form floral sprays. The tape is used to neaten the stems, and the stamens, available in many colours, form the centres of the flowers.

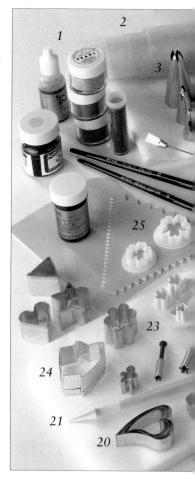

Papers There are several papers used in cake decorating. Greaseproof paper is used for making piping bags and for drying sugar-frosted flowers and fruits, while baking parchment is used for spreading melted chocolate and for icing run-outs.

Cutters Small cocktail cutters are useful for making cut-out shapes from chocolate, sugarpaste and marzipan. Blossom cutters, available in different shapes and sizes, are good for making small flowers, while a special frill cutter can be used to cut out quick-and-easy frills.

1 *food colourings*
2 *greaseproof paper and baking parchment*
3 *piping nozzles*
4 *fabric piping bag*
5 *nozzle brush*
6 *paintbrushes*
7 *icing turntable*
8 *florist's wire*
9 *stamens*
10 *florist's tape*
11 *straight-edge ruler*
12 *cake pillars*
13 *cake pillar supports*
14 *crimping tools*
15 *food colouring pens*
16 *flower nail*
17 *frill cutter*
18 *textured rolling pin*
19 *foam pad*
20 *shaped cutters*
21 *modelling tool*
22 *plunger cutters*
23 *dual blossom cutter*
24 *cocktail cutters*
25 *plain and serrated side scrapers*

*M*arzipan

With its smooth, pliable texture, marzipan has been popular for centuries in cake making, especially for large cakes such as wedding and christening cakes. It is also excellent for making a variety of cake decorations. The following recipe is sufficient to cover the top and sides of an 18 cm/7 inch round or a 15 cm/6 inch square cake. Make half the amount if only the top is to be covered.

2 ▲ Add the lemon juice, almond essence and enough beaten egg to mix to a soft but firm dough. Gather together with your fingers to form a ball.

INGREDIENTS
Makes 450 g/1 lb
225 g/8 oz/2¼ cups ground almonds
115 g/4 oz/1 cup icing sugar, sifted
115 g/4 oz/½ cup caster sugar
1 tsp lemon juice
2 drops almond essence
1 size 4 egg, beaten

STORING
The marzipan will keep for up to four days, wrapped in clear film in an airtight container, and stored in the refrigerator.

1 ▲ Put the ground almonds, icing and caster sugars into a bowl and mix together.

3 ▲ Knead the marzipan on a work surface lightly dusted with sifted icing sugar until smooth.

Using Marzipan
Marzipan is applied to the sides and top of a cake, particularly rich fruit cakes, to prevent moisture seeping through the cake and to provide a smooth under-coat for the top covering of royal icing or sugarpaste icing.

Once the marzipan has been applied, leave it to dry for a day or two before applying the icing. For a richer taste you can mix up your own marzipan. However, if you have any concerns about using raw eggs in uncooked recipes, especially in light of current health warnings, do buy ready-made marzipan. It is very good quality, does not contain raw egg and is available in two colours, white and yellow. White is the best choice if you want to add your own colours and create different moulded shapes.

Marzipan can be used as an attractive cake coating in its own right as well as providing a base for other icings.

Sugarpaste Icing

Sugarpaste icing has opened up a whole new concept in cake decorating. It is wonderfully pliable, easy to make and use, and can be coloured, moulded and shaped in the most imaginative fashion. Though quick to make at home, shop-bought sugarpaste, also known as easy-roll or ready-to-roll icing, is very good quality and handy to use. This recipe makes sufficient to cover the top and sides of an 18 cm/7 inch round or a 15 cm/6 inch square cake.

INGREDIENTS
Makes 350 g/12 oz
1 size 3 egg white
1 tbsp liquid glucose, warmed
350 g/12 oz/3 cups icing
sugar, sifted

STORING
The icing will keep for up to a week, wrapped in clear film or a plastic bag and stored in the refrigerator. Bring to room temperature before using. If a thin crust forms, trim off before using or it will make the icing lumpy. Also, if the icing dries out or hardens, knead in a little boiled water to make it smooth and pliable again.

1 Put the egg white and glucose in a bowl. Stir together with a wooden spoon to break up the egg white.

2 ▲ Add the icing sugar and mix together with a palette knife or knife, using a chopping action, until well blended and the icing begins to bind together.

3 Knead the mixture with your fingers until it forms a ball.

4 ▲ Knead the sugarpaste on a work surface lightly dusted with sifted icing sugar for several minutes until smooth, soft and pliable. If the icing is too soft, knead in some more sifted icing sugar until it is firm and pliable.

Tip

Ready-made shop-bought sugarpaste does not contain raw egg, so do use if you prefer to avoid uncooked egg in recipes in light of current health warnings.

Tinted or left pure white, sugarpaste icing can be used to cover cakes, and moulded to make decorations to suit any shape of cake.

Royal Icing

Royal icing has gained a regal position in the world of icing. Any special occasion cake which demands a classical, professional finish uses this smooth, satin-like icing. The following recipe makes sufficient to cover the top and sides of an 18 cm/7 inch round or a 15 cm/6 inch square cake.

INGREDIENTS
Makes 675 g/1½ lb
3 size 3 egg whites
about 675 g/1½ lb/6 cups icing sugar, sifted
1½ tsp glycerine
few drops lemon juice
colouring (optional)

STORING
Royal icing will keep for up to three days in an airtight container, stored in the refrigerator. Stir the icing well before using.

Tips

• Always sift the icing sugar before using, to get rid of any lumps.
• Never add more than the stated amount of glycerine. Too much will make the icing crumbly and too fragile to use.
• A little lemon juice is added to prevent the icing from discolouring, but too much will make the icing become hard.

2 ▲ Add the icing sugar gradually in small quantities, beating well with a wooden spoon between each addition. Add sufficient icing sugar to make a smooth, white, shiny icing with the consistency of very stiff meringue. It should be thin enough to spread, but thick enough to hold its shape.

3 ▲ Beat in the glycerine, lemon juice and food colouring, if using.

4 It is best to let the icing sit for about 1 hour before using. Cover the surface with a piece of damp clear film or a lid so the icing does not dry out. Before using, stir the icing to burst any air bubbles. Even when working with royal icing, always keep it covered.

1 ▲ Put the egg whites in a bowl and stir lightly with a wooden spoon to break them up.

Royal Icing Using Pure Albumen Powder

If you are concerned about current health warnings advising against the use of raw eggs in uncooked recipes, try the following recipe.

INGREDIENTS
Makes 450 g/1 lb
450 g/1 lb/4 cups icing sugar, sifted
6 tbsp water
12.5g/½ oz/7 tsp pure albumen powder

STORING
This royal icing will keep for up to a week in an airtight container, stored in a cool place.

1 Mix the pure albumen powder with the water. Leave to stand for 15 minutes, then stir until the powder dissolves.

2 Sieve the albumen solution into a mixing bowl. Add half the icing sugar and beat until smooth. Add the remaining sugar and beat again for 12–14 minutes or until smooth.

3 Adjust the consistency as needed, adding a little more icing sugar for a stiffer icing or a little water for a thinner one. If storing, transfer to an airtight container, cover the surface of the royal icing with clear film and then close the lid.

ICING CONSISTENCIES

For flat icing

▲ The recipes on the opposite page are for a consistency of icing suitable for flat icing a rich fruit cake covered in marzipan. When the spoon is lifted out of the icing, it should form a sharp point, with a slight curve at the end, known as a 'soft peak'.

For peaking

▲ Make the royal icing as before, but to a stiffer consistency so that when the spoon is lifted out of the bowl the icing stands in straight peaks.

For piping

For piping purposes, the icing needs to be slightly stiffer than for peaked icing so that it forms a fine, sharp peak when the spoon is lifted out. This allows the icing to flow easily for piping, at the same time enabling it to keep its definition.

For run-outs

For elegant and more elaborate cakes, you may want to pipe outlines of shapes and then fill these in with different coloured icing. These are known as run-outs. For the outlines, you need to make the icing to a piping consistency, while for the insides you need a slightly thinner icing with a consistency of thick cream, so that with a little help it will flow within the shapes. Ideally the icing should hold its shape and be slightly rounded after filling the outlines.

The right consistency

If you need to change the consistency of your icing, add a little sifted icing sugar to make it stiffer, or beat in a little egg white for a thinner icing. Be sure to do this carefully, as a little of one or the other will change the consistency fairly quickly.

A traditional look for a classic royal icing. This square rich fruit cake has been marzipanned and then flat iced with three, ultra-smooth layers of royal icing. It is simply, but elegantly, decorated with piped borders, a crisp, white ribbon and fresh roses.

Butter Icing

The creamy, rich flavour and silky smoothness of butter icing are popular with both children and adults. The icing can be varied in colour and flavour and makes a decorative filling and coating for sponge and Madeira cakes or Swiss rolls. Simply swirled, or more elaborately piped, butter icing gives a delicious and attractive finish. The following quantity makes enough to fill and coat the sides and top of a 20 cm/8 inch sponge cake.

INGREDIENTS
Makes 350 g/12 oz
75 g/3 oz/6 tbsp butter, softened,
or soft margarine
225 g/8 oz/2 cups icing sugar, sifted
1 tsp vanilla essence
2–3 tsp milk

STORING
The icing will keep for up to three days, in an airtight container stored in the refrigerator.

1 ▲ Put the butter or margarine, icing sugar, vanilla essence and 1 tsp of the milk in a bowl.

2 ▲ Beat with a wooden spoon or an electric mixer, adding sufficient extra milk to give a light, smooth and fluffy consistency.

FLAVOURINGS
The following amounts are for a single quantity of icing. Increase or decrease the amounts proportionally as needed.
Chocolate *Blend 1 tbsp cocoa powder with 1 tbsp hot water. Allow to cool before beating into the icing.*
Coffee *Blend 2 tsp instant coffee powder or granules with 1 tbsp boiling water. Allow to cool before beating into the icing.*
Lemon, orange or lime *Substitute the vanilla essence and milk for lemon, orange or lime juice and 2 tsp of finely grated citrus zest. Omit the zest if using the icing for piping. Lightly colour the icing with the appropriate shade of food colouring, if wished.*

Generous swirls of butter icing give a mouth-watering effect to a cake.

Glacé Icing

*This icing can be made in just a few minutes
and can be varied by adding a few drops of food colouring or
flavouring. The following quantity makes enough to cover the top
and decorate a 20 cm/8 inch round sponge cake.*

INGREDIENTS
Makes 225 g/8 oz
*225 g/8 oz/2 cups icing sugar
2–3 tbsp warm water or fruit juice
food colouring, optional*

STORING
*Not suitable for storing.
The icing must be used
immediately after making.*

1 ▲ Sift the icing sugar into a mixing
bowl to get rid of any lumps.

2 ▲ Using a wooden spoon, gradually
stir in enough water to make an
icing with the consistency of thick
cream. Beat until the icing is smooth. It
should be thick enough to coat the back
of the spoon. If it is too runny, beat in a
little more sifted icing sugar.

3 To colour the icing, beat in a few
drops of food colouring. Use the
icing immediately for coating or piping.

*Drizzled or spread, glacé icing can
quickly turn a plain cake into
something special.*

Fudge Frosting

A rich, darkly delicious frosting, this can transform a simple sponge cake into one worthy of a very special occasion. Spread fudge frosting smoothly over the cake or swirl it. Or be even more elaborate with a little piping - it is very versatile. The following amount will fill and coat the top and sides of a 20 cm/8 inch or 23 cm/9 inch round sponge cake.

INGREDIENTS
Makes 350 g/12 oz
50 g/2 oz plain chocolate
225 g/8 oz/2 cups icing sugar, sifted
50 g/2 oz/4 tbsp butter or margarine
3 tbsp milk or single cream
1 tsp vanilla essence

STORING
Not suitable for storing. The icing must be used immediately after making.

1 ▲ Break or chop the chocolate into small pieces. Put the chocolate, icing sugar, butter, milk and vanilla essence in a heavy-based saucepan.

2 ▲ Stir over a very low heat until the chocolate and butter or margarine melt. Remove from the heat and stir until evenly blended.

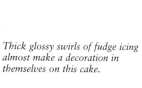

3 ▲ Beat the icing frequently as it cools until it thickens sufficiently to use for spreading or piping. Use immediately and work quickly once it has reached the right consistency.

Thick glossy swirls of fudge icing almost make a decoration in themselves on this cake.

Satin Chocolate Icing

Shiny as satin and smooth as silk, this dark chocolate icing can be poured over a sponge cake. A few fresh flowers, pieces of fresh fruit, simple chocolate shapes or white chocolate piping add the finishing touch. Use this recipe to cover a 20 cm/8 inch square or a 23 cm/ 9 inch round quick-mix sponge or Madeira cake.

INGREDIENTS
Makes 225 g/8 oz
175 g/6 oz plain chocolate
150 ml/¼ pint/⅔ cup single cream
½ tsp instant coffee powder

STORING
*Not suitable for storing.
The icing must be used immediately
after making.*

Tip
Before using the icing, place the cake on a wire rack positioned over a baking sheet or a piece of greaseproof paper. This will avoid unnecessary mess.

2 ▲ Stir over a very low heat until the chocolate melts and the mixture is smooth and evenly blended.

3 Remove from the heat and immediately pour the icing over the cake, letting it slowly run down the sides to coat it completely. Spread the icing with a palette knife as necessary, working quickly before the icing has time to thicken.

Satin chocolate icing brings a real touch of sophistication to the most humble of cakes.

1 ▲ Break or chop the chocolate into small pieces. Put the chocolate, cream and coffee in a small heavy-based saucepan. Place the cake to be iced on a wire rack.

overing Cakes

Covering cakes with icing – whether marzipan, royal or sugarpaste – not only provides a wonderful surface for decorating but also helps to keep the cake moist. The icings need to be applied with care to ensure that the finish is beautifully smooth. Always plan ahead; it will take several days to marzipan and royal ice a cake, allowing for the drying out times.

Marzipanning a Cake for Sugarpaste Icing

Marzipan can be applied as an icing in its own right, but is mainly used as a base for sugarpaste or royal icing. Unlike a cake covered in royal icing which traditionally has sharp, well defined corners, a cake covered in sugarpaste has much smoother lines with rounded corners and edges. There are therefore two different techniques depending on how you wish to ice the cake.

1 If the cake is not absolutely flat, fill any hollows or build up the top edge (if it is lower than the top of the cake) with a little marzipan. Brush the top of the cake with a little warmed and sieved apricot jam.

2 ▲ Lightly dust a work surface with icing sugar. Knead the marzipan into a smooth ball. Roll out to a 5 mm/ ¼ inch thickness and large enough to cover the top and sides of the cake, allowing about an extra 7.5 cm/3 inches all around for trimming. Make sure the marzipan does not stick to the work surface and moves freely.

3 ▲ Lift the marzipan using your hands, or place it over a rolling pin to support it, and position over the top of the cake. Drape the marzipan over the cake to cover it evenly.

4 ▲ Smooth the top with the palm of your hand to eliminate any air bubbles. Then carefully lift up the edges of the marzipan and let them fall against the sides of the cake, being careful not to stretch the marzipan. Ensure the marzipanned sides are flat and there are no creases – all the excess marzipan should fall on to the work surface. Use the palms of your hands to smooth the sides and eliminate air bubbles.

5 ▲ With a sharp knife, trim the excess marzipan, cutting it flush with the base of the cake.

6 ▲ With your hands, work in a circular motion over the surface of the marzipan to give it a smooth finish. Spread a little royal icing over the middle of a cake board and place the cake in the centre to secure. Lay a piece of greaseproof paper over the top to protect the surface, then leave for at least 12 hours to dry before covering with icing.

Marzipanning a Round Cake for Royal Icing

1 ▲ If the cake is not absolutely flat, fill any hollows or build up the top edge (if it is lower than the top of the cake) with a little marzipan.

2 Brush the top of the cake with warmed and sieved apricot jam.

3 Lightly dust a work surface with icing sugar. Using one-third of the marzipan, knead it into a ball. Roll out to a round 5 mm/¼ inch thickness and 1 cm/½ inch larger than the top of the cake. Make sure that the marzipan does not stick to the work surface and moves freely.

4 ▲ Invert the top of the cake on to the marzipan. Trim the marzipan almost to the edge of the cake. With a small metal palette knife, press the marzipan inwards so it is flush with the edge of the cake.

▶ The method for marzipanning a square cake for royal icing is the same as for a round one, except for the sides. Measure the length and height of the sides with string and roll out the marzipan in four separate pieces, using the string measurements as a guide.

5 Carefully turn the cake the right way up. Check the sides of the cake. If there are any holes, fill them with marzipan to make a flat surface. Brush the sides with apricot jam.

6 Knead the remaining marzipan and any trimmings (making sure there are no cake crumbs on the work surface) to form a ball. For the sides of the cake, measure the circumference with a piece of string, and the height of the sides with another piece.

7 ▲ Roll out a strip of marzipan to the same thickness as the top, matching the length and width to the measured string. Hold the cake on its side, being careful to touch the marzipanned top as lightly as possible. Roll the cake along the marzipan strip, pressing the marzipan into position to cover the sides. Trim if necessary to fit.

8 ▲ Smooth the joins together with a palette knife. Spread a little royal icing into the middle of a cake board and place the cake in the centre to secure. Lay a piece of greaseproof paper very loosely over the top to protect the surface, then leave for at least 24 hours to dry before covering with icing.

Tip

When buying marzipan, it is best to choose the white kind for covering a cake, as the bright yellow marzipan may discolour pale coloured sugarpaste or royal icing.

Covering a Round Cake with Royal Icing

A cake which is coated with royal icing is always covered with marzipan first. The marzipan should be applied one to two days before the royal icing so it has time to dry out slightly, giving a firm surface on which to work. The royal icing is then built up in two or three layers, each one being allowed to dry out before covering with the next. The final coat should be perfectly flat and smooth, with no air bubbles.

ip

It is difficult to calculate the exact amount of icing required, but if you work with 450 g/1 lb/⅔ quantity batches, it should always be fresh. While working, keep the royal icing in a bowl and cover with a clean, damp cloth or clear film so it does not dry out.

1 The icing should be of 'soft peak' consistency. Put about 2 tbsp of icing in the centre of the marzipanned cake (the amount will depend on the size of cake you are icing).

2 ▲ Using a small palette knife, spread the icing over the top of the cake, working back and forth with the flat of the knife to eliminate any air bubbles. Keep working the icing in this way until the top of the cake is completely covered. Trim any icing that extends over the edge of the cake with the palette knife.

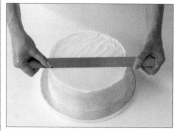

3 ▲ Position a straight-edge ruler on the top edge of the cake furthest away from you. Slowly and smoothly pull the ruler across the surface of the icing, holding it at a slight angle. Do this without stopping to prevent ridges forming. You may need several attempts to get a smooth layer, in which case simply re-spread the top of the cake with icing and try again.

4 ▲ Trim any excess icing from the top edges of the cake with the palette knife to give a straight, neat edge. Leave the icing to dry for several hours, or overnight, in a dry place before continuing.

5 ▲ Place the cake on a turntable. To cover the sides, spread some icing on to the side of the cake with a palette knife. Rock the knife back and forth as you spread the icing to eliminate air bubbles. Rotate the turntable as you work your way around the cake.

6 ▲ Using a plain side-scraper, hold it firmly in one hand against the side of the cake at a slight angle. Turn the turntable round in a continuous motion and in one direction with the other hand, while pulling the scraper smoothly in the opposite direction to give a smooth surface to the iced sides. When you have completed the full turn, carefully lift off the scraper to leave a neat join. Trim off any excess icing from the top edge and the cake board.

7 Leave the cake to dry, uncovered, then apply the icing in the same way to give the cake two or three more coats of icing. For a really smooth final layer, use a slightly softer consistency of icing.

Covering a Square Cake

The method is essentially the same as for icing a round cake.

1 Cover the top with icing as for the round cake. Leave to dry.

2 ▲ Cover the sides as for the round cake, but work on one side at a time and allow the icing to dry out before continuing with the next side. You will not need a turntable. Simply pull the scraper firmly and smoothly across each side in a single movement, repeating if necessary, for a really smooth finish.

3 ▲ Trim off any excess icing from the cake board with a knife.

4 Leave the cake to dry, uncovered, then apply the icing in the same way to give the cake two or three more coats of icing. For a really smooth final layer, use a slightly softer consistency.

This colourful Christmas Tree cake shows an interesting version of peaked, or rough, icing. The fruit cake is first covered with coloured marzipan and left to dry for 12 hours, then royal icing is peaked around the lower half of the sides. The decorations are also made of coloured marzipan.

Rough Icing a Cake

Peaking the icing to give it a rough appearance, like that of snow, is a much quicker and simpler way of applying royal icing to a cake. It is also much quicker to apply as you only need one covering of icing.

1 ▲ Spread the icing evenly over the cake, bringing the icing right to the edges so the cake is completely covered.

2 ▲ Starting at the bottom of the cake, press the flat side of a palette knife into the icing, then pull away sharply to form a peak. Repeat until the whole cake is covered with peaks. Alternatively, flat ice the top of the cake and rough ice the sides - or vice versa.

Covering with Sugarpaste Icing

Sugarpaste icing is a quick, professional way to cover a cake. Although fruit cakes are usually covered with marzipan first, this is not necessary if you are using a sponge base. The sugarpaste can be applied in one coating, unlike royal icing which requires several coats for a really smooth finish. Keep the icing white or knead in a little food colouring to tint. Ready-made sugarpaste is extremely good quality and is available in various colours for fast and professional results.

1 Carefully brush a little water or sherry over the marzipanned surface to help the icing stick to the marzipan. (If you miss a patch, unsightly air bubbles may form.)

2 ▲ Lightly dust a work surface with icing sugar. Roll out the sugarpaste to a 5 mm/¼ inch thickness and large enough to cover the top and sides of the cake plus a little extra for trimming. Make sure the icing does not stick to the surface and moves freely.

3 ▲ Lift the sugarpaste using your hands, or place it over a rolling pin to support it, and position over the top of the cake. Drape the sugarpaste over the cake to cover it evenly.

4 ▲ Dust your hands with a little cornflour. Smooth the top and sides of the cake with your hands, working from top to bottom, to eliminate any air bubbles.

5 ▲ With a sharp knife, trim off the excess sugarpaste, cutting flush with the base of the cake.

6 Spread a little royal icing into the middle of a cake board and place the cake in the centre to secure.

Tip

To avoid damaging the surface of the cake while you move it, slide the cake to the edge of the work surface and support it underneath with your hand. Lift it and place on the cake board.

Covering Awkward Shapes

Although most shapes of cake can be covered smoothly with one piece of sugarpaste icing, there are some which need to be covered in sections. A cake baked in a ring mould is one such. The top and outer side of the cake is covered with two identical pieces of sugarpaste, and the inner side with a third piece.

1 ▲ Measure half of the outer circumference of the cake with a piece of string, then measure the side and rounded top with another piece of string.

2 ▲ Take three-quarters of the sugarpaste icing and cut in half. Keep the remaining icing well wrapped until needed. Brush the marzipan lightly with water. Roll out each half of the icing into a rectangle, matching the string measurements. Cover the top and side of the cake in two halves.

3 Measure the circumference and the height of the inner side with two pieces of string. Roll out the reserved sugarpaste icing into a rectangle matching the string measurements, and use to cover the inside of the ring. Trim the sugarpaste to fit and press the joins together securely.

FOOD COLOURINGS & TINTS

Food colourings and tints for cake making are available today in almost as large a range as those found on an artist's palette. This has opened up endless possibilities for the cake decorator to create the most imaginative and colourful designs. Liquid colours are only suitable for marzipan and sugarpaste icing if a few drops are required to tint the icing a very pale shade. If used in large amounts they will soften the icings too much. So for vibrant, stronger colours, as well as for subtle sparkling tints, use pastes or powders, available from cake icing specialists. When choosing colours for icings, ensure that they are harmonious, and complement your design.

Colouring icings

How you apply the colour to an icing depends on whether it is in liquid form, a paste or powder. While working with the colourings it is best to stand them on a plate or washable board so they do not mark your work surface. When using cocktail sticks for transferring the colour to the icing, select a fresh stick for each colour so the colours do not become mixed.

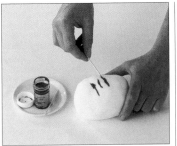

1 ▲ Add liquid colour to the icing a few drops at a time until the required shade is reached. Stir into softer icings, such as butter, royal or glacé.

2 ▲ To colour firmer icings, such as sugarpaste and marzipan, use paste colourings. Dip a cocktail stick into the colouring and streak it on to the surface of a ball of the icing.

4 ▲ To create subtle tints in specific areas, brush powdered colourings on to the surface of the icing.

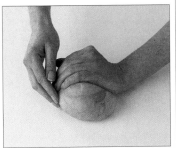

3 ▲ Knead thoroughly until the colour is evenly worked in and there is no streaking. Add sparingly at first, remembering that the colour becomes more intense as the icing stands, then leave for about 10 minutes to see if it is the shade you need.

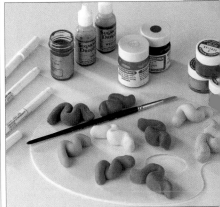

A cake decorator's palette – a vivid array of food colourings to help bring out the artist in you.

ecorating with Royal Icing

Of all the icings, royal icing is probably the most complex and hardest to work with. But once the techniques are mastered, it provides a classic backdrop for both traditional as well as more contemporary cake designs. Traditionally it is used for decorating white wedding and Christmas cakes, but as colour is being introduced more and more into cake decorating, royal icing can now be used in many imaginative ways. This chapter demonstrates how to introduce a modern look using a wide variety of classic techniques.

Making and Using Piping Bags

A piping bag is an essential tool when working with royal icing. You can buy piping bags made of washable fabric and icing syringes, which are ideal for the beginner or for piping butter icing in bold designs. However, for more intricate piping, particularly if using several icing colours and nozzles, home-made greaseproof paper or baking parchment piping bags are more practical and flexible to handle. Make up several ahead of time, following the instructions given here, then fit them with straight-sided nozzles. Do not use nozzles with ridges as they do not have such a tight fit in the bag. To prevent the icing drying out when working with several bags, cover the nozzle ends with a damp cloth when not in use.

2 ▶ With the point of the triangle facing away from you, hold the triangle with your thumb in the middle of the longest edge. Take the left corner and bring it over to meet the point of the triangle, as shown.

3 ▼ Hold in position and bring the remaining corner round and back over to meet the other two points, forming a cone shape. Holding all the points together, position them to make the cone tight and the point of it sharp, as shown.

1 ▲ Cut out a 25 cm/10 inch square of greaseproof paper or baking parchment. Fold it in half diagonally to make a triangle.

4 ▲ With the cone open, turn the points neatly inside the top edge, creasing firmly down. Secure the cone with a staple.

5 For using with a nozzle, cut off the pointed end of the bag and position the nozzle so it fits snugly into the point. Half-fill the bag with icing and fold over the top to seal. To use without a nozzle, add the icing, seal, then cut a small straight piece off the end of the bag to pipe lines.

6 For ease and control, it is important to hold the bag in a relaxed position. You may find it easier to hold it with one or both hands. For one hand, hold the bag between your middle and index fingers and push out the icing with your thumb.

7 ▲ If using both hands, simply wrap the other hand around the bag in the same manner, so both thumbs can push the icing out.

8 ▲ To pipe, hold the bag so the nozzle is directly over the area you want to pipe on. The bag will be held straight or at an angle, depending on the shape you are piping. Gently press down with your thumb on the top of the bag to release the icing, and lift your thumb to stop the flow of icing. Use a small palette knife to cut off any excess icing from the tip of the nozzle as you lift the bag from each piped shape, to keep the shapes neat.

Royal icing is the perfect icing for piping. This cake shows how you can achieve pretty effects with shells, stars, lines and beads. Piped roses in full bloom complement the colour chosen for the top of the cake, and the petal tips have been highlighted with food colouring. Carry the design on to the cake board for a classic celebratory cake.

Piping Shapes

Royal icing gives cakes a professional finish, and is often used in decorating to give a formal and ornate character to a cake. However, simple piping skills can easily be achieved given a little practice. This section shows you how, with just a few piping nozzles, you can enhance the look of your cakes. Remember that the icing must be of the correct consistency – not too firm or it will be difficult to squeeze out of the piping bag, and not too soft or the piping will not hold its shape. Small nozzles are used for the delicate designs made with royal icing. Larger ones are more suitable for butter icing and frostings.

Stars, swirls and scrolls

PIPING TWISTED ROPES AND LEAVES

For the ropes, fit nozzles Nos 43 or 44, or a writing nozzle, into a greaseproof paper piping bag and half-fill with icing. Hold the bag at a slight angle and pipe in a continuous line with even pressure, twisting the bag as you pipe. For leaves, you can use a No 18 petal nozzle or simply cut off the point of the bag in the shape of an arrow. Place the tip of the bag on the cake, holding the bag at a slight angle. Pipe out the icing, then pull away quickly to make the tapering end of a leaf.

Twisted ropes and leaves

PIPING STARS

For a simple star shape, choose a star-shaped nozzle in a size to suit your design. Hold the piping bag upright directly over the area to be iced. Gently squeeze the bag to release the icing and to form a star. Pull off quickly and sharply, keeping the bag straight, to give a neat point to the star.

PIPING SWIRLS

Choose a star-shaped nozzle in a size to suit your design. Hold the piping bag directly over the area to be iced. Pipe a swirl in a circular movement, then pull off quickly and sharply, keeping the bag straight to leave a neat point.

PIPING SCROLLS

Choose star or rope nozzles in a size to suit your design. Hold the piping bag at a slight angle and place the tip of the nozzle on the cake. Pipe the icing lightly upwards and outwards, then come down in a circular movement, tailing off the icing so the end rests on the cake to make a scroll. The action is a little like piping a large 'comma'. For a reverse scroll, repeat as before, but pipe in the opposite direction, going inwards to reverse the shape. A scroll border can be particularly effective if you alternate two colours of icing.

PIPING CORNELLI

Cornelli is a fun technique which can be carried out in one or more colours. It is a little like doodling. Use writing nozzles Nos 1 or 2 and pipe a continuous flow of icing, squiggling the lines in the shape of W's and M's.

PIPING SIMPLE EMBROIDERY

Piped embroidery is very fine work, requiring writing nozzles Nos 0 or 1. Keep the design simple and work in one or several colours. Pipe little circles, lines and dots to make a delicate pattern for your cake. Look at textile embroidery designs for some ideas.

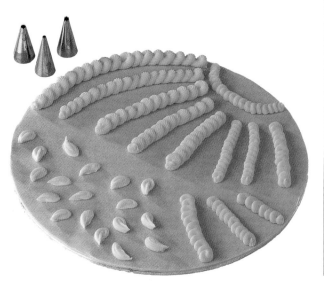

Cornelli and simple embroidery

PIPING DOTS OR BEADS

Use writing nozzles Nos 1, 2 or 3. Hold the piping bag directly over the area you wish to pipe. Press out the icing so it forms a bead, then release the pressure on the bag and take it off gently to one side. The smaller size nozzle will make simple dots. Neither dots nor beads should end in a sharp point. If this happens, lightly press any sharp points back into the bead with a small damp brush, or try making the icing a little softer.

PIPING SHELLS

Use star nozzles Nos 5 or 8. Rest the tip of the nozzle on the cake and pipe out a little icing to secure it to the surface. Gently squeeze out the icing while lifting the bag slightly up and then down, ending with the nozzle back on the surface of the cake. Pull off to release the icing. Repeat, allowing the beginning of the next shell to touch the end of the first one and continue in this way until you have completed a continuous line of shells.

PIPING LINES

Use a writing nozzle, remembering that the smaller the hole, the finer the line. Hold the bag at an angle, rest the nozzle on the cake and pipe out a little icing to secure it to the surface. Pipe the icing, lifting the bag slightly as you work, so it is just above the surface of the cake. Continue to pipe, allowing the line of piping to fall in a straight line. Do not pull or the line will break. At the end of the line, release the pressure, rest the nozzle on the surface of the cake and pull off to break the icing. The line can be varied by curving or looping it.

PIPING TRELLISES

To pipe trellises, use the same technique as above to pipe a set of parallel lines. Then overpipe a set in the opposite direction for squares, or horizontally across the lines for diamonds. You can also get different effects by using different widths of writing nozzles.

PIPING ZIGZAGS

Use a No 2 or 3 writing nozzle and pipe either one continuous zigzag, or stop and start at the end of each point to make them sharper.

Dots and beads

Lines, trellises and zigzags

Shells

Piped Sugar Pieces

These little piped sugar pieces are very fragile and have the appearance of fine lace. They must be made ahead of time, and left to dry. The sugar pieces need to be handled carefully, and it is a good idea to make plenty in case of breakages.

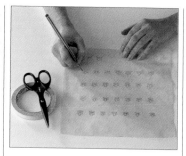

1 ▲ On a piece of greaseproof paper, draw your chosen design several times with pencil. The designs should be kept fairly small.

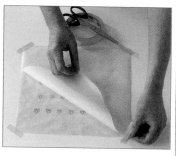

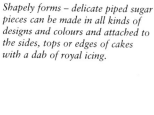

2 ▲ Tape the paper to the work surface or a flat board and secure a piece of greaseproof paper or baking parchment over the top. Tape the paper down at the corners with masking tape.

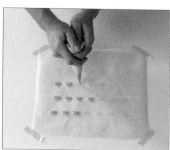

3 ▲ Fit a piping bag with a No 1 writing nozzle. Half-fill with royal icing, and fold over the top to seal. Pipe over each design, carefully following the pencilled lines with a continuous thread of icing. Repeat, piping as many pieces as you need plus a few extra in case of any breakages.

4 Leave to dry for at least two hours. Remove from the paper by carefully turning it back and lifting off each piece with a palette knife. When dry, store in a box between layers of tissue paper.

Shapely forms – delicate piped sugar pieces can be made in all kinds of designs and colours and attached to the sides, tops or edges of cakes with a dab of royal icing.

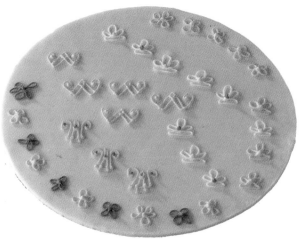

Simple Piped Flowers

To make these pretty piped flowers, you will need a petal nozzle – either small, medium or large depending on how big you want the flowers to be – a paper piping bag, a cocktail stick and a flower nail. Make the flowers ahead of time and, when dry, store in a box between layers of tissue paper.

ROSE

1 For a tightly formed rose, make a fairly firm icing. Colour the icing, or leave it white. Fit the petal nozzle into a paper piping bag, half-fill with royal icing and fold over the top to seal.

2 Hold the piping bag so the wider end of the nozzle is pointing into what will be the base of the flower, and hold a cocktail stick in the other hand. Pipe a small cone shape around the tip of a cocktail stick. Pipe a petal half way around the cone, lifting it so it is at an angle and curling outwards, not flat, and turning the cocktail stick at the same time.

3 ▲ Repeat with more petals so they overlap each other slightly. The last petals can lie flatter and be more open. Remove the rose from the cocktail stick by threading the stick through a large hole on a grater. The rose will rest on the grater. Leave until dry and firm.

PANSY

1 Colour the icing. Fit the petal nozzle into a paper piping bag, half-fill with royal icing and fold over the top to seal. Cut out a small square of greaseproof paper and secure to the flower nail with a little icing.

2 ▲ Holding the nozzle flat, pipe the petal shape in a curve, turning the flower nail at the same time. Pipe five petals in all. Pipe beads of yellow icing in the centre with a small writing nozzle, or use stamens.

3 Remove the paper from the flower nail, but leave the pansy on the paper until it is dry and firm. Coloured details can be added by painting with food colouring, or using food colouring pens, once the flower has dried. Lift the pansy from the paper by carefully slipping a palette knife underneath the base of the flower.

COLOURED SUMMER FLOWERS

1 Colour the icing. Make up the flowers in a variety of shades for a colourful arrangement. Fit the petal nozzle into a paper piping bag, half-fill with royal icing and fold over the top to seal. Cut out a small square of greaseproof paper and secure to the flower nail with a little icing.

2 ▲ Pipe five flat petals in a circle so they slightly overlap each other. Pipe beads of yellow icing in the centre of each flower or sprinkle with hundreds and thousands. Leave to dry and add coloured details as for the pansy.

Bouquet of iced blossoms, including roses, pansies and bright summer flowers – arrangements of piped flowers make colourful cake decorations.

Run-outs

Designs for run-outs can be as complicated or as simple as you like. It is best to start off with a fairly solid shape for your first attempt, as these decorations can be quite fragile to handle. Always make a few more run-outs than you think you will need in case of breakages.

1 Make up the royal icings to the correct consistencies: a stiffer one for the outline, and a softer one for filling in (see the basic recipe for Royal Icing). Leave the icing to stand, preferably overnight, to allow any air bubbles to come to the surface. Stir the icing before using. On a piece of greaseproof paper, draw your chosen design several times.

2 ▲ Tape the paper to the work surface or a flat board and lay a piece of baking parchment over the top. Tape the paper down at the corners with masking tape.

3 ▲ Fit a paper piping bag with a No 1 writing nozzle, and half-fill with the stiffer icing for piping the outline. Carefully pipe over the outline of your design with a continuous thread of icing.

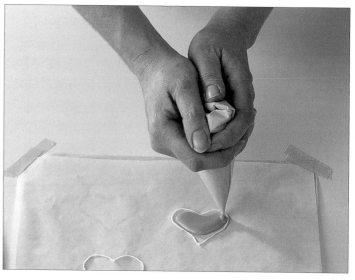

4 ▲ Add the softer icing for filling in into a second paper piping bag. Cut the pointed end off the bag in a straight line. Do not make it too big, or the icing will flow out too quickly. Pipe the icing into the outlines to fill, working from the outline into the centre, being careful not to touch the outline or it may break. To prevent air bubbles forming, keep the end of the bag in the icing. The icing should look overfilled and rounded, as it will shrink slightly as it dries.

5 ▲ You now need to work quickly while the icing is still soft. Move a paintbrush carefully through the icing to fill in any gaps and to ensure it goes right to the edge of the outline, keeping the icing smooth. If any air bubbles do appear, smooth them out with the brush or burst with a pin.

6 ▲ Leave the run-outs on the paper to dry; the drying time will vary depending on their size, but leave for at least one day and preferably longer. When completely dry, remove by carefully slipping a palette knife under the shapes and easing them off the paper. Decorative details can then be piped on to the dried run-outs. Allow these to dry before using or storing.

7 Store the run-outs in a box between layers of greaseproof paper.

When royal icing is presented in bright colours it takes on a lively new look. The hearts and brilliant butterflies are made using the run-out technique. The wings are made separately, then joined with a line of piping to form the body of each butterfly. This also secures them to the cake. Piped sugar pieces, scroll borders and polka dots complete the design.

$\mathscr{D}$ecorating with Sugarpaste Icing

As a covering, sugarpaste icing gives a softer look to a cake than royal icing. It is much quicker to work with, requiring only one rolled out layer. This is then placed in position so it curves itself over the edges of the cake. Because it is so pliable, sugarpaste can also be used for a wide range of decorative effects. When making sugarpaste decorations, always wrap any icing you are not using immediately in clear film to stop it drying out.

Marbling

As an alternative to covering a cake in a single colour, sugarpaste icing can be marbled for a multi-coloured effect. Use several colours and keep them quite vibrant, or use one or two delicate tones. Marbled sugarpaste icing can also be used to make effective moulded flowers and other modelled decorations.

3 ▲ On a work surface lightly sprinkled with icing sugar, roll out the sugarpaste icing to reveal the marbled effect.

5 ▲ Twist the colours together and knead for several seconds until the strips of colour are fused together but retain their individual colours.

1 ▲ Form the sugarpaste icing into a smooth roll or ball. Dip the end of a cocktail stick into the food colouring and dab a few drops on to the icing. Repeat with more colours if wished.

4 ▲ Alternatively, for a very bold interweaving of colours, use the following technique. Divide the sugarpaste icing into three or four equal portions, depending on how many colours you want to use. Colour them with food colouring. Divide each colour into four or five portions and roll out with your hands into sausage shapes. If you like, you could even put two colours together to make an instant marbled sausage. Place the different-coloured sausages side-by-side on the work surface.

6 ▲ Roll out the marbled icing on a work surface lightly dusted with icing sugar.

2 ▲ Knead the sugarpaste icing just a few times. The colouring should look very patchy.

Crimping

Crimping tools are similar to large tweezers with patterned ends and are available in a good variety of styles. Crimping is a very quick and efficient way of giving decorative edges and borders to sugarpaste-coated cakes – the effect is similar to the embroidery technique of smocking. For a simple finish to the crimped cake, top with a small posy of edible flowers, a ribbon, or other bought decorations.

1 ▲ Cover the cake with sugarpaste icing. For crimping, the icing must still be soft, so do not allow it to dry out before decorating. Dip the crimping tool in a little cornflour.

2 ▼ Position the crimping tool on the cake in the place you wish to start the design and squeeze the teeth together to make the pattern.

3 ▲ Slowly release the crimper so as not to tear the icing. Repeat the pattern, either touching the last one or spacing them evenly apart. The pattern can be varied by using different crimping tools.

4 ▲ The same technique can be used to crimp decorative designs down the sides of a cake. If applying sugarpaste frills to a cake, crimp the edges for a neat and pretty finish.

Embossing

Special embossing tools can be purchased from cake icing specialists, but you can also use any other patterned items such as cookie stamps, cutters or icing nozzles.

1 ▲ Cover the cake with sugarpaste icing. For embossing, the icing must still be soft, so do not allow it to dry out. Brush a little cornflour on to the embossing tool and press firmly on to the soft icing. Repeat, brushing with cornflour each time.

2 ▲ To add colour, brush a little powdered food colouring on to the embossing tool instead of the cornflour and press on to the icing as before. Highlights can also be added with food colouring pens, as shown.

3 ▲ Textured rolling pins are also available from cake icing specialists. Cover the cake with sugarpaste icing as before and smooth over with your hand. Roll over the surface of the icing with the textured rolling pin. This rolling pin gives a basketweave effect.

Modelling

Sugarpaste is wonderfully adaptable, and can be used to model almost any shape you can think of. Choose small objects, such as flowers, fruits, vegetables, animals, or whatever is going to suit your cake. Using this technique, every cake you make will be unique. Remember to dust the work surface lightly with icing sugar before you start, to prevent sticking. Leave the modelled shapes to dry on greaseproof paper, before applying to the cake.

SMART TEDDY BEAR

▲ Mould each part of the bear's body separately in cream-coloured sugarpaste icing. Roll out the waistcoat to fit the body and cut out the bow tie in purple icing. Mould the buttons and eyes in black icing. Attach the head to the body with a little water, pressing together to secure. Brush the body lightly with water and wrap the waistcoat round, folding back the top two corners. Attach the arms, legs and ears with a little water, pressing to secure, then bend into shape. Attach the bow tie, buttons and eyes with a little water, then paint on any details such as nose and mouth with brown food colouring.

FROSTY SNOWMAN

▲ Mould the snowman's body, head and arms in white sugarpaste icing. Roll out the scarf in red icing, cutting the ends with a sharp knife to represent the tassels. Shape two small balls of blue icing for the eyes, one of red for the nose and two of black for buttons. Using black icing, shape the hat in two pieces, as shown. Attach the head to the body with a little water, then the arms, pressing lightly to secure. Attach the scarf, eyes, nose, buttons and hat in the same way.

HUNGRY RABBIT

▼ Mould the rabbit's body and head, legs, tail and ears in light brown sugarpaste icing. Shape two small balls of blue icing for the eyes. Attach the tail, legs and ears to the rabbit's body with a little water, pressing lightly to secure. Paint the nose and details on the eyes with brown food colouring. For the carrots, shape long ovals out of orange icing, tapering at one end, then make markings on them with the back of a knife. Attach small pieces of green icing on to the ends.

CAT ON A MAT

▲ Mould and shape the cat's body, head, legs, tail and ears in grey marbled sugarpaste icing. Shape two small ovals in black for the eyes and a small pink ball for the nose. Roll out a piece of green icing for the mat. Attach the head to the body with a little water, then the legs, tail, ears, eyes and nose, pressing lightly to secure and bending into shape where necessary. Press four short lengths of florist's wire into the head to represent whiskers (these must be removed before serving the cake). Paint the mouth with black food colouring and place the cat on the mat.

Let your imagination run riot when it comes to using sugarpaste icing. All the inhabitants of this water-lily pond are moulded or cut out of sugarpaste. The water lilies are formed with a small petal-shaped cocktail cutter, then bent into shape. The lily pads are formed with a small round cutter, and then snipped with a knife to make them more lifelike. A blossom cutter creates the flowers on the grassy bank, and the irises, bulrushes, frog and goldfish are modelled by hand.

Cut-out Shapes

Cut-out Borders

Using a variety of shaped cutters, sugarpaste icing can be stamped out to make all kinds of colourful shapes for decorating cakes.

1 Colour the sugarpaste icing to the desired shade, then roll out evenly on a work surface lightly dusted with icing sugar.

2 ▲ Dip the ends of the cutter in icing sugar and cut out the shapes. Leave to dry flat on greaseproof paper, then attach the shapes to the cake with a little royal icing.

The sky's the limit – use cutters or make your own templates for creating a variety of cut-out images.

Borders on the cutting edge – cut-out shapes can also be positioned around the edge of a cake to add a decorative border. Make the borders in bold or delicate designs so that they fit the character of the cake.

1 ▲ Roll out the sugarpaste icing thinly and cut out with a medium-sized cutter – a round, fluted biscuit cutter has been used here. Leave whole or cut in half, depending on the shape.

2 ▲ Use smaller cutters to cut out inside shapes for a filigree effect, or make up your own shapes and use templates cut out of card.

3 Leave the shapes to dry flat on greaseproof paper, then attach them around the top edges of the cake with a little royal icing.

Plunger Blossoms

A special plunger blossom cutter, available in different sizes, is used to make these dainty flowers. The cutter contains a plunger for ejecting the delicate shapes once they have been cut out.

1 ▲ Roll out the icing thinly on a work surface lightly dusted with icing sugar. Dip the cutter in cornflour and cut out the flower shapes.

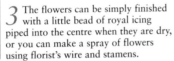

2 ▲ The flower should remain on the end of the cutter. To remove the flower, hold the cutter on a foam pad and depress the plunger. As it goes into the foam it will bend the flower into shape and release it.

3 The flowers can be simply finished with a little bead of royal icing piped into the centre when they are dry, or you can make a spray of flowers using florist's wire and stamens.

4 ▲ To make a spray, push a pin through the centre of each flower. Leave the flowers to dry on the foam.

5 ▲ When dry, pipe a little royal icing on to a stamen and thread it through the hole. This will hold it in position. Repeat with all the flowers.

6 ▲ When the individual flowers are completely dry, twist a piece of florist's wire on to the end of each stamen. Group the flowers and twist the wires together to make a spray.

This pretty Teddy Bear Christening cake is simply decorated with a modelled bear and delicate plunger blossoms.

Frills

Sugarpaste frills give a particularly elaborate finish to a cake and are especially appropriate for decorating wedding, christening and anniversary cakes. Try layering two different coloured frills together for a very special occasion.

1 ▲ Roll out the sugarpaste icing thinly on a work surface lightly dusted with icing sugar. Use a special frill cutter to cut out the rings for the frills. One ring will make one large or two smaller frills.

2 ▲ Position the end of a wooden cocktail stick over about 5 mm/ ¼ inch of the outer edge of the ring. Roll the stick back and forth firmly around the edge with your finger. The edge will become thinner and start to frill. Continue in this way until the ring is completely frilled.

3 ▲ Using a sharp knife, cut through the ring once to open it up. Gently ease it open. For shorter frills, cut the ring in half to make two frills.

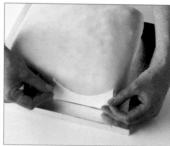

4 ▲ Cut out a template the size of the opened frill and hold against the side of a covered cake. Mark with a pin to show where to attach the frill, and repeat all around the cake.

5 ▲ To attach the frill, either pipe a line of royal icing on to the cake or brush a line of water. Carefully secure the frill on to the line of royal icing or water. Overlay with a second frill in the same or a different coloured icing if wished. Repeat around the cake. The top edge of each frill can be decorated with piping or with a crimping tool.

Tip

If you do not have a special frill cutter you can use individual pastry cutters instead. Use a 7.5–10 cm/ 3–4 inch plain or fluted cutter to cut out the outer circle and a 4–5 cm/ 1½–2 inch plain cutter to cut out the inner circle.

Design Variations

1 ▲ Looped frills look very pretty attached to the cake 'upside-down' as shown here. They are made and attached in the same way as described for looped frills, except that you need to cut out a larger hole from the middle of the ring to make the frills thinner. They will drape more effectively this way.

2 ▲ Frills look equally attractive applied diagonally to the cake sides at regular intervals. They are made and attached to the cake in exactly the same way as described for looped frills, although each ring will probably be large enough to make two frills.

Plaques

A plaque can simply be a plain cut-out shape, or it can be more decorative with, for example, a frilled edge and delicate piping work. Use a plaque as a focal point on a cake to dedicate it to someone special, for weddings, christenings, anniversaries and birthdays, or as a base on which to paint a picture with food colourings.

2 ▲ Using royal or glacé icing, pipe on a decoration or name. Alternatively, write or draw on the plaque with a food colouring pen, or with food colourings and a fine paintbrush.

3 ▲ For a frilled plaque, cut out the shape as described above. While the icing is still soft, position the end of a wooden cocktail stick over about 5 mm/¼ inch of the outer edge of the plaque. Roll the stick back and forth firmly around the edge with your finger. The edge will become thinner and start to frill. Continue until the edge of the plaque is completely frilled.

1 ▲ For a plain plaque, roll out the sugarpaste thinly on a work surface lightly dusted with icing sugar. Dip a cutter (round, oval, heart-shaped or fluted) in a little cornflour. Cut out the shape and leave it to dry flat on greaseproof paper.

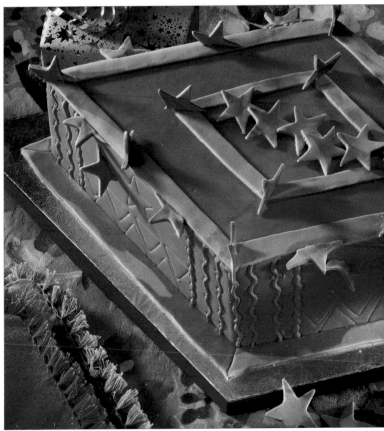

Endlessly versatile, sugarpaste icing can be embossed, crimped, cut out and marbled, techniques which are all displayed on this unusual diamond-shaped cake. Small cutters have been used for the embossed pattern on the sides, and different crimping tools for the designs at the corners. 'Paprika' food colouring has been used for the sugarpaste covering for a contemporary terracotta shade, and the trimmings have been marbled with a little blue icing both for the unusual cut-out edging and the star decorations.

Decorating with Marzipan

Marzipan can be a decorative icing in its own right, or it can provide a firm undercoat for a royal icing or sugarpaste icing covering. It is extremely pliable, and the white variety in particular takes colour well.

Marzipan can be moulded and shaped, crimped and embossed, and cut out or modelled into all kinds of animal shapes, figures, flowers, fruits, and even edible Christmas decorations, to name just a few possibilities.

Embossing

A 'pattern in relief' can be created on cakes by using special embossing tools, or any piece of kitchen equipment that will leave a patterned indentation on the marzipan. To make the embossed picture more interesting, paint on highlights with food colouring.

1 Cover the cake with marzipan, then emboss straight away before the icing dries. Dust the embossing tool with a little cornflour, press firmly into the marzipan, then lift off carefully to reveal the pattern. Alternatively, for a coloured design, brush a little powdered food colouring on to the embossing tool instead of the cornflour and press on to the marzipan as before.

2 ▼ Paint on coloured highlights with food colouring, if you wish.

Very simple versions of crimping and embossing have been applied to the marzipan top of this Simnel cake. The edges are crimped – or fluted – with the fingers and the top is embossed using the back of the fork.

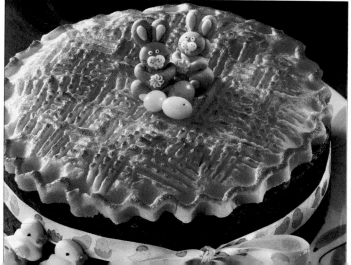

Crimping

As with sugarpaste icing, marzipan can be crimped to give simple, pretty edgings and patterns to cakes.

1 Cover a cake with marzipan, but do not allow to dry out. To prevent the crimping tool from sticking, dip it in a little cornflour.

2 Place the crimping tool on the edge of the cake where it is to be decorated and then squeeze the teeth together to make the design. Slowly release the crimping tool, being careful not to let it open quickly or it will tear the marzipan.

3 ▲ Re-position the crimper and repeat to complete the design. You can decorate both the top and base edges of the cake, or the whole side of the cake, if you wish. The crimping tool can also be used to make a pattern on top of the cake.

Marzipan Cut-outs

Small flower and other shaped cutters can be purchased from cake icing specialists for cutting out marzipan shapes. Aspic, cocktail or biscuit cutters can also be used. Once you have cut out the basic shapes, you can decorate them with different coloured marzipan trims, small sweets or piping. Here are some ideas for cut-out marzipan flowers.

COLOURFUL BLOSSOMS

▲ Colour the marzipan to the desired shades. Roll out evenly on a work surface lightly dusted with icing sugar. Dip the ends of a leaf cutter or a small round cutter in icing sugar, and cut out five petals for each flower. Overlap the petals in a circle, securing with a little water. Shape small balls of yellow or orange marzipan and place one in the centre of each flower.

FRILLY BLOSSOMS AND LEAVES

▲ Colour and roll out the marzipan as for the Colourful Blossoms. For each flower, cut out two circles using two fluted cutters, one slightly smaller than the other. (The sizes will depend on the size of flower you are making.) To frill the edges, position the end of a wooden cocktail stick over 3 mm/1/8 inch of the outer edge of each circle. Roll the stick firmly back and forth around the edges with your finger so the edges become thinner and begin to frill. Continue until the circles are completely frilled.

Place the smaller frill on top of the larger, and lightly press together to secure. Take a small ball of the deeper shade of marzipan and press through a fine sieve. Cut off the marzipan which has been pushed through the sieve and place in the centre of the flower.

Cut out leaves from green marzipan with a leaf cutter. Bend the leaves slightly to make them look more lifelike. Larger leaves can be left to bend over the handle of a wooden spoon until firm.

VIOLETS

▲ Colour the marzipan purple and roll out as for the Colourful Blossoms. Cut out each flower with a four-petal cocktail cutter. With a little yellow marzipan, shape small balls and then position in the centre of each flower.

Creative cut-outs – marzipan can be used in unusual ways to make imaginative shapes and borders.

Modelling

Marzipan is a wonderful icing to use for modelling. Work with either coloured marzipan, or use white and highlight it with colour after shaping. If colouring your own marzipan, tint it to the required shade, then paint on extra tones and details when the model is assembled to make the objects more life-like. Here are just a few suggestions for shaping fruits and vegetables.

RED-HOT CHILLI PEPPERS

▲ Colour equal portions of marzipan red and green. Mould the chilli shapes, tapering them to a point towards the ends. Shape the stems from green marzipan and attach to the chillies, pressing together lightly to secure.

BUNCH OF GRAPES

▲ Colour the marzipan purple. Shape a cone for the main body of the grape bunch, then mould small individual balls for the grapes. Mould the stem, using a little brown marzipan. Arrange the grapes until the cone is completely covered. Use a little water if necessary to make them stick and press lightly to secure. Make a small indentation in the top of the cone and press in the stem to secure.

RIPE BANANAS

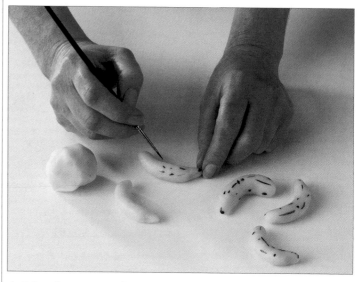

▲ Colour the marzipan yellow or use yellow marzipan. Mould and bend small pieces of the icing into the shapes of bananas. Paint on highlights with brown food colouring.

ROSY APPLES

▲ Colour the marzipan green for the apples and brown for the stems. Shape the green marzipan into rounds and make an indent at one end with a modelling tool. Shape small pieces of brown icing for the stems. Paint a rosy bloom on the apples with red food colouring and press the stems into the indents.

More familiar as an undercoat for a cake, marzipan should not be neglected as a decoration in itself. It takes colour well, and when used to coat this light fruit ring cake, it should certainly not be covered up. Marzipan's plasticity also makes it ideal for moulding flowers, such as this colourful collection of roses, and for twisting into ropes to make a colourful edging.

Plaiting and Weaving

Use these techniques with marzipan to make colourful edgings and decorations for cakes.

CANDY-STRIPE ROPE

1 Take two pieces of different coloured marzipan. On a work surface lightly dusted with icing sugar, roll out two or three ropes of even length and width with your fingers.

2 ▲ Pinch the ends together at the top, then twist into a rope. Pinch the other ends to seal neatly.

PLAIT

1 Take three pieces of different coloured marzipan. On a work surface lightly dusted with icing sugar, roll out three ropes of even length and width with your fingers.

2 ▲ Pinch the ends together at the top, then plait the ropes neatly and pinch the other ends to seal neatly.

MARZIPAN TWIST

1 Colour the marzipan (working with one or two colours). On a work surface lightly dusted with icing sugar, roll out each piece of marzipan to a 5 mm/¼ inch thickness, then cut each piece into 1 cm/½ inch wide strips.

2 ▲ Take two different coloured strips and pinch the ends together at the top. Twist the strips together, joining on more strips with water, if needed.

BASKET-WEAVE

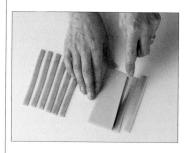

1 ▲ On a work surface lightly dusted with icing sugar, roll out a piece of marzipan (or work with two colours and roll out each one separately) to a 5 mm/¼ inch thickness. Cut into 5 mm/¼ inch wide strips.

2 ◄ Arrange the strips, evenly spaced, in parallel lines, then weave the strips in and out. Alternate the colours if using two, as shown. This decoration looks stunning on top of a cake. The edges can be trimmed to fit the shape of the cake.

Marzipan Roses

Not only do these roses smell sweet, they taste good too. Though they may look difficult to make, marzipan roses are quite simple to mould. For a formally decorated cake, shape the roses in a variety of colours and sizes, then arrange flamboyantly on top.

1 ▲ Take a small ball of coloured marzipan and form it into a cone shape. This forms the central core which supports the petals.

2 ▲ To make each petal, take a small piece of marzipan about the size of a large pea, and work it with your fingers to a petal shape which is slightly thicker at the base. If the marzipan sticks, dust your fingers in icing sugar or cornflour.

3 ▲ Wrap the petal around the cone as shown. Press the petal to the cone to secure. Bend the ends of the petal back slightly, to curl.

4 ▲ Mould the next petal in the same way and attach as before, so it just overlaps the first one. Curl the ends back slightly. Repeat with several more petals, making them slightly bigger until you have the size of rose you want. Overlap each petal and curl the ends back as before. Make sure all the petals are securely attached, then cut off the base of the cone. This provides a flat surface so the rose will stand on the cake.

5 For rosebuds, make just a few smaller petals and do not curl the ends back.

6 To add more detail to the rose, paint tints on to the petals using a paintbrush and food colouring. Leave to stand on greaseproof paper until firm.

Blooming roses – moulded roses can add glamour to any cake.

ecorating with Butter Icing

Butter icing is very quick to make up and is easy to use for quick and simple decorations. It can be used to sandwich cakes together, or to coat the top and sides with a thick, creamy layer of icing. To make your butter-iced cakes a little more individual, texture the icing on the tops or sides – or both if you wish. To finish, you can pipe the icing in swirls.

Cake Sides

For decorating cake sides, all you need is a plain or serrated scraper, depending on whether you want a smooth or a textured finish to the icing. If you have an icing turntable, it will make icing cake sides a much simpler task, but it is not essential.

Here a chocolate-flavoured and green-coloured butter icing have been realistically swirled to imitate tree bark and leaves in this delightful novelty cake idea.

1 ▲ Secure the cake to a cake board with a little icing. Cover the top and sides of the cake with icing and put it on an icing turntable. Using a plain or serrated scraper, hold it with one hand firmly against the side of the cake at a slight angle.

2 ▲ Turn the turntable round in a steady continuous motion and in one direction with the other hand, while pulling the scraper smoothly in the opposite direction to give a smooth or serrated surface to the iced sides. When you have completed the full turn, stop the turntable and carefully lift off the scraper to leave a neat join. Trim off any excess icing from the top edge and the cake board.

Cake Tops

More intricate patterns can be made on the tops of cakes with a few simple tools. Use a small palette knife, a plain or serrated scraper or a fork to give a silky smooth finish to the cake, or to make a variety of patterned ridges or some deep, generous swirls.

SWIRLS

1 ▲ Spread the icing smoothly over the top of the cake, then work over the icing with the tip of a palette knife from side to side to create a series of swirled grooves.

2 For a more formal appearance, draw the tip of a palette knife through the swirled grooves in evenly spaced lines.

2 ▲ Pull out lines with the tip of the knife, radiating out from a central point to the edge of the cake.

RIDGED SPIRAL

1 Spread the icing smoothly over the top of the cake, then place the cake on a turntable.

2 ▲ Hold a serrated scraper at a slight angle, pointing it towards the centre of the cake. Rotate the cake with your other hand, while moving the scraper sideways to make undulations and a ridged spiral pattern.

FEATHERED SPIRAL

1 Spread the icing smoothly over the top of the cake and place the cake on a turntable. Rotate the turntable slowly, drawing the flat tip of a palette knife in a continuous curved line, starting from the edge of the cake and working in a spiral into the centre.

RIDGED SQUARES

1 Spread the icing smoothly over the top of the cake. Pull a fork across the cake four or five times, depending on the size of the cake, to produce groupings of evenly spaced lines.

2 ▲ Pull the fork across the cake four or five times as before, but at right angles to the first lines, to give a series of large squares.

DIAMONDS

1 Spread the icing smoothly over the top of the cake. Then lightly dredge with cocoa powder, if using white or lightly tinted butter icing, or icing sugar if using chocolate icing.

2 ▲ Draw a series of lines with the flat side of a knife to expose the butter icing and to make a diamond pattern over the top.

Piping with Butter Icing

The butter icing needs to be of the correct consistency for piping. To check, dip a palette knife and then lift out – the icing should form a sharp point. If too stiff, the icing will be difficult to pipe, if too soft, it will not hold its shape. Add a little extra milk or fruit juice if the consistency is too stiff, or more icing sugar if it is too thin.

DRAMATIC TOUCHES

Piping butter icing in bold, swirling designs with large nozzles can produce dramatic effects.

1 ▲ Cover the top of the cake with a smooth, thin layer of butter icing and smooth the sides with a plain scraper. Using a No 13 plain piping nozzle fitted in a material piping bag, pipe large overlapping spirals to cover the top of the cake. For each spiral, start in the centre and work outwards, until they are the required size.

2 ▼ Pipe large beads of icing around the edges of the cake, using a large writing nozzle. Lightly sprinkle the spirals with either a little sifted cocoa or icing sugar, depending on the colour of the butter icing.

DAINTY DESIGNS

For a more delicate effect, use small nozzles to pipe shapes such as dots and beads, stars or scrolls, as demonstrated for royal icing.

1 Cover the top of the cake with a smooth, thin layer of butter icing. Make a ridged pattern with a serrated scraper around the sides of the cake and a swirled spiral with a palette knife over the top.

2 Using a writing nozzle fitted in a paper piping bag, pipe loops and beads of icing in a contrasting colour.

3 ▲ Pipe beads of icing at the ends of each loop in the same colour as used to cover the cake.

BASKET-WEAVE DESIGN

Butter icing can be piped very effectively with a ribbon nozzle to make a basket-weave design. You can use different colours for the vertical and horizontal lines.

1 Fit a ribbon nozzle into a paper piping bag. Add the icing and fold over the top of the bag to secure. Pipe a vertical line the length of the area you wish to cover with basket weave.

2 Pipe 2 cm/$^3/_4$ inch horizontal lines over the vertical line (slightly longer each side than the width of the vertical line) at 1 cm/$^3/_8$ inch intervals.

3 ▲ Pipe another vertical line so that it just covers one end of all the horizontal lines.

4 ▲ Fill in the spaces between the horizontal lines with an alternating row of horizontal lines to make the basket-weave design. Repeat until the area you wish to cover is completed.

Few can resist the glossy smoothness of butter icing. If you add flavouring and food colouring, the colour of the icing should reflect the taste, as with this tangy lemon-iced cake. Use a serrated scraper to create ridges in the icing on the sides and a palette knife to make the swirled and feathered effect on the top of the cake. Finish off with generous swirls of piped white butter icing.

Decorating with Glacé Icing

Using white and coloured glacé icing, simple but effective patterns can be created for decorating sponges, Madeira cakes or Swiss rolls. To vary the ideas shown here using one colour of icing, make up two colours of icing and pipe them alternately. Glacé icing sets quickly but needs to be very soft to create the following designs, so make a batch just before you want to decorate the cake and work quickly before it hardens.

Cobweb, Feather and Fan Icing

Cobweb, feather and fan effects are created using the same basic technique. For the cobweb, the coloured lines are piped in circles. For the fan, the colour is applied in straight lines and the skewer is pulled across in radiating lines. For feather icing the skewer is pulled at right angles through them.

COBWEB ICING

1 Make the glacé icing, colour a portion and put in a paper piping bag, as for feather icing. Coat the top of the cake evenly with the remaining white icing.

2 ▲ Work quickly before the icing has a chance to set. Pipe evenly spaced circles on top of the icing, starting from the centre of the cake and moving towards the edge.

3 ▲ Using a skewer, pull it in straight lines from the edge of the cake to the centre so that it is evenly divided into four sections.

4 ▲ Working from the centre of the cake to the edge, pull the skewer between the four lines to divide the cake evenly into eight. Leave to set.

For an effective Spider's web cake, use the cobweb icing technique. First cover the cake with yellow glacé icing. Pipe a continuous spiral of black glacé icing, then draw a skewer down from the top at regular intervals.

FEATHER ICING

1 Make the glacé icing (see Basic Icing Recipes). Put 2 tbsp of the icing in a small bowl and colour with a little food colouring.

2 Fit a paper piping bag with a No 2 writing nozzle, then spoon in the coloured icing and fold over the top of the bag to secure.

3 ▼ Coat the top of the cake evenly with the remaining white icing. Working quickly so the icing does not set, pipe the coloured icing in straight lines across the cake. You may find it easier to work from the centre outwards when doing this.

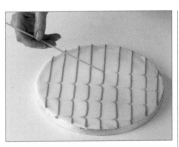

4 ▲ Using a skewer, pull it at right angles through the coloured lines in one direction, leaving an even spacing between the lines.

5 ▲ Working in the space between the lines, pull the skewer in the opposite direction, to give a feather pattern. Leave to set.

FAN ICING

1 Make the glacé icing, colour a portion and put in a paper piping bag. Ice the top of the cake as for the Feather and Cobweb techniques.

2 Working quickly so the icing does not set, pipe the coloured icing in evenly spaced straight lines across the cake. You may find it easier to work from the centre outwards.

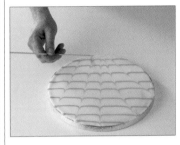

3 ▲ Using a skewer, pull it through the coloured lines, starting from a point at one edge of the cake and radiating the lines out from it.

4 ▲ Working in the space between the lines, pull the skewer through the piped lines in the opposite direction to give a fan pattern. Leave to set.

Squiggle Icing

Marbling Flowers and Leaves

Here a random patterning of icing, similar to cornelli (see Decorating with Royal Icing), is lightly feathered or marbled. The technique is shown here using white icing on a chocolate-tinted background, but would be equally effective using one or two colours on a white icing background.

1 Make the glacé icing. Put 2 tbsp of the icing into a paper piping bag fitted with a No 2 writing nozzle, and colour the rest with cocoa mixed with a little water. Coat the top of the cake evenly with the chocolate icing.

2 ▲ Working quickly before the icing has a chance to set, pipe haphazard squiggles all over the top of the cake in a continuous line.

3 ▼ Using a cocktail stick, pull it through the lines in short, swirling movements and in different directions, to create a random feathered effect.

The feathering technique can also be used to give a marbled effect to piped decorations. The technique has been used here for a pretty flower and leaf design. The method is also effective for holly leaves, with the lines being pulled outwards to create the spiky points on the leaves.

1 Make the glacé icing, colour a small portion green and a portion red and put each in a paper piping bag fitted with a No 2 writing nozzle. Coat the top of the cake evenly with the remaining white icing.

2 ▲ Working quickly before the icing sets, pipe a floral design on to the cake, piping circles for flowers in the red icing, and ovals for leaves in the green icing.

3 ▲ To marble the flowers, pull a skewer through the lines from the outer edge almost to the middle. The number of petals will be determined by the number of lines you pull. Do the same for the leaves.

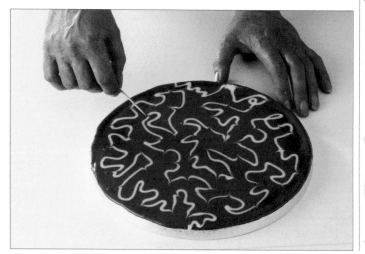

Tip

If the top of the cake is not perfectly flat for piping on, simply turn the cake upside down and use the flat base as the top.

Piping with Glacé Icing

All kinds of imaginative designs can be created, using the following method, to decorate the tops and edges of cakes.

This cake is covered with white glacé icing and the side is then coated with green-tinted desiccated coconut. The bold, exotic flowers are piped in red and green glacé icing and then marbled with a small cocktail stick, before the white or coloured icings have time to set, for a delicate finish.

1 Make the glacé icing, reserving a few tablespoons for piping. Coat the top of the cake evenly with the remaining icing (either white or coloured) and leave to set.

2 Divide the reserved icing into two equal portions and colour each in contrasting but complementary shades. Spoon the icings into two separate paper piping bags, each fitted with a No 2 writing nozzle. Use one colour to pipe geometric shapes or other simple designs over the icing.

3 ▲ Pipe a border around the edge of the cake with the other colour.

ecorating with Chocolate

Nothing adds a luxurious touch to a cake quite like chocolate, whether it is poured over to form a glossy icing, or piped, shaved, dipped or curled. There are several types of chocolate to choose from, and all should be used with care. Couverture is the best and used for professional chocolate work, but it is expensive and requires particularly careful handling. For the following techniques, good-quality baking or eating chocolate is suitable. Chocolate-flavoured cake covering is easy to use but is inferior both in taste and texture.

Chocolate decorations can look particularly interesting if different kinds of chocolate – dark, milk and white – are used in combination. White chocolate can be coloured, but make sure you use powdered food colouring for this as liquid colourings will thicken it. Store chocolate decorations in the refrigerator in a plastic container between layers of greaseproof paper until ready to use. Also, handle the decorations as little as possible with your fingers, as they will leave dull marks on the shiny surface of the chocolate.

Melting

For most of the decorations described in this section, the chocolate must be melted first.

1 ▼ Break the chocolate into small pieces and place in a bowl set over a pan of hot water. Do not allow the bowl to touch the water and do not let the water boil; the chocolate will spoil if overheated. Melt the chocolate slowly and stir occasionally. Be careful not to let water or steam near the chocolate or it will become too thick.

2 ▲ When the chocolate is completely melted, remove the pan from the heat and stir.

Coating Cakes

1 ▲ Stand the cake on a wire rack. It is a good idea to place a sheet of greaseproof paper or a baking sheet underneath the rack to catch any chocolate drips. Pour the chocolate icing over the cake quickly, in one smooth motion, to coat the top and sides.

2 Use a palette knife to smooth the chocolate over the sides, if necessary. Allow the chocolate to set, then coat with another layer, if wished.

Piping with Chocolate

Chocolate can be piped directly on to a cake, or it can be piped on to baking parchment to make run-outs, small outlined shapes or irregular designs. After melting the chocolate, allow it to cool slightly so it just coats the back of a spoon. If it still flows freely it will be too runny to hold its shape when piped. When it is the right consistency, you then need to work fast as the chocolate will set quickly.

CHOCOLATE OUTLINES

Pipe the chocolate in small, delicate shapes to use as elegant decorations on cakes. Or pipe random squiggles and loosely drizzle a contrasting chocolate over the top.

1 Melt 115 g/4 oz chocolate and allow to cool slightly. Tape a piece of baking parchment to a baking sheet or flat board.

2 ▼ Fill a paper piping bag with the chocolate. Cut a small piece off the pointed end of the bag in a straight line. Pipe your chosen shape in a continuous line, and repeat or vary. Leave to set in a cool place, then carefully lift off the paper with a palette knife.

PIPING ON TO CAKES

This looks effective on top of a cake iced with coffee glacé icing.

1 Melt 50 g/2 oz each of white and dark chocolate in separate bowls and allow to cool slightly. Place the chocolates in separate paper piping bags. Cut a small piece off the pointed end of each bag in a straight line.

2 ▲ Hold each piping bag in turn above the surface of the cake and pipe the chocolates all over. Here, the chocolates have been piped in overlapping semi-circles of different sizes. Try your own designs, too.

CHOCOLATE LACE CURLS

Make lots of these curly shapes and store them in a cool place ready for using as cake decorations. Try piping the lines in contrasting colours of chocolate to vary the effect.

1 ▲ Melt 115 g/4 oz chocolate and allow to cool slightly. Cover a rolling pin with baking parchment and attach it with tape. Fill a paper piping bag with the chocolate and cut a small piece off the pointed end in a straight line.

2 ▲ Pipe lines of chocolate backwards and forwards over the baking parchment, as shown.

3 ▲ Leave the chocolate lace curls to set in a cool place, then carefully peel off the paper.

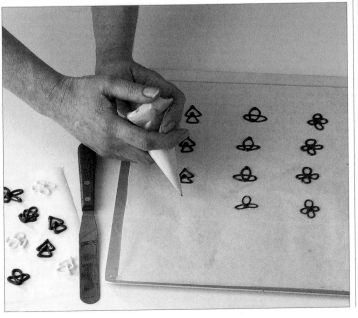

Marbling Chocolate — Chocolate Run-Outs

Here, dark chocolate is swirled over a white glacé-iced cake for a stunningly simple effect. Before melting the chocolate, make the icing, then work very quickly while both the chocolate and the icing are still soft.

The same basic method used for making royal icing run-outs is used here with chocolate. Try piping the outline in one colour of chocolate and filling in the middle with another.

1 Melt 50 g/2 oz of dark chocolate. Coat the top of the cake evenly with white glacé icing.

2 ▲ Spoon the chocolate into a paper piping bag, cut a small piece off the pointed end in a straight line and then quickly pipe the chocolate in large, loose loops.

3 ▼ Pull a cocktail stick through the chocolate in short, swirling movements and in different directions, to create a random marbled effect.

1 ▲ Tape a piece of greaseproof paper to a baking sheet or flat board. Draw around a shaped biscuit cutter on to the paper, or trace or draw a shape of your choice freehand. Repeat the design several times.

2 Secure a piece of baking parchment over the top of the pencilled design. Tape it down securely at the corners with masking tape.

3 ▲ Fill two paper piping bags with melted chocolate. Cut a small piece off the pointed end of one of the bags in a straight line and pipe over the outline of your design in a continuous thread.

4 ▲ Cut the end off the other bag, slightly wider than before, and pipe the chocolate to fill in the outline so it looks slightly rounded. Leave to set in a cool place, then carefully lift off the paper with a palette knife.

Chocolate icing and decorating techniques are demonstrated in all their glory on this sumptuous chocolate gâteau. The cake is covered with fudge frosting. A neat ring of cocoa is then dusted around the edge, using a round stencil to protect the centre of the cake. The cake is decorated with mottled white and plain chocolate leaves. Chocolate curls adorn the top, and haphazardly piped white chocolate shapes, loosely overpiped with dark chocolate, complete the ultimate chocoholic extravaganza.

Chocolate Leaves

Chocolate Cut-Outs

Chocolate leaves are made by coating real leaves with dark, white or milk chocolate or any combination of the three. Choose small freshly-picked leaves with simple shapes and well-defined veins, such as rose leaves. Leave a short stem on the leaves so you have something to hold.

You can make abstract shapes, or circles, squares and diamonds, by cutting them out freehand with a sharp knife. Alternatively, use a large biscuit cutter or ruler as a guide, or cut out the shapes with small biscuit or cocktail cutters. These shapes look equally attractive whether evenly positioned around the sides of the cake, spaced apart or overlapping each other, or simply arranged haphazardly.

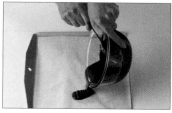

1 ▲ Wash and dry the leaves well on kitchen paper. Melt 115 g/4 oz chocolate. Using a paintbrush, brush the underside of each leaf with chocolate. Take care not to go over the edge of the leaf or the chocolate will be difficult to peel off.

1 ▲ Cover a baking sheet with baking parchment and tape down at each corner. Melt 115 g/4 oz dark, milk or white chocolate. Pour the chocolate on to the baking parchment.

3 ▲ Press the cutter firmly through the chocolate and lift off the paper with a palette knife. Try not to touch the surface of the chocolate or you will leave marks on it.

4 ▲ The finished shapes can be left plain or piped with a contrasting chocolate if you wish.

2 ▲ Using different chocolates for a mottled effect, brush the leaves in the same way, partly with plain or milk and partly with white chocolate.

3 Place the leaves chocolate-side up on baking parchment. Leave to set.

2 ▲ Spread the chocolate evenly with a palette knife. Allow to stand until the surface is firm enough to cut, but not so hard that it will break. It should no longer feel sticky when touched with your finger.

5 ▲ Abstract shapes can be cut with a knife freehand. They look particularly effective pressed on to the sides of a butter iced cake.

4 ▲ Carefully peel the leaf from the chocolate, handling the chocolate as little as possible. if the chocolate seems too thin, re-coat with more melted chocolate. Leave to set.

Chocolate-dipped Fruit and Nuts

Use small, fresh fruit such as strawberries, grapes and kumquats for dipping, and whole nuts such as almonds, cashews, brazils or macadamias. Make sure that the fruit and nuts are at room temperature, or the chocolate will set too quickly.

1 Line a baking sheet with baking parchment. Wash the fruit and dry well on kitchen paper. Hold the fruit by its stem, then dip into the chocolate. You can either coat the piece of fruit completely, or just dip half of it, leaving the line of chocolate straight or at a slight angle. Remove the fruit, shake it gently and let any excess chocolate fall back into the bowl. Place on baking parchment and leave to set.

2 ▲ For nuts, place a nut on the end of a long kitchen fork or dipping fork. Lower into the chocolate and coat completely. Lift out of the chocolate and shake off any excess, then leave to set as for fruit. To coat just half of the nut, hold it between your fingers and dip part way into the chocolate.

3 For a two-tone effect, melt dark and white chocolate in separate bowls. Dip the fruit or nuts into one colour to coat completely, then, when set, half-dip into the other colour.

Chocolate Curls

1 Melt 115 g/4 oz chocolate. Pour the chocolate on to a firm, smooth surface such as a marble, wood or plastic laminate, set on a slightly damp cloth to prevent slipping. Spread the chocolate evenly over the surface with a large palette knife.

2 ▲ Leave the chocolate to cool slightly. It should feel just set, but not hard. Hold a large sharp knife at a 45° angle to the chocolate and push it along the chocolate in short sawing movements from right to left and left to right to make curls.

3 ▲ Remove the curls by sliding the point of the knife underneath each one and lifting off. Leave until firm.

Chocolate Shavings

The quickest way to turn chocolate into a decoration is simply to grate or shave it. The chocolate should be at room temperature for this.

1 ▲ For fine shavings, grate the chocolate on the coarse side of a grater. For coarser shavings, peel off curls with a vegetable peeler.

This sophisticated heart-shaped cake is a wonderful idea for Valentine's Day or to celebrate an engagement. It is completely covered with rich, dark chocolate curls.

COLOUR EFFECTS

*If you think of the surface of a cake as an artist's canvas, it opens up
all sorts of decorating ideas using painting and drawing techniques.
This is made possible by the wide range of colours available in the form
of food colourings and food colouring pens.*

Using Stencils

Cards with stencil patterns on them can be found at cake icing specialists or at stationers, or you can make your own stencils out of thin card.

1 Coat the cake with sugarpaste, royal or marzipan icing and leave to dry.

2 ▲ Lay the stencil over the surface of the cake. Dip a dry, clean paintbrush into powdered food colouring and dab into the stencil. Lift off the stencil to reveal the design. You could also fill in the colour with a food colouring pen.

Flicking

Use one colour or several. This is almost a decoration in itself.

1 Cover the cake with sugarpaste, royal or marzipan icing and leave to dry. Place the cake on a fairly large sheet of greaseproof paper to protect the work surface.

2 ▲ Water down the food colouring, and then load up the end of the paintbrush with the colour. Position the brush over the area you wish to colour, then flick your wrist in the direction of the cake, so the colour falls on to it in small beads.

Linework

Food colouring pens are a quick way to add simple line designs to the tops and sides of cakes. Use a ruler to achieve straight lines, and a pair of compasses for large curved lines.

1 Cover the cake and leave to dry. Royal icing gives the firmest surface for the pens. Work out the design.

2 ▲ For small circles, curves or semi-circles, draw around the edge of a plain round cutter.

3 ▼ Add details to the design with small dots.

Painting and Drawing

Food colourings can be used like water-colours and food colouring pens like crayons or felt-tip pens on iced cakes. Let the icing dry before applying the design. Before working on the cake, you might find it easier to practise on a spare piece of icing. When painting different colours next to each other, allow the first colour to dry before applying the second to prevent colours running into each other – unless that is the effect you wish to achieve.

1 ▲ Dilute food colourings with a little water or use straight from the bottle. A small plastic palette is useful for mixing the colours. Work out the design and either paint it straight on to the cake, or draw it out first with a food colouring pen.

2 ▲ Food colouring pens look like felt-tip pens, but are filled with edible food colourings. They are a speedy way to add lively highlights to designs. They can also be used to colour in patterned borders, to draw personalized pictures or to write messages on cakes.

3 ▶ Look to the great artists, such as Matisse and Picasso, for inspiration, either for a painting style or theme.

Stippling

This is normally used as a background decoration, so it is best to keep the colours delicate. Try blending two soft shades together.

1 Cover the cake with sugarpaste, royal or marzipan icing and leave until the icing is dry.

2 ▲ Water down the food colouring and apply with a dry, clean piece of sponge or kitchen paper, by dabbing it on to the surface of the cake.

Powdered Tints

These can be brushed on dry, either with a paintbrush for detail, or with a clean, dry piece of sponge when you wish to cover larger areas.

1 Cover the cake with sugarpaste, royal or marzipan icing and leave until the icing is dry.

2 ▲ Draw on the design with different coloured food colouring pens, and then brush in the colours with powdered tints.

Using Bought Decorations

When you want to put a cake together in a hurry for a last-minute celebration, or even if you do not have much time to spend on decorating cakes, remember there are all kinds of easy-to-use edible items and ready-to-use decorations that can be found in supermarkets, health food shops, and in confectionery and specialist cake icing shops.

Edible Decorations

Here are just some of the delicious edible decorations which can be used for quick-and-easy cake decorating. Keep a few of these in your cupboard, ready for an impromptu celebration cake.

Sweets Choose small, colourful, simple shapes such as jelly babies, jelly beans, coloured chocolate beans, chocolate buttons, liquorice allsorts, chocolate-coated espresso beans, yogurt-coated nuts and raisins, small moulded chocolate shapes or sugared almonds. These are just a few of the sweets which, used with imagination and flair, turn a cake into something special.
Jellied Shapes Packaged jellied orange and lemon slices are also useful, either whole or cut into wedges, as are jelly diamonds, available in several colours.
Nuts Use these chopped or whole, plain or toasted, for decorating the tops and to coat the sides of cakes.
Glacé and Crystallized Fruits Glacé cherries and angelica are probably the most familiar of these popular quick cake decorations, but there are many other tasty varieties to choose from, such as pineapple and ginger – even diced papaya. Depending on their size, the fruits can be halved, sliced, chopped or cut into shapes ready for arranging on the cake.
Coconut Desiccated coconut is another useful cake decoration, particularly as it can also be tinted with a few drops of food colouring to give an attractive coating for the sides of a cake. Other more unusual kinds of coconut are also available; such as coconut threads, coconut chips and coconut slices. All can be used raw or toasted.

Marzipan Fruits and Sugar Flowers Both can be bought ready-made if you do not wish to shape your own.
Citrus Fruits Fresh lemon, lime and orange zest can be transformed into attractive cake decorations. Cut off thin, curly strips of rind with a sharp knife or zester. Alternatively, use tiny aspic cutters to cut out shapes from the rinds, but be careful not to include the white pith. The shapes can be grouped together or linked to form a border around the cake.

MAKING PATTERNS WITH EDIBLE DECORATIONS

2 ▲ This jazzy design is ideal for a child's cake. It is made from whole and halved coloured chocolate beans.

1 ▲ Arrange jelly diamonds and jellied orange slices on a square or round cake to form a pretty stylized design such as the one shown.

3 ▲ Sugared almonds, flaked toasted almonds and silver balls add life to any cake iced in pastel shades, and are ideal for Easter.

Decorative edibles help to make cake decorating fun as well as easy.

Sweet Flowers

Edible decorations can be used in different combinations to make attractive floral designs for cakes.

1 ▲ Use jelly diamonds for the petals and leaves, slices of dolly mixtures for the centres and strips of angelica for the stems.

2 ▲ Arrange halved coloured chocolate beans, cut-side down, to form a flower. Use different colours, with a silver ball for the centre.

3 ▲ Dip blanched whole almonds in melted chocolate to form the petals of a flower, then arrange with a chocolate button or chocolate bean for the centre.

Stencilling

For this technique you can use icing sugar, cocoa or even finely ground nuts to create the stencilling effect.

1 ▲ For a quick stencilled pattern, lay a patterned doiley on the cake and sift icing sugar over the top. Lift off the doiley to reveal the pattern. The centre can be cut out of the doiley to create another stencilled area. For maximum contrast, use icing sugar on a chocolate cake and cocoa on a plain cake.

2 ▼ Another stencilling method is to lay strips of paper over the cake, either in straight lines, diagonally or in a lattice pattern. Use fairly thick paper so it lies flat. For more dramatic effects, cut out strips of paper in wavy, zigzag or other geometric patterns.

It's time to have fun. Load up a paintbrush with orange food colouring and then flick it over a sugarpaste-iced cake. Cut out bears with the icing and paint on their features. Line up jelly teddy bears, jelly beans and other colourful sweets, paint a bright design on the iced board and you have a cake that is surprisingly easy to decorate.

Ribbon Decorations

Stripy ones, dotty ones, sparkly ones, wide and pencil-thin ones – ribbons are a lovely way to add height, colour and a special celebratory look to a cake. They can be wrapped around the cake, using varying widths and colours for different effects, made into simple shapes, or threaded into the icing. Tiny coloured bows can be purchased from cake icing specialists, or you can make your own decorations as suggested here.

RIBBON CURLS

OVALS

RIBBON LOOPS

These look pretty if one or several loops are attached to florist's wire, or if alternating colours are looped together.

1 Use thin ribbon, about 5 mm/¼ inch wide. Make two or three small loops of ribbon.

2 ▲ Using a piece of florist's wire, twist it around the ends of the ribbon to secure the loops together. Trim the ends of the ribbon. The wire will form a stem for the loops, so cut it to the required length and use it to put the loops in position on the cake. The loops must be removed from the cake before serving.

▲ Use a thin piece of gift wrapping ribbon, about 5 mm/¼ inch wide, and cut into the chosen lengths. Run the blade of a pair of scissors or a sharp knife down the length of the ribbons to make them curl.

MULTIPLE CURLS

▲ Use a thick piece of gift wrapping ribbon, about 2 cm/¾ inch wide, and cut into the chosen lengths. Tear the ribbon into four or five thin strips, almost to the end. Run the blade of a pair of scissors or a sharp knife down the length of each strip to curl.

▲ Hold both ends of a thin piece of ribbon. With your left hand bring the end up and twist it over to cross and form an oval with two straight ends hanging down. Where the ribbon crosses, secure with a little royal icing. Cut the ends diagonally to neaten.

RIBBON DESIGNS

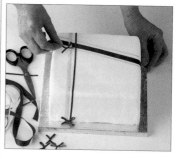

▲ Use combinations of colours and widths of ribbons and bows to create special patterns on the tops and sides of cakes. Secure with a little royal icing.

A riot of ribbons – let the colours or patterns of ribbon you choose complement the shade and design of the cake without dominating it.

RIBBON INSERTION

This technique looks much more difficult than it actually is. A cake covered with sugarpaste icing provides the best surface for this decoration. Leave the icing to dry until it is soft underneath and just firm on the top.

1 ▲ Work out your design for the number and size of slits, and whether the design is to be straight or curved. Draw the design on a piece of greaseproof paper.

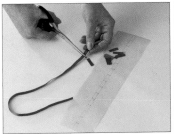

2 ▲ Cut pieces of ribbon which are fractionally longer than the size of each slit.

3 ▲ Secure the template to the cake with pins. Cut through the drawn lines to make the slits in the icing using a scalpel. Remove the template.

4 ▲ With the aid of a pointed tool, insert one end of the ribbon into the first slit and the other end into the second slit.

5 ▲ Leave a space and repeat, filling all the slits with the pieces of ribbon in the same way.

Sugar-frosting Flowers and Fruit

Something as simple as a spray of fresh sugar-frosted flowers or a grouping of small fruits is often all that is needed to decorate a cake. When frosting flowers choose ones that are edible, such as pansies, primroses, violets, roses, freesias, tiny daffodils or nasturtiums.

FLOWERS

Sugar-frosted flowers keep surprisingly well, and you may want to make the most of springtime primroses and violets to liven up cakes later in the year. Once the flowers are dry, store them in a single layer between sheets of tissue paper in a small box. Keep the box in a cool, dry place.

1 ▲ Lightly beat an egg white in a small bowl, and sprinkle some caster sugar on to a plate. Dry the flower on kitchen paper. If possible, leave some stem attached. Evenly brush both sides of the petals with the egg white.

2 ▲ Holding the flower by its stem over a plate lined with kitchen paper, sprinkle it evenly with the sugar, then shake off any excess.

3 ▲ Place on a flat board or wire rack covered with kitchen paper and leave to dry in a warm place.

FRUITS

When frosting fruits, choose really fresh ones which are small and firm such as kumquats, cherries, grapes or strawberries. Frosted fruits will only keep as long as the fruits themselves stay fresh. Place on a lined tray and keep in the refrigerator. Eat within two days.

1 Wash the fruit and pat dry on kitchen paper.

2 ▲ Lightly beat an egg white in a small bowl, and sprinkle some caster sugar on to a plate. Hold the fruit by the stem if possible and evenly brush all over with the egg white.

Frosty florals – whole flowers or individual petals can be frosted in the same way.

Sometimes the simplest cakes can be the most elegant. The stark white background of sugarpaste icing is all that is needed to show off a sweeping spray of frosted flowers, an interlocking design of ribbons and a few ribbon curls and bows.

3 ▲ Holding the fruit over a plate lined with kitchen paper, sprinkle it evenly with the sugar, then shake off any excess.

4 Place on a flat board or wire rack covered with kitchen paper and leave to dry in a warm place.

Frosty fruits – make a pile of these luscious fruits for a stunning centrepiece on a cake.

Classic Cakes

This chapter includes innovative interpretations and designs for much-loved favourites which are a must for every cake-maker's basic repertoire. From simply decorated sponge cakes, to delicious dessert cakes and sumptuous gâteaux, there are recipes here for every taste and every occasion.

Black Forest Gâteau

A perfect gâteau for a special occasion tea party, or for serving as a sumptuous dessert at a dinner party.

INGREDIENTS
Serves 10–12
5 size 3 eggs
175 g/6 oz/³/₄ cup caster sugar
50 g/2 oz/¹/₂ cup plain flour, sifted
50 g/2 oz/¹/₃ cup cocoa
powder, sifted
75 g/3 oz/6 tbsp butter, melted

For the Filling
5–6 tbsp Kirsch
575 ml/1 pint/2¹/₂ cups double cream
1 x 425 g/15 oz can black cherries,
drained, stoned and chopped

To Decorate
225 g/8 oz plain chocolate
15–20 fresh cherries, preferably
with stems
sifted icing sugar (optional)

STORING
This cake is not suitable for storing.

1 Preheat the oven to 180°C/350°F/ Gas 4. Grease two deep 20 cm/8 inch round cake tins, line the bases with greaseproof paper and grease the paper.

2 ▲ Place the eggs and sugar in a large mixing bowl and beat with an electric mixer for about 10 minutes or until the mixture is thick and pale.

3 Sift together the flour and cocoa powder, then sift again into the whisked mixture. Fold in very gently, then slowly trickle in the melted butter and continue to fold in gently.

4 Divide the mixture between the tins and smooth the surfaces. Bake in the centre of the oven for about 30 minutes, or until springy to the touch. Leave in the tin for about 5 minutes, then turn out on to a wire rack, peel off the lining paper and leave to cool.

5 ▲ Cut each cake in half horizontally and lay on a work surface. Sprinkle the four layers with the Kirsch.

6 ▲ In a large bowl, whip the cream until it holds soft peaks. Transfer two-thirds of the cream to another bowl and stir in the chopped cherries. Place a layer of cake on a serving plate or cake board and spread over one-third of the filling. Top with another layer of cake and continue layering, finishing with a layer of cake.

7 Use the remaining whipped cream to cover the top and sides of the gâteau, spreading it evenly with a knife.

8 To decorate the gâteau, melt the chocolate in a bowl over a pan of hot water, or in a double boiler. Spread the chocolate out on to a plastic chopping board and allow to set.

9 ▲ Using a long sharp knife, scrape along the surface of the melted chocolate to make thin shavings and use these to cover the sides of the cake and to decorate the top. Finish by arranging the cherries on top of the gâteau. Dust with sifted icing sugar, if wished.

Tip
If liked, the cherries can be coated or half-coated in chocolate before arranging on the cake. To do this, reserve 2–3 tbsp of the melted chocolate and dip the cherries into it. Allow the dipped cherries to set on greaseproof paper.

Crunchy-topped Madeira Cake

Traditionally served with a glass of Madeira wine in Victorian England, this light sponge still makes a perfect tea-time treat.

INGREDIENTS
Serves 8–10
200 g/7 oz/14 tbsp butter, softened
finely grated zest of 1 lemon
150 g/5 oz/³/₄ cup caster sugar
3 size 3 eggs
75 g/3 oz/³/₄ cup plain flour, sifted
150 g/5 oz/1¹/₄ cups self-raising flour, sifted

For the Topping
3 tbsp clear honey
115 g/4 oz/³/₄ cup plus 2 tbsp chopped mixed peel
50 g/2 oz/¹/₂ cup flaked almonds

STORING
This cake can be kept for up to three days in an airtight container.

1 Preheat the oven to 180°C/350°F/ Gas 4. Grease a 450 g/1 lb loaf tin, line the base and sides with greaseproof paper and grease the paper.

2 ▲ Place the butter, lemon zest and sugar in a mixing bowl and beat until light and fluffy. Beat in the eggs, one at a time, until evenly blended.

3 ▲ Sift together the flours, then stir into the egg mixture. Transfer the cake mixture to the prepared tin and smooth the surface.

4 ▲ Bake in the centre of the oven for 45–50 minutes or until a skewer inserted into the centre of the cake comes out clean. Leave the cake in the tin for about 5 minutes. Turn out on to a wire rack, peel off the lining paper and leave to cool completely.

5 ▲ To make the topping, place the honey, chopped mixed peel and almonds in a small saucepan and heat gently until the honey melts. Remove from the heat and stir briefly to coat the peel and almonds, then spread over the top of the cake. Allow to cool completely before serving.

Cherry Batter Cake

This colourful tray bake looks pretty cut into neat squares or fingers.

INGREDIENTS
Serves 8–10
225 g/8 oz/2 cups self-raising flour
1 tsp baking powder
75 g/3 oz/6 tbsp butter, softened
150 g/5 oz/²⁄₃ cup soft light
brown sugar
1 size 3 egg, lightly beaten
150 ml/¹⁄₄ pint/ ²⁄₃ cup milk

For the Topping
1 x 680g/1¹⁄₂ lb jar black cherries or
blackcurrants, drained
175 g/6 oz/³⁄₄ cup soft light
brown sugar
50 g/2 oz/¹⁄₂ cup self-raising flour
50 g/2 oz/4 tbsp butter, melted
sifted icing sugar, to decorate
whipped cream, to serve (optional)

STORING
*This cake can be kept for up to two
days in an airtight container.*

1 Preheat the oven to 190°C/375°F/
Gas 5. Grease a 33 x 23 cm/13 x
9 inch Swiss roll tin, line the base and
sides with greaseproof paper and grease
the paper.

2 To make the base, sift the flour and
baking powder into a mixing bowl.
Add the butter, sugar, egg and milk.
Beat the mixture until the batter
becomes smooth, then turn into the
prepared tin and smooth the surface.

3 ▲ Scatter the drained fruit evenly
over the batter mixture.

4 ▲ Mix together the remaining
topping ingredients and spoon
evenly over the fruit. Bake in the centre
of the oven for about 40 minutes, or
until golden brown and the centre is
firm to the touch.

5 Leave to cool, then dredge with
icing sugar. Serve with whipped
cream, if wished.

Chestnut Cake

An Italian speciality, this is definitely a cake to mark an occasion. Rich, moist and heavy, it can be made up to a week in advance and kept, undecorated, wrapped and stored in an airtight container. Allow the cake to come to room temperature before serving.

INGREDIENTS
Serves 8–10
150 g/5 oz/1¼ cups plain flour
pinch of salt
225 g/8 oz/1 cup butter, softened
150 g/5 oz/¾ cup caster sugar
439 g/15½ oz can chestnut purée
9 size 3 eggs, separated
7 tbsp dark rum
300 ml/½ pint/1¼ cups
double cream

To Decorate
marrons glacés, chopped
icing sugar, sifted

STORING
Once decorated, do not store.

1 Preheat the oven to 180°C/350°F/
Gas 4. Grease a 21 cm/8½ inch
springform cake tin, line the base with
greaseproof paper and grease the paper.

2 Sift together the flour and salt, and
set aside. Place the butter and
three-quarters of the sugar in a bowl
and beat until fluffy.

3 ▲ Fold in two-thirds of the chestnut
purée, alternating with the egg yolks,
and beat. Fold in the flour and salt.

4 ▲ Whisk the egg whites in a clean,
dry bowl until stiff. Beat a little of
the egg whites into the chestnut
mixture, until evenly blended, then
fold in the remainder.

5 ▲ Transfer the cake mixture to
the prepared tin and smooth the
surface. Bake in the centre of the oven
for about 1¼ hours, or until a skewer
inserted into the centre of the cake
comes out clean.

6 Place the cake, still in the tin, on a
wire rack. Using a skewer, pierce
holes evenly all over the cake. Sprinkle
4 tbsp of the rum over the top, then
allow the cake to cool completely.

7 ▲ Remove the cake from the tin,
peel off the lining paper and cut
horizontally into two layers. Place the
bottom layer on a serving plate. Whisk
the cream in a mixing bowl with the
remaining rum, sugar and chestnut
purée until thick and smooth.

8 To assemble the cake, spread two-
thirds of the chestnut cream mixture
over the bottom layer and place the other
layer on top. Spread some of the
remaining chestnut cream over the top
and sides of the cake, then fill a
greaseproof paper piping bag, fitted with
a star nozzle, with the rest of the chestnut
mixture. Pipe big swirls around the
outside edge of the cake. Decorate with
the marrons glacés and sifted icing sugar.

Tip

In order to have the most control
over a piping bag, it is important to
hold it in a relaxed position. You
may find it easier to hold it with
one or both hands.

Strawberry Cream Gâteau

Fresh raspberries also work well for this recipe.

INGREDIENTS
Serves 8–10
2 egg yolks
4 size 3 eggs
finely grated zest of 1 lemon
115 g/4 oz/½ cup caster sugar
115 g/4 oz/1 cup plain flour, sifted
115 g/4 oz/½ cup butter, melted

For the Strawberry Cream
225 g/8 oz/1½ cups fresh
strawberries, washed, dried
and hulled
275 ml/½ pint/1¼ cups double cream
50 g/2 oz/½ cup icing sugar
1 tbsp strawberry liqueur or Kirsch

STORING
This cake can be kept for up to two days in the refrigerator.

1 Preheat the oven to 150°C/300°F/ Gas 2. Grease a 20 cm/8 inch round cake tin, line the base with greaseproof paper and grease the paper.

2 Place the eggs yolks, egg, lemon zest and sugar in a mixing bowl and beat with an electric mixer for about 10 minutes or until thick and pale. Add the flour and melted butter. Whisk for a further minute, then transfer to the prepared cake tin.

3 ▲ Bake in the centre of the oven for 30–35 minutes or until a skewer inserted into the centre of the cake comes out clean. Turn out on to a wire rack, peel off the lining paper and leave to cool completely.

4 ▲ To make the strawberry cream, place all but one of the strawberries in a food processor or blender and purée until smooth. Place the double cream in a mixing bowl and whisk until it holds peaks. Fold the purée into the cream with the icing sugar and liqueur.

5 ▲ Place the cooled cake on a plate and spread the strawberry cream evenly over the top and sides, making swirls for an attractive finish. Decorate with the sliced reserved strawberry.

Upside-down Pear & Ginger Cake

A light spicy sponge topped with glossy baked fruit and ginger. This is also good served warm for pudding.

INGREDIENTS
Serves 6–8
1 x 900 g/2 lb can pear
halves, drained
8 tbsp finely chopped stem ginger
8 tbsp ginger syrup from the jar
175 g/6 oz/1½ cups self-raising flour
½ tsp baking powder
1 tsp ground ginger
175 g/6 oz/¾ cup soft light
brown sugar
175 g/6 oz/¾ cup butter, softened
3 size 3 eggs, lightly beaten

STORING
This cake is not suitable for storing.

1 Preheat the oven to 180°C/350°F/ Gas 4. Grease a deep 20 cm/8 inch round cake tin, line the base with greaseproof paper and grease the paper.

2 ▲ Fill the hollow in each pear with half the chopped ginger. Arrange the pear halves, flat sides down, over the base of the cake tin, then spoon half the ginger syrup over the top.

3 Sift the flour, baking powder and ground ginger into a mixing bowl. Stir in the soft brown sugar and butter, then add the eggs and beat together for 1–2 minutes until level and creamy.

4 ▲ Carefully spoon the mixture into the tin and smooth the surface.

5 ▲ Bake in the centre of the oven for about 50 minutes, or until a skewer inserted in the centre of the cake comes out clean. Leave the cake to cool in the tin for about 5 minutes. Turn out on to a wire rack, peel off the lining paper and leave to cool completely. Add the reserved chopped ginger to the pear halves and drizzle over the remaining ginger syrup.

One-stage Victoria Sandwich

Originally made in an oblong shape, today's Victoria sandwich is made using a variety of different flavourings and decorations, and is baked and cut into all sorts of shapes and sizes. Use this basic recipe to suit the occasion.

INGREDIENTS
Serves 6–8
175 g/6 oz/1½ cups self-raising flour
pinch of salt
175 g/6 oz/¾ cup butter, softened
175 g/6 oz/¾ cup caster sugar
3 size 3 eggs

To Finish
4–6 tbsp raspberry jam
caster sugar or icing sugar

STORING
This cake can be kept for up to three days in an airtight container.

1 Preheat the oven to 180°C/375°F/ Gas 4. Grease two deep 18 cm/7 inch round cake tins, line the bases with greaseproof paper and grease the paper.

2 ▲ Place all the ingredients in a mixing bowl and whisk together using an electric hand whisk. Divide the mixture between the prepared tins and smooth the surfaces. Bake in the centre of the oven for 25–30 minutes, or until a skewer inserted into the centre of the cakes comes out clean. Turn out on to a wire rack, peel off the lining paper and leave to cool completely.

3 ▲ Place one of the cakes on a serving plate and spread with the raspberry jam. Place the other cake on top, then dredge with caster or icing sugar, to serve.

Variation
Makes 8–10 iced fancies

1 ▲ Place the cake mixture in a greased and lined 23 × 33 cm/9 × 13 inch Swiss roll tin and smooth the surface. Bake in the centre of the oven for 25–30 minutes, or until a skewer inserted into the centre of the cake comes out clean. Turn out on to a wire rack, peel off the lining paper and leave to cool completely.

2 ▲ Cut the cake into individual sized shapes, such as fingers, diamonds, squares or small rounds, using a knife or biscuit cutters. Using one quantity of Butter Icing, cover with decorative piping. You can flavour or colour the butter icing by substituting orange or lemon juice for the milk and/or adding a few drops of food colouring.

3 For alternative decorations, you could try a selection of the following: glacé cherries, angelica, jellied fruits, grated chocolate, chopped or whole nuts, or choose one of your own ideas.

Tip

To make the decorative stencilled pattern with icing sugar shown here, cut out star shapes from paper. Lay the paper stars over the top of the cake and then dredge with icing sugar. Remove the paper shapes carefully to reveal the stencilled pattern. You could also use a paper doily as a stencil.

Flourless Fruit Cake

A really easy recipe which everyone will enjoy. Children can have fun crushing the cornflakes and helping you to beat the ingredients together.

INGREDIENTS
Serves 12–15

1 x 450 g/1 lb jar mincemeat
350 g/12 oz/2 cups dried mixed fruit
115 g/4 oz/1 cup no-soak dried apricots, chopped
115 g/4 oz/1 cup no-soak dried figs, chopped
115 g/4 oz/¹/₂ cup glacé cherries, halved
115 g/4 oz/1 cup walnut pieces
225 g/8 oz/8–10 cups cornflakes, crushed
4 size 3 eggs, lightly beaten
1 x 410 g/14¹/₂ oz can evaporated milk
1 tsp ground mixed spice
1 tsp baking powder
mixed glacé fruits, chopped, to decorate

STORING
This cake can be kept for up to a week in an airtight container.

1 Preheat the oven to 150°C/300°F/ Gas 2. Grease a 25 cm/10 inch round cake tin, line the base and sides with a double thickness of greaseproof paper and grease the paper.

2 Put all the ingredients into a large mixing bowl. Beat together well.

3 ▲ Turn into the prepared tin and smooth the surface with the back of a spoon.

4 ▲ Bake in the centre of the oven for about 1³/₄ hours, or until a skewer inserted in the centre of the cake comes out clean. Allow the cake to cool in the tin for 10 minutes, then turn out on to a wire rack, peel off the lining paper and leave to cool completely. Decorate with the chopped glacé fruits.

Tip

This cake may be iced and marzipanned to make a Christmas or birthday cake. A useful recipe for anyone who needs to avoid eating wheat flour.

Exotic Celebration Gâteau

Use any tropical fruits you can find to make a spectacular display of colours and tastes.

INGREDIENTS
Serves 8–10
175 g/6 oz/³⁄₄ cup butter, softened
175 g/6 oz/³⁄₄ cup caster sugar
3 size 3 eggs, beaten
250 g/9 oz/2¼ cups self-raising flour
2–3 tbsp milk
6–8 tbsp light rum
425 ml/³⁄₄ pt/scant 2 cups
double cream
25 g/1 oz/¼ cup icing sugar, sifted

To Decorate
450 g/1 lb mixed fresh exotic and
soft fruits, such as figs, redcurrants,
star fruit, kiwi fruit, etc.
6 tbsp apricot jam, warmed
and sieved
2 tbsp warm water
sifted icing sugar

STORING
*This cake can be kept for up to two
days in the refrigerator.*

1 Preheat the oven to 190°C/375°F/
Gas 5. Grease and flour a deep
20 cm/8 inch ring mould.

2 ▲ Place the butter and sugar in a
mixing bowl and beat until light
and fluffy. Gradually beat in the eggs,
then fold in the flour with the milk.

3 Spoon the cake mixture into
the prepared tin and smooth the
surface. Bake in the centre of the oven
for about 45 minutes, or until a skewer
inserted into the centre of the cake
comes out clean. Turn out on to a wire
rack and leave to cool completely.

4 ▲ Place the cake on a serving plate,
then use a thin skewer to make
holes randomly over the cake. Drizzle
over the rum and allow to soak in.

5 ▲ Place the cream and icing sugar
in a mixing bowl and beat with an
electric mixer until the mixture holds
soft peaks. Spread all over the top and
sides of the cake.

6 Arrange the fruits attractively in the
hollow centre of the cake, allowing
the fruits to overhang the edges a little.
Mix together the apricot jam and water,
then use to brush evenly over the fruit.
Sift over a little icing sugar, to decorate.

Carrot and Almond Cake

Made with grated carrots and ground almonds, this unusual fat-free sponge makes a delicious afternoon treat.

INGREDIENTS

Serves 8–10

5 size 3 eggs, separated
finely grated zest of 1 lemon
300 g/10 oz/1⅓ cups caster sugar
350 g/12 oz/5–6 carrots, peeled and finely grated
225 g/8 oz/1¼ cups ground almonds
115 g/4 oz/1 cup self-raising flour, sifted
sifted icing sugar, to decorate
marzipan carrots, to decorate (optional)

STORING

This cake can be kept for up to two days in an airtight container.

Tip

To make the marzipan carrots, knead a little orange food colouring into 115 g/4 oz marzipan until evenly blended. On a work surface lightly dusted with icing sugar, divide the marzipan into even-sized pieces, about the size of small walnuts. Mould into carrot shapes and press horizontal lines along each carrot with a knife blade. Press a tiny stick of angelica into the end of each piece to resemble the carrot top. Position the marzipan carrots on the cake, to decorate.

1 Preheat the oven to 190°C/375°F/ Gas 5. Grease a deep 20 cm/8 inch round cake tin, line the base with greaseproof paper and grease the paper.

2 ▲ Place the egg yolks, lemon zest and sugar in a bowl. Beat with an electric mixer for about 5 minutes, until the mixture is thick and pale.

3 ▲ Mix in the grated carrot, ground almonds and flour and stir until evenly combined.

4 In a clean, dry bowl, whisk the egg whites until stiff. Using a large metal spoon or rubber spatula, mix a little of the whisked egg whites into the carrot mixture, then fold in the rest.

5 ▲ Spoon the mixture into the prepared cake tin and bake in the centre of the oven for about 1¼ hours, or until a skewer inserted into the centre of the cake comes out clean. Leave the cake in the tin for about 5 minutes, then turn out on to a wire rack, peel off the lining paper and leave to cool completely.

6 ▲ Decorate with sifted icing sugar and marzipan carrots.

Vegan Chocolate Gâteau

It isn't often that vegans can indulge in a slice of chocolate cake and this one tastes so delicious, they'll all be back for more!

INGREDIENTS
Serves 8–10
300 g/10 oz/2¹/₂ cups self-raising
wholemeal flour
50 g/2 oz/¹/₃ cup cocoa powder
3 tsp baking powder
250 g/9 oz/1¹/₄ cups caster sugar
few drops of vanilla essence
9 tbsp sunflower oil
350 ml/12 fl oz/1¹/₂ cups water
sifted cocoa powder, to decorate
25 g/1 oz/¹/₄ cup chopped nuts,
to decorate

For the Chocolate Fudge
50 g/2 oz/¹/₄ cup vegan (soya)
margarine
3 tbsp water
250 g/9 oz/2¹/₃ cups icing sugar
2 tbsp cocoa powder
1 – 2 tbsp hot water

STORING
This cake can be kept for up to two days in the refrigerator.

1 Preheat the oven to 170°C/325°F/ Gas 3. Grease a deep 20 cm/8 inch round cake tin, line the base and sides with greaseproof paper and grease the paper.

2 Sift the flour, cocoa powder and baking powder into a large mixing bowl. Add the caster sugar and vanilla essence, then gradually beat in the sunflower oil and water to make a smooth batter.

3 Pour the cake mixture into the prepared tin and smooth the surface with the back of a spoon.

4 ▲ Bake in the centre of the oven for about 45 minutes or until a skewer inserted into the centre of the cake comes out clean. Leave in the tin for about 5 minutes, then turn out on to a wire rack, peel off the lining paper and leave to cool. Cut the cake in half.

5 ▲ To make the chocolate fudge, place the margarine and water in a pan and heat gently until the margarine has melted. Remove from the heat and add the sifted icing sugar and cocoa powder, beating until smooth and shiny. Allow to cool until firm enough to spread and pipe.

6 ▲ Place the bottom layer of cake on a serving plate and spread over two-thirds of the chocolate fudge mixture. Top with the other layer of cake. Fit a piping bag with a star nozzle, fill with the remaining chocolate fudge and pipe stars over the cake. Sprinkle with cocoa powder and chopped nuts.

*G*orgeous Chocolate Cake

This recipe will definitely make you famous.
Make sure you serve it with paper and pens, as everyone will want
to take down the recipe.

INGREDIENTS
Serves 8–10
175 g/6 oz/¾ cup butter, softened
115 g/4 oz/½ cup caster sugar
250 g/9 oz/9 squares plain
chocolate, melted
200 g/7 oz/2⅓ cups ground
almonds
4 size 3 eggs, separated
115 g/4 oz/4 squares white
chocolate, melted, to decorate

STORING
This cake can be kept for up to four
days in an airtight container.

4 ▲ Place the remaining butter and remaining melted plain chocolate in a saucepan. Heat very gently, stirring constantly, until melted. Pour over the cake, allowing the topping to coat the sides too. Leave to set for at least an hour. To decorate, fill a piping bag with the melted white chocolate and snip the end. Drizzle all around the edges to make a double border. Use any remaining chocolate to make leaves (see Trailing Orchid Wedding cake, steps 2 and 3).

3 ▲ Whisk the egg whites in another clean, dry bowl until stiff. Fold them into the chocolate mixture, then transfer to the prepared tin and smooth the surface. Bake for 50–55 minutes or until a skewer inserted into the centre of the cake comes out clean. Leave the cake in the tin for about 5 minutes, then turn out on to a wire rack, peel off the lining paper and leave to cool completely.

*T*ip

Place a large sheet of greaseproof paper or a baking sheet under the wire rack before pouring the chocolate topping over the cake. This will catch all the drips and keep the work surface clean.

1 Preheat the oven to 180°C/350°F/ Gas 4. Grease a deep 21 cm/8½ inch springform cake tin, then line the base with greaseproof paper and grease the paper.

2 ▲ Place 115 g/4 oz/½ cup of the butter and all the sugar in a mixing bowl and beat until light and fluffy. Add two thirds of the plain chocolate, the ground almonds and the egg yolks and beat until evenly blended.

*M*ocha-hazelnut Battenberg

The traditional Battenberg cake originated in Germany when the Prince of Battenberg married Queen Victoria's daughter, Beatrice. This recipe is a variation of the original theme.

INGREDIENTS
Serves 6–8
115 g/4 oz/¹/₂ cup butter, softened
115 g/4 oz/¹/₂ cup caster sugar
2 size 3 eggs
115 g/4 oz/1 cup self-raising
flour, sifted
50 g/2 oz/²/₃ cup ground hazelnuts
2 tsp coffee essence
1 tbsp cocoa powder

To Finish
7 tbsp apricot jam, warmed
and sieved
225 g/8 oz yellow marzipan
50 g/2 oz/²/₃ cup ground hazelnuts
sifted icing sugar, for rolling out
ground hazelnuts, to decorate

STORING
This cake can be kept for up to three days in an airtight container.

1 Preheat the oven to 180°C/350°F/ Gas 4. Grease an 18 cm/7 inch square cake tin, line the base with greaseproof paper and grease the paper.

2 ▲ Place the butter and sugar in a bowl and beat until fluffy. Gradually beat in the eggs, then fold in the flour. Transfer mixture to another bowl.

3 ▲ Stir the ground hazelnuts into one half of the cake mixture and the coffee essence and cocoa powder into the other half.

4 ▲ Prepare a strip of foil to fit the width and height of the cake tin, then place the mocha-flavoured cake mixture in one half of the tin. Position the strip of foil down the centre, then spoon the hazelnut-flavoured cake mixture into the other half of the tin. Smooth the surface of both mixtures.

5 Bake for 30–35 minutes or until a skewer inserted into the centre of both halves comes out clean. Leave the cakes to cool in the tin for about 5 minutes, then turn out on to a wire rack, peel off the lining paper and leave to cool completely.

6 ▲ Separate the cakes and cut each one in half lengthways. Take one portion of the mocha-flavoured cake and brush along one long side with a little apricot jam. Sandwich this surface with a portion of the hazelnut-flavoured cake. Brush the top of the cakes with apricot jam and position the other portion of mocha-flavoured cake on top of the hazelnut base. Brush along the inner long side with apricot jam and sandwich with the final portion of hazelnut-flavoured cake. Set aside.

7 Knead the marzipan on the work surface to soften, then knead in the ground hazelnuts until evenly blended. On the work surface lightly dusted with icing sugar, roll out the marzipan into a rectangle large enough to wrap around the cake, excluding the ends.

8 Brush the long sides of the cake with apricot jam, then lay the cake on top of the marzipan. Wrap the marzipan around the cake, sealing the edge neatly. Place the cake on a serving plate, seal-side down, and pinch the edges of the marzipan to give an attractive finish. Score the top surface with a knife and sprinkle with ground hazelnuts.

Greek New Year Cake

A gold coin wrapped in foil is baked into this cake and tradition holds that good luck will come to the person who finds it.

INGREDIENTS
Serves 8–10
275 g/10 oz/2½ cups plain flour
2 tsp baking powder
50 g/2 oz/⅔ cup ground almonds
225 g/8 oz/1 cup butter, softened
175 g/6 oz/¾ cup plus 2 tbsp caster
sugar, plus a little extra
4 size 3 eggs
150 ml/¼ pint/⅔ cup fresh orange juice
50 g/2 oz/½ cup blanched almonds
1 tbsp sesame seeds

STORING
This cake can be kept for up to four days in an airtight container.

1 ▲ Preheat the oven to 180°C/350°F/ Gas 4. Grease a 23 cm/9 inch square cake tin, line the base and sides with greaseproof paper and grease the paper.

2 ▲ Sift the flour and baking powder into a mixing bowl and stir in the ground almonds.

3 ▲ In another mixing bowl, cream together the butter and sugar until light and fluffy. Beat in the eggs, one at a time, using an electric mixer. Fold in the flour mixture, alternating with the orange juice, until evenly combined.

4 ▲ Add a coin wrapped in foil if you wish to make the cake in the traditional manner, then spoon the cake mixture into the prepared tin and smooth the surface. Arrange the almonds on top, then sprinkle over the sesame seeds. Bake in the centre of the oven for 50–55 minutes or until a skewer inserted into the centre of the cake comes out clean. Leave to cool in the tin for about 5 minutes, then turn out on to a wire rack, peel off the lining paper and leave to cool completely. Serve cut into diamond shapes.

Simnel Cake

A traditional cake for Easter.

INGREDIENTS
Serves 10–12
225 g/8 oz/1 cup butter, softened
225 g/8 oz/1 cup caster sugar
4 size 3 eggs, beaten
550 g/1¼ lb/3 cups mixed dried fruit
115 g/4 oz/½ cup glacé cherries
3 tbsp sherry (optional)
275 g/10 oz/2½ cups plain flour, sifted
3 tsp ground mixed spice
1 tsp baking powder
675 g/1½ lb yellow marzipan
1 egg yolk, beaten
ribbons and sugared eggs,
to decorate

STORING
This cake can be kept for up to two weeks in an airtight container.

1 Preheat the oven to 160°C/325°F/ Gas 3. Grease a deep 20 cm/8 in round cake tin, line with a double thickness of greaseproof paper and grease the paper.

2 Place the butter and sugar in a large mixing bowl and beat until light and fluffy. Gradually beat in the eggs. Stir in the dried fruit, glacé cherries and sherry, if using.

3 ▲ Sift together the flour, mixed spice and baking powder, then fold into the cake mixture. Set aside.

4 ▲ Cut off half of the marzipan and roll out on a work surface lightly dusted with icing sugar to a 20 cm/ 8 inch round. Spoon half of the cake mixture into the prepared tin and smooth the surface with the back of a spoon. Place the marzipan round on top, then add the other half of the cake mixture and smooth the surface.

5 Bake in the centre of the oven for about 2½ hours or until golden and springy to the touch. Leave the cake in the tin for about 15 minutes, then turn out on to a wire rack, peel off the lining paper and leave to cool completely.

6 ▲ Roll out the other half of the marzipan to a round to fit on top of the cooled cake. Brush the top of the cake with a little of the egg yolk and position the marzipan round on top. Flute the edges of the marzipan and, if liked, make a decorative pattern on top with a fork. Brush with more egg yolk.

7 Put the cake on a baking sheet and place under a grill for 5 minutes or until the top is lightly browned. Leave to cool completely before decorating with ribbons and sugared eggs.

hocolate Gâteau Terrine

A spectacular finale to a special-occasion meal.
You'll find this is well worth the time and effort to make.

INGREDIENTS
Serves 10–12
115 g/4 oz/¹/₂ cup butter, softened
few drops of vanilla essence
115 g/4 oz/¹/₂ cup caster sugar
2 size 3 eggs
115 g/4 oz/1 cup self-raising
flour, sifted
50 ml/2 fl oz/¹/₄ cup milk
25 g/1 oz/¹/₂ cup desiccated
coconut, to decorate
fresh bud roses, or other flowers,
to decorate

For the Light Chocolate Filling
115 g/4 oz/¹/₂ cup butter, softened
2 tbsp icing sugar, sifted
75 g/3 oz/3 squares plain
chocolate, melted
225 ml/8 fl oz/1 cup double cream,
lightly whipped

For the Dark Chocolate Filling
115 g/4 oz/4 squares plain
chocolate, chopped
115 g/4 oz/¹/₂ cup butter
2 size 3 eggs
2 tbsp caster sugar
225 ml/8 fl oz/1 cup double cream,
lightly whipped
50 g/2 oz/¹/₂ cup cocoa powder
1 tbsp dark rum (optional)
2 tbsp gelatine powder dissolved in
2 tbsp hot water

For the White Chocolate Topping
225 g/8 oz/8 squares white
chocolate
115 g/4 oz/¹/₂ cup butter

STORING
This cake is not suitable for storing.

1 Preheat the oven to 180°C/350°F/
Gas 4. Grease a 900 g/2 lb loaf tin,
line the base and sides with greaseproof
paper and grease the paper.

2 To make the cake, place the butter,
vanilla essence and sugar in a
mixing bowl and beat until light and
fluffy. Add the eggs, one at a time,
beating well after each addition. Sift the
flour again and fold it and the milk into
the cake mixture.

3 Transfer the cake mixture to the
prepared tin and bake in the centre
of the oven for 25–30 minutes or until
a skewer inserted into the centre of the
cake comes out clean. Leave the cake in
the tin for about 5 minutes, then turn
out on to a wire rack, peel off the lining
paper and leave to cool completely.

4 ▲ To make the light chocolate
filling, place the butter and icing
sugar in a mixing bowl and beat until
creamy. Add the chocolate and cream
until evenly blended. Cover and set
aside in the refrigerator, until required.

5 To make the dark chocolate filling,
place the chocolate and butter in a
small saucepan and heat very gently,
stirring frequently, until melted. Set
aside to cool. Place the eggs and sugar
in a bowl and beat with an electric
mixer until thick and frothy. Fold in the
chocolate mixture, cream, cocoa, rum and
dissolved gelatine until evenly blended.

6 ▲ To assemble the terrine, wash
and dry the loaf tin, then line with
clear film, allowing plenty of film to
hang over the edges. Using a long
serrated knife, cut the cake horizontally
into three even layers.

7 ▲ Spread two of the layers with the
light chocolate filling, then place
one of these layers, filling side up, in the
base of the tin.

8 Cover with half of the dark
chocolate filling, then chill for about
10 minutes. Place the second light
chocolate-topped layer in the terrine,
filling side up. Spread over the
remaining dark chocolate filling, then
chill for another 10 minutes. Top with
the remaining layer of cake and chill the
terrine again for about 10 minutes.

9 To make the white chocolate
topping, place the chocolate and
butter in a small saucepan and heat very
gently, stirring frequently, until melted
and well blended. Allow to cool
slightly.

10 To finish the terrine, turn it out
on to a wire rack, removing the
clear film. Trim the edges with a long,
sharp knife, then pour over the white
chocolate topping, spreading it evenly
over the sides. Sprinkle the coconut
over the top and sides. Allow to set
before transferring the terrine to a
serving plate and decorating with fresh
bud roses.

Lemon and Apricot Cake

This more-ish cake is topped with a crunchy layer of flaked almonds and pistachio nuts, and is soaked in a tangy lemon syrup after baking to keep it really moist.

INGREDIENTS
Serves 10–12
175 g/6 oz/³/₄ cup butter, softened
175 g/6 oz/1¹/₂ cups self-raising
flour, sifted
¹/₂ tsp baking powder
175 g/6 oz/³/₄ cup caster sugar
3 size 3 eggs, lightly beaten
finely grated zest of 1 lemon
175 g/6 oz/1¹/₂ cups no-soak dried
apricots, finely chopped
75 g/3 oz/1 cup ground almonds
40 g/1¹/₂ oz/¹/₃ cup pistachio
nuts, chopped
50 g/2 oz/¹/₃ cup flaked almonds
15 g/¹/₂ oz/2 tbsp whole pistachio nuts

For the Syrup
freshly squeezed juice of 1 lemon
3 tbsp caster sugar

STORING
This cake can be kept for up to three days in an airtight container.

1 Preheat the oven to 180°C/350°F/
Mark 4. Grease a 900 g/2 lb loaf
tin, line the base and sides with
greaseproof paper and grease the paper.

2 Place the butter together with the
sifted flour and baking powder into
a mixing bowl, then add the sugar, eggs
and lemon zest. Beat for 1–2 minutes
until smooth and glossy, and then stir in
the apricots, ground almonds and the
chopped pistachio nuts.

3 ▲ Spoon the mixture into the
prepared tin and smooth the surface.
Sprinkle with the flaked almonds and
the whole pistachio nuts. Bake in the
centre of the oven for about 1¹/₄ hours,
or until a skewer inserted into the centre
of the cake comes out clean. Check the
cake after about 45 minutes and cover
with a piece of foil when the top is nicely
brown. Leave the cake to cool in the tin.

4 ▲ To make the lemon syrup, put
the lemon juice and caster sugar
into a small saucepan and heat gently,
stirring until the sugar has dissolved.

5 ▲ Spoon the syrup over the cake.
When the cake is completely
cooled, turn it carefully out of the tin
and peel off the lining paper.

Gooseberry Cake

*This cake is delicious served warm
with fresh whipped cream.*

INGREDIENTS
Serves 6–8
115 g/4 oz/¹/² cup butter
165 g/5¹/² oz/1¹/³ cups self-raising flour
1 tsp baking powder
2 size 3 eggs, beaten
115 g/4 oz/¹/² cup caster sugar
1–2 tsp rose water
pinch of freshly grated nutmeg
1 x 115 g/4 oz jar gooseberries in
syrup, drained, juice reserved
caster sugar, to decorate
whipped cream, to serve

STORING
*This cake can be kept for up to
three days in an airtight container.*

1 Preheat the oven to 180°C/350°F/
Gas 4. Grease an 18 cm/7 inch
square cake tin, line the base and sides
with greaseproof paper and then grease
the paper.

2 Place the butter in a medium
saucepan and melt over a gentle
heat. Remove the pan from the heat,
transfer the melted butter to a mixing
bowl and allow to cool.

3 ▲ Sift together the flour and
baking powder and add to the
melted butter. Beat in the eggs, one at a
time, the sugar, rose water and grated
nutmeg, to make a smooth batter.

4 ▲ Mix in 1–2 tbsp of the reserved
gooseberry juice, then pour half of
the batter mixture into the prepared tin.
Scatter over the gooseberries. Pour over
the remaining batter mixture, evenly
covering the gooseberries.

5 Bake in the centre of the oven for
about 45 minutes, or until a skewer
inserted into the centre of the cake
comes out clean.

6 ▲ Leave in the cake tin for about
5 minutes, then turn out on to a
wire rack, remove the lining paper and
allow to cool for a further 5 minutes.
Dredge with caster sugar and serve
immediately with whipped cream,
or leave the cake to cool completely
before decorating and serving.

Jewel Cake

*This pretty tea-time cake is excellent
served as an afternoon treat with tea or coffee.*

INGREDIENTS
Serves 10–15
115 g/4 oz/¹/₂ cup mixed coloured
glacé cherries, halved, washed
and dried
50 g/2 oz/¹/₄ cup stem ginger in
syrup, chopped, washed and dried
50 g/2 oz/¹/₃ cup chopped mixed peel
115 g/4 oz/1 cup self-raising flour
75 g/3 oz/³/₄ cup plain flour
25 g/1 oz/3 tbsp cornflour
175 g/6 oz/³/₄ cup butter
175 g/6 oz/³/₄ cup caster sugar
3 size 3 eggs
finely grated zest of 1 orange

To Decorate
175 g/6 oz/1¹/₂ cups icing sugar, sifted
2–3 tbsp freshly squeezed
orange juice
50 g/2 oz/¹/₄ cup mixed coloured
glacé cherries, chopped
25 g/1 oz/2¹/₂ tbsp mixed
peel, chopped

STORING
*This cake can be kept for up to two
days in an airtight container.*

Tip

To ring the changes, bake the cake
in a 18 cm/7 inch round cake tin, if
wished. Use the same quantities of
ingredients and follow the method
as described here. Decorate with
crystallized citrus fruits instead of
the glacé cherries and mixed peel.

1 Preheat the oven to 180°C/350°F/
Gas 4. Grease a 900 g/2 lb loaf tin,
line the base and sides with greaseproof
paper and grease the paper.

2 ▲ Place the cherries, stem ginger
and mixed peel in a plastic bag with
25 g/1 oz/1 tbsp of the self-raising
flour and shake to coat evenly. Sift
the remaining flours and cornflour
into a small bowl.

3 ▲ Place the butter and sugar in a
mixing bowl and beat until light
and fluffy. Beat in the eggs, one at a
time, until evenly blended. Fold in the
sifted flours with the orange zest, then
stir in the dried fruit.

4 ▲ Transfer the cake mixture to the
prepared tin and bake in the centre
of the oven for about 1¹/₄ hours, or until
a skewer inserted into the centre of the
cake comes out clean. Leave the cake in
the tin for about 5 minutes, then turn
out on to a wire rack, peel off the lining
paper and leave to cool completely.

5 ▲ To decorate the cake, place the
icing sugar in a mixing bowl. Stir
the orange juice and mix until smooth.
Drizzle the icing over the cake. Mix
together the chopped glacé cherries and
mixed peel in a small bowl, then use to
decorate the cake. Allow the icing to set
before serving.

Vegan Dundee Cake

Containing no eggs or other dairy products, this cake is a rare treat for vegans. There are several different types of dairy-free margarines on the market, many of which are suitable for baking with.

INGREDIENTS

Serves 8–10
350 g/12 oz/3 cups plain
wholemeal flour
1 tsp ground mixed spice
175 g/6 oz/³/₄ cup vegan
(soya) margarine
175 g/6 oz/³/₄ cup plus 2 tbsp dark
muscavado sugar
175 g/6 oz/1 cup sultanas
175 g/6 oz/1 cup currants
175 g/6 oz/1 cup raisins
75 g/3 oz/¹/₃ cup chopped mixed peel
150 g/5 oz/³/₃ glacé cherries, halved
finely grated zest of 1 orange
2 tbsp ground almonds
25 g/1 oz/¹/₄ cup blanched
almonds, chopped
125 ml/4 fl oz/¹/₂ cup soya milk
75 ml/3 fl oz/6 tbsp sunflower oil
2 tbsp malt vinegar
1 tsp bicarbonate of soda

To Decorate
mixed nuts, such as pistachios,
pecans and macadamia, glacé
cherries and angelica
4 tbsp clear honey, warmed

STORING
This cake can be kept for up to one
week in an airtight container.

1 Preheat the oven to 150°C/300°F/
Gas 2. Grease a deep 20 cm/8 inch
square loose-bottom cake tin, line with
a double thickness of greaseproof paper
and grease the paper.

2 ▲ Sift the flour and mixed spice into
a large mixing bowl, adding the bran
left in the sieve. Rub the margarine into
the flour until it resembles fine
breadcrumbs. Stir in the sugar, dried
fruits, mixed peel, cherries, orange zest
and ground and blanched almonds.

3 ▲ Warm 50 ml/2 fl oz/¹/₄ cup of the
soya milk in a saucepan, then add
the sunflower oil and vinegar. Dissolve
the bicarbonate of soda in the rest of the
milk, then combine the two mixtures
and stir into the dry ingredients.

4 ▲ Spoon the cake mixture into the
prepared tin and smooth the
surface. Bake in the centre of the oven
for about 2¹/₂ hours or until a skewer
inserted into the centre of the cake
comes out clean. Leave the cake in the
tin for about 5 minutes, then turn out
on to a wire rack, peel off the lining
paper and leave to cool completely.

5 Place the mixed nuts, glacé cherries
and angelica on top of the cake,
then brush with the warmed honey.

Autumn Cake

Greengages, plums or stoned semi-dried prunes
are delicious in this recipe.

INGREDIENTS
Serves 6–8
115 g/4 oz/½ cup butter, softened
150 g/5 oz/¾ cup caster sugar
3 size 3 eggs, beaten
75 g/3 oz/1 cup ground hazelnuts
150 g/5 oz/1¼ cup shelled pecan
nuts, chopped
50 g/2 oz/½ cup plain flour
1 tsp baking powder
½ tsp salt
675 g/1½ lb stoned plums,
greengages or semi-dried prunes
4 tbsp lime marmalade
1 tbsp lime juice
2 tbsp blanched almonds, chopped,
to decorate

STORING
This cake is not suitable for storing.

1 Preheat the oven to 180°C/350°F/
Gas 4. Grease a 23 cm/9 inch
round, fluted tart tin.

2 ▲ Place the butter and sugar in a
mixing bowl and beat with an
electric mixer until light and fluffy.
Gradually beat in the eggs, alternating
with the ground hazelnuts, until evenly
combined.

3 Stir in the pecan nuts, then sift in
the flour, baking powder and salt.
Fold in until evenly combined, then
transfer the mixture to the prepared tin.

4 ▲ Bake in the centre of the oven for
45–50 minutes or until a skewer
inserted into the centre of the cake
comes out clean.

5 ▲ Remove from the oven and
carefully arrange the fruit on top.
Return to the oven and bake for a
further 10–15 minutes until the fruit
has softened. Transfer to a wire rack to
cool completely then remove the cake
from the tin.

6 Place the marmalade and lime juice
in a small saucepan and warm
gently. Brush over the fruit, then
sprinkle with the almonds. Allow to set,
then chill before serving.

 utumn Passionettes

Perfect for a tea party or packed lunch, this passion cake mixture can also be made as one big cake to serve for a celebration or as a dessert.

INGREDIENTS
Makes 24
150 g/5 oz/³/₄ cup butter, melted
200 g/7 oz/⁷/₈ cup soft light brown sugar
115 g/4 oz/1 cup carrots, peeled and finely grated
50 g/2 oz/1 cup dessert apples, peeled and finely grated
pinch of salt
1–2 tsp ground mixed spice
2 size 3 eggs
200 g/7 oz/1³/₄ cups self-raising flour
2 tsp baking powder
115 g/4 oz/1 cup shelled walnuts, finely chopped

For the Topping
175 g/6 oz/³/₄ cup full-fat soft cheese
4–5 tbsp single cream
50 g/2 oz/¹/₂ cup icing sugar, sifted
25 g/1 oz/¹/₄ cup shelled walnuts, halved
2 tsp cocoa powder, sifted

STORING
Both the large and small cakes can be kept for up to four days in an airtight container.

1 Preheat the oven to 180°C/350°F/ Gas 4. Arrange 24 fairy cake paper cases in bun tins and put to one side.

2 ▲ Place the butter, sugar, carrots, apples, salt, mixed spice and eggs in a mixing bowl and beat well to combine.

3 ▲ Sift together the flour and baking powder into a small bowl, then sift again into the mixing bowl. Add the chopped walnuts and fold in until evenly blended.

4 ▲ Fill the paper cases half-full with the cake mixture, then bake for 20–25 minutes, or until a skewer inserted into the centres of the cakes comes out clean.

5 Leave the cakes in the tins for about 5 minutes, before transferring them to a wire rack to cool completely.

6 ▲ To make the topping, place the full-fat soft cheese in a mixing bowl and beat in the cream and icing sugar until smooth. Put a dollop of the topping in the centre of each cake, then decorate with the walnuts. Dust with sifted cocoa powder and allow the icing to set before serving.

Tip

To make one big cake, which will serve 6–8, grease a 20 cm/8 inch fluted American bundt cake tin and line the base with greaseproof paper. Grease the paper. Place all of the cake mixture in the tin and bake for about 1¹/₄ hours, or until a skewer inserted into the centre of the cake comes out clean. Leave the cake in the tin for about 5 minutes. Turn out on to a wire rack, peel off the lining paper and leave to cool completely. Decorate with the topping mixture, walnuts and sifted cocoa powder.

Apple Crumble Cake

In the autumn use windfall apples. Served
warm with thick cream or custard this cake doubles as a dessert.

INGREDIENTS
Serves 8–10
For the Topping
75 g/3 oz/¾ cup self-raising flour
½ tsp ground cinnamon
40 g/1½ oz/3 tbsp butter
25 g/1 oz/2 tbsp caster sugar

For the Base
50 g/2 oz/4 tbsp butter, softened
75 g/3 oz/6 tbsp caster sugar
1 size 3 egg, beaten
115 g/4 oz/1 cup self-raising
flour, sifted
2 cooking apples, peeled, cored
and sliced
50 g/2 oz/⅓ cup sultanas

To Decorate
1 red dessert apple, cored, thinly
sliced and tossed in lemon juice
2 tbsp caster sugar, sifted 1
pinch of ground cinnamon

STORING
This cake can be kept for up to two
days in an airtight container.

1 Preheat the oven 180°C/350°F/
Gas 4. Grease a deep 18 cm/7 inch
springform tin, line the base with
greaseproof paper and grease the paper.

2 ▲ To make the topping, sift the
flour and cinnamon into a mixing
bowl. Rub the butter into the flour until
it resembles breadcrumbs, then stir in
the sugar. Set aside.

3 ▲ To make the base, put the butter,
sugar, egg and flour into a bowl and
beat for 1–2 minutes until smooth.
Spoon into the prepared tin.

4 ▲ Mix together the apple slices and
sultanas and spread them evenly
over the top. Sprinkle with the topping.

5 Bake in the centre of the oven for
about 1 hour. Cool in the tin for 10
minutes before turning out on to a wire
rack and peeling off the lining paper.
Serve warm or cool, decorated with
slices of red dessert apple and caster
sugar and cinnamon sprinkled over.

Summer Strawberry Shortcake

A summer-time treat. Serve with a cool glass
of pink sparkling wine for a truly refreshing dessert.

INGREDIENTS
Serves 6–8
225 g/8 oz/2 cups plain flour
1 tbsp baking powder
½ tsp salt
50 g/2 oz/4 tbsp caster sugar
50 g/2 oz/4 tbsp butter, softened
150 ml/¼ pint/⅔ cup milk
300 ml/½ pint/1¼ cups double cream
450 g/1 lb fresh strawberries, halved
and hulled

STORING
This cake is not suitable for storing.

1 Preheat the oven to 220°C/425°F/
Gas 7. Grease a baking sheet, line
the base with greaseproof paper and
grease the paper.

2 ▲ Sift the flour, baking powder and
salt together into a large mixing
bowl. Stir in the sugar, cut in the butter
and toss into the flour mixture until it
resembles coarse breadcrumbs. Stir in
just enough milk to make a soft dough.

3 ▲ Turn out the dough on to a
lightly floured work surface and
pat, using your fingers, into a 30 ×
15 cm/12 × 6 inch rectangle. Using a
template, cut out two 15 cm/6 inch
rounds, indent one of the rounds
dividing it into eight equal portions,
and place them on the baking sheet.

4 ▲ Bake in the centre of the oven
for 10–15 minutes or until slightly
risen and golden. Leave the shortcake
on the baking sheet for approximately
5 minutes, then transfer to a wire rack,
peel off the lining paper and leave to
cool completely.

5 Place the cream in a mixing bowl
and whip with an electric mixer
until it holds soft peaks. Place the
unmarked shortcake on a serving plate
and spread or pipe with half of the
cream. Top with two-thirds of the
strawberries, then the other shortcake.
Use the remaining cream and
strawberries to decorate the top layer.
Chill the cake for at least 30 minutes
before serving.

Fresh Fruit Genoese

This Italian classic, 'Genovese con Panne e Frutta',
can be made with any type of soft fresh fruit.

INGREDIENTS
Serves 8–10
For the Sponge
175 g/6 oz/1¹/₂ cups plain flour, sifted
pinch of salt
4 size 3 eggs
115 g/4 oz/¹/₂ cup caster sugar
6 tbsp orange-flavoured liqueur

For the Filling and Topping
600 ml/1 pint/2¹/₂ cups double cream
4 tbsp vanilla sugar
450 g/1 lb fresh soft fruit, such as
raspberries, blueberries, cherries, etc.
150 g/5 oz/1¹/₄ cups shelled pistachio
nuts, finely chopped
4 tbsp apricot jam, warmed and
sieved, to glaze

STORING
This cake is not suitable for storing.

ip

To save time and money, use
shop-bought chopped mixed nuts
to coat the sides of the gâteau
instead of pistachios.

1 Preheat the oven to 180°C/350°F/
Gas 4. Grease a 21 cm/8¹/₂ inch
round springform cake tin, line the
base with greaseproof paper and grease
the paper.

2 ▲ Sift the flour and salt together
three times, then set aside.

3 Place the eggs and sugar in a mixing
bowl and beat with an electric
mixer for about 10 minutes or until
thick and pale.

4 ▲ Sift the reserved flour mixture
into the mixing bowl, then fold in
very gently. Transfer the cake mixture
to the prepared tin. Bake in the centre
of the oven for 30–35 minutes or until
a skewer inserted into the centre of the
cake comes out clean. Leave the cake in
the tin for about 5 minutes, then turn
out on to a wire rack, peel off the lining
paper and leave to cool completely.

5 Cut the cake horizontally into two
layers, and place the bottom layer
on a serving plate. Sprinkle the orange-
flavoured liqueur over both layers.

6 ▲ Place the double cream and
vanilla sugar in a mixing bowl and
beat with an electric mixer until it
holds peaks.

7 ▲ Spread two-thirds of the cream
mixture over the bottom layer of
cake and top with half the fruit. Place
the second layer of the cake on top and
spread the remaining cream over the
top and sides.

8 Using a knife, lightly press the
chopped nuts evenly around the
sides. Arrange the remaining fresh fruit
on top and brush over a light glaze
using the apricot jam.

Marbled Spice Cake

This cake is baked in a fluted ring-shaped tin called a kugelhupf mould from Germany and Austria to give it a pretty shape.

INGREDIENTS
Serves 8–10

75 g/3 oz/6 tbsp butter, softened
115 g/4 oz/½ cup caster sugar
2 size 3 eggs, lightly beaten
few drops of vanilla essence
130 g/4½ oz plain flour
1½ tsp baking powder
3 tbsp milk
3 tbsp black treacle
1 tsp ground mixed spice
½ tsp ground ginger
175 g/6 oz/1⅛ cups icing sugar,
    sifted, to decorate

STORING
This cake can be kept for up to two days in an airtight container.

1 Preheat the oven to 180°C/350°F/ Gas 4. Grease and flour a 900 g/2 lb kugelhupf mould or ring-shaped cake tin.

2 Cream the butter and sugar together in a bowl until light and fluffy. Beat in the egg and vanilla essence.

3 ▲ Sift together the flour and baking powder, then fold into the mixture, alternating with the milk, until evenly combined.

4 Spoon about one-third of the mixture into a small bowl and stir in the treacle and spices.

5 ▲ Drop alternating spoonfuls of the light and dark mixtures into the tin. Run a knife or skewer through them to give a marbled effect.

6 ▲ Bake in the centre of the oven for about 50 minutes or until a skewer inserted into the centre comes out clean. Leave in the tin for 10 minutes before turning out on to a wire rack to cool.

7 ▲ To decorate, stir enough warm water into the icing sugar to make a smooth icing. Spoon quickly over the cake. Allow to set before serving.

Tip
If you do not have a kugelhupf mould or a ring-shaped cake tin, use a 20 cm/8 inch round cake tin.

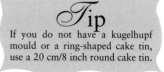

Apricot Brandy-snap Roulade

A magnificent combination of soft and crisp textures, this cake looks impressive and is easy to prepare.

INGREDIENTS
Serves 6–8
4 size 3 eggs, separated
½ tbsp fresh orange juice
115 g/4 oz/½ cup caster sugar
175 g/6 oz/2 cups ground almonds
4 brandy-snap biscuits, crushed,
to decorate

For the Filling
150 g/5 oz canned apricots, drained
300 ml/½ pint/1¼ cups double cream
25 g/1 oz/4 tbsp icing sugar

STORING
This cake is not suitable for storing.

3 ▲ Whisk the egg whites until they hold stiff peaks. Fold the egg whites into the almond mixture, then transfer to the Swiss roll tin and smooth the surface. Bake in the centre of the oven for about 20 minutes or until a skewer inserted into the centre comes out clean. Leave to cool in the tin, covered with a clean, just-damp cloth.

4 ▲ To make the filling, place the apricots in a blender or food processor and purée until smooth. Place the cream and icing sugar in a mixing bowl and whip until the cream holds soft peaks. Fold in the apricot purée.

5 Spread out the crushed brandy-snaps, on a sheet of greaseproof paper. Spread about one-third of the cream mixture over the cake, then invert it on to the crushed brandy-snaps. Peel away the lining paper.

6 Use the remaining cream mixture to cover the cake, then, using the greaseproof paper as a guide, tightly and neatly roll up the roulade from a short end. Transfer to a serving dish, sticking on any extra pieces of crushed brandy-snaps.

1 ▲ Preheat the oven to 190°C/375°F/ Gas 5. Grease a 33 × 23 cm/13 × 9 inch Swiss roll tin, line the base with greaseproof paper and grease the paper.

2 Place the egg yolks, orange juice and sugar in a mixing bowl and beat with an electric mixer for about 10 minutes until thick and pale. Fold in the ground almonds.

Special
Occasion Cakes

*Here you will find inspired ideas for christenings, Christmas,
Hallowe'en, Easter, birthdays and Valentine's day. Employing
an imaginative variety of decorating techniques, the recipes
range from a sumptuous chocolate-iced anniversary cake to a
wonderful royal-iced wedding extravaganza.*

Teddy Bear Christening Cake

To personalise the cake, make a simple plaque for the top and pipe or write the name of the new baby with a food colouring pen.

INGREDIENTS
Serves 30
20 cm/8 inch square Light
Fruit Cake
3 tbsp apricot jam, warmed
and sieved
900 g/2 lb marzipan
800 g/1¾ lb/2⅓ x quantity
Sugarpaste Icing
peach, yellow, blue and brown
food colourings
115 g/4oz/¹⁄₆ quantity Royal Icing

MATERIALS AND EQUIPMENT
25 cm/10 inch square cake board
crimping tool
blossom cutter or plunger
foam pad
7.5 cm/3 inch round cutter
frill cutter
wooden cocktail stick
peach ribbon
small blue ribbon bow

STORING
*The finished cake can be stored
for up to four weeks in an
airtight container.*

1 Brush the cake with the apricot jam. Roll out the marzipan on a work surface lightly dusted with icing sugar, then use to cover the cake. Leave to dry for 12 hours.

2 Colour 500 g/1¼ lb of the sugarpaste icing peach. Roll out the icing. Brush the marzipan with a little water and cover the cake with the icing.

3 ▲ Position the cake on the cake board. Using a crimping tool dipped in cornflour, crimp the top and bottom edges of the cake.

4 Divide the remaining sugarpaste into three portions. Leave one-third white and colour one-third yellow. Cut the remaining third in half and colour one portion peach and the other blue.

5 ▲ To make the flowers, roll out the peach and blue sugarpaste thinly on a work surface lightly dusted with icing sugar. Dip the end of the blossom cutter or a plunger in cornflour and cut out small and larger flowers. Place a small ball of peach icing in the centre of the blue flowers; and a small ball of blue icing in the centre of the peach flowers. Secure with water, if necessary. Leave the flowers to dry on a foam pad for several hours or overnight. Gather together the blue icing trimmings and set aside, wrapped in clear film.

6 ▲ Make the teddy bear with the yellow icing. Shape the head, body, arms and ears of the bear and press together with a little water to secure. Make the button for the chest out of a little blue icing. Paint on highlights, such as eyes, nose and mouth, with brown food colouring. Leave the bear to dry on a piece of greaseproof paper for several hours or overnight.

7 To make the blanket, roll out the blue icing and cut out a circle with the 7.5 cm/3 inch round cutter. Slice off a small piece, about 1 cm/½ inch, to give a straight line for the top. Set aside. Roll out the white icing thinly and, using the frill cutter, cut out a ring. Put the end of the wooden cocktail stick over about 5 mm/¼ inch of the outer edge of the ring. Roll the stick around the edge firmly back and forth with your finger so the edge becomes thinner and begins to frill. Continue until the ring is completely frilled. Using a sharp knife, cut through the ring once to open it up. Gently ease it open.

8 ▲ Brush the edge of the blue blanket with water and secure the white frill on to the edge.

9 Decorate the cake with the ribbon. Position the bear on top and lay the blanket over it, securing with a little water or royal icing. Secure the flowers with a little royal icing and then the bow to the bear's neck in the same way.

*R*ose Blossom Wedding Cake

The traditional white wedding cake, with its classic lines and elegant piping, is still a favourite choice for many brides and grooms.

INGREDIENTS
Serves 80
23 cm/9 inch square Rich Fruit Cake
15 cm/6 inch square Rich Fruit Cake
75 ml/7 tbsp apricot jam, warmed
and sieved
1.5 kg/3½ lb marzipan
1.5 kg/3½ lb/2⅓ x quantity Royal
Icing, to coat
675 g/1½ lb/1 quantity Royal Icing,
to pipe
pink and green food colourings

MATERIALS AND EQUIPMENT
28 cm/11 inch square cake board
20 cm/8 inch square cake board
No 1 writing and No 42 nozzles
several greaseproof paper
piping bags
thin pink ribbon
8 pink bows
3–4 cake pillars
about 12 miniature roses
few fern sprigs

STORING
*The finished cake can be kept
for up to three months in an
airtight container.*

1 Brush the cakes with the apricot jam and cover with marzipan, allowing 450 g/1 lb marzipan for the 15 cm/6 inch cake and the remainder for the 23 cm/ 9 inch cake. Place the cakes on the cake boards and leave to dry for 12 hours.

2 Make the royal icing for coating the cake. Secure the cakes to the cake boards with a little of the icing. Flat ice the cakes with three or four layers of smooth icing, allowing each layer to dry overnight before applying the next. The royal icing should be very dry before assembling the cake, so it can be made to this stage and stored in cardboard cake boxes for several days.

3 Make the royal icing for piping, and colour a small amount pale pink and another small portion pale green. To make the piped sugar pieces, draw the double-triangle design on a piece of greaseproof paper several times. You will need 40 pieces, but make extra in case of breakages. Tape the paper to a baking sheet or flat board and secure a piece of baking parchment over the top. Tape it down at the corners.

4 ▲ Fit a piping bag with a No 1 writing nozzle. Half-fill with white royal icing and fold over the top to seal. Pipe over each design, carefully following the outlines with a continuous thread of icing. Spoon a little of the pink icing and a little of the green icing into separate paper piping bags fitted with No 1 writing nozzles. Pipe pink dots on the corners of the top triangle in each design and green on the corners of the bottom triangle in each design. Leave to dry for at least two hours.

5 Mark four triangles on the top and side of each cake with a pin. Work from the centre of each side, so each triangle is 6 cm/2½ inches wide at the base and 4 cm/1½ inches high on the smaller cake, and 7.5 cm/3 inches wide at the base and 5 cm/2 inches high on the larger cake. Fit a paper piping bag with a clean No 1 writing nozzle and half-fill with some of the white icing. Using the pin marks as a guide, pipe double lines to outline the triangles.

6 ▲ Using the same nozzle, pipe cornelli inside all the triangles.

7 ▲ Fit a piping bag with a No 42 nozzle and half-fill with white icing. Pipe shells around the top and bottom edges of each cake, but not within the triangles.

8 Using the piping bags fitted with No 1 writing nozzles and filled with pink and green icing, pipe dots on the corners of each cake.

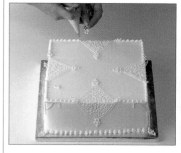

9 ▲ Remove the piped sugar pieces from the paper by carefully turning it back and lifting off each piece with a palette knife. Secure them to the cake and cake board with a little icing.

10 Decorate the cake with the ribbon and bows. Just before serving, assemble the cake with the cake pillars and decorate with the roses and fern sprigs.

*F*lickering Birthday Candle Cake

Stripy icing candles are flickering and ready to blow out on this birthday celebration cake for all ages.

INGREDIENTS
Serves 15–20
*20 cm/8 inch square Madeira Cake
1 quantity Butter Icing
3 tbsp apricot jam, warmed and sieved
800 g/1¾ lb/2⅓ x quantity
Sugarpaste Icing
pink, yellow, purple and jade
food colourings
edible silver balls, to decorate*

MATERIALS AND EQUIPMENT
*23 cm/9 inch square cake board
leaf cutter
small round cutter
pink and purple food colouring pens
5 mm/¼ inch wide jade-
coloured ribbon*

STORING
*The finished cake can be stored
for up to one week in an
airtight container.*

1 Cut the cake horizontally into three layers, using a long serrated knife. Sandwich the layers together with the butter icing and brush the cake with the apricot jam. Roll out 500 g/1¼ lb of the sugarpaste icing on a work surface lightly dusted with icing sugar and use to cover the cake. Position on the cake board.

2 Divide the remaining sugarpaste into four portions and colour one portion pink, one portion yellow, one portion pale purple and one portion jade. Roll out the jade icing and cut into six 1 cm/½ inch wide strips of slightly different lengths, but each long enough to go over the side and on to the top of the cake. Make a diagonal cut at one end of each strip.

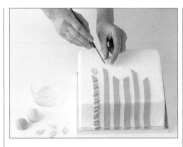

3 ▲ Roll out the yellow icing and cut out six candle flames with the leaf cutter. Place a silver ball in each flame. Set aside the remaining yellow icing, wrapped in clear film. Arrange the candles on top of the cake, securing with a little water. Mould small strips, fractionally longer than the width of each candle, from the yellow and purple icings. Arrange alternate colours on the candles at a slight angle, securing with water. Position the flames at the end of each jade strip, also securing with water.

4 ▲ Roll out the pink and remaining purple icings, then cut out wavy pieces with a sharp knife. Attach to the cake, above the candles, with a little water. Gather together the pink icing trimmings and roll into a ball.

5 ▲ Using the leftover yellow and pink icings, make the decorations for the sides of the cake. Roll out the yellow icing and cut out circles with the small round cutter or the end of a piping nozzle. Make small balls from the pink icing and attach to the yellow circles with a little water. Press a silver ball in the centre of each pink ball.

6 Arrange the decorations around the bottom edge of the cake, securing with water.

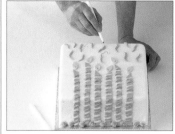

7 ▲ Using food colouring pens, draw wavy lines and dots coming from the purple and pink wavy icings. Decorate the sides of the cake board with the ribbon, securing at the back with a little softened sugarpaste.

*J*azzy Chocolate Gâteau

This cake is made with Father's Day in mind, though really it can be made for anyone who loves chocolate.

INGREDIENTS
Serves 12–15
2 x quantity chocolate-flavour Quick-Mix Sponge Cake mix
75 g/3 oz/3 squares plain chocolate
75 g/3 oz/3 squares white chocolate
½ quantity Fudge Frosting
½ quantity Glacé Icing
1 tsp weak coffee
8 tbsp chocolate hazelnut spread

MATERIALS AND EQUIPMENT
2 x 20 cm/8 inch round cake tins
greaseproof paper piping bag
No 1 writing nozzle

STORING
The finished cake can be kept for up to three days in the refrigerator.

1 Preheat the oven to 160°C/325°F/ Gas 3. Grease the cake tins, line the bases with greaseproof paper and grease the paper. Divide the cake mixture evenly between the tins and smooth the surfaces. Bake in the centre of the oven for 20–30 minutes, or until firm to the touch. Turn out on to a wire rack, peel off the paper and leave to cool completely.

2 Meanwhile, cover a large baking sheet or board (or two smaller ones) with baking parchment and tape it down at each corner. Melt each chocolate in separate bowls over pans of hot water, stirring until smooth, then pour on to the baking parchment. Spread out the chocolates evenly with a palette knife. Allow to cool until the surfaces are firm enough to cut, but not so hard that they will break. The chocolate should no longer feel sticky when touched with your finger.

3 ▲ Cut out haphazard shapes of chocolate and set aside.

4 ▲ Make the fudge frosting and, when cool enough to spread, use to sandwich the two cakes together. Place the cake on a stand or plate.

5 Make the glacé icing, using 1 tsp weak coffee (to colour it very slightly) along with enough water to form a spreading consistency, and spread on top of the cake almost to the edges. Spread the side of the cake with enough chocolate hazelnut spread to cover.

6 ▲ Arrange the chocolate pieces around the side of the cake, pressing into the hazelnut spread to secure.

7 To decorate, spoon about 3 tbsp of the chocolate hazelnut spread into a piping bag fitted with a No 1 nozzle and pipe 'jazzy' lines over the glacé icing.

Mother's Day Bouquet

A piped bouquet of flowers can bring as much pleasure as a fresh one for a Mother's Day treat.

INGREDIENTS
Serves 8–10
1 quantity Quick-Mix Sponge Cake mix
2 x quantity Butter Icing green, blue, yellow and pink food colourings

MATERIALS AND EQUIPMENT
2 x 18 cm/7 inch round cake tins
serrated scraper
5 greaseproof paper piping bags
No 3 writing and petal nozzles

STORING
The finished cake can be kept for up to three days in an airtight container in the refrigerator.

1 Preheat the oven to 160°C/325°F/ Gas 3. Grease the cake tins, line the bases with greaseproof paper and grease the paper. Divide the cake mixture evenly between the tins and smooth the surfaces. Bake in the centre of the oven for about 20 minutes or until firm to the touch. Turn out on to a wire rack, peel off the lining paper and leave to cool.

2 ▲ Place one of the cakes on paper on a turntable. Use half to two-thirds of the butter icing to sandwich the cakes together and to coat the top and sides. Coat the top using a palette knife and the sides using the scraper.

3 Transfer the cake to a serving plate, then divide the remaining butter icing into four bowls and colour one portion green, one portion blue, one portion yellow and one portion pink. Spoon the blue icing into a greaseproof paper piping bag fitted with the No 3 writing nozzle. Pipe the vase on top of the cake in lines and beads.

4 ▲ Spoon the green icing into a fresh piping bag fitted with a clean No 3 writing nozzle. Pipe the flower stems coming out of the vase.

5 Spoon the pink icing into a fresh piping bag fitted with the petal nozzle. Pipe pink petals on the ends of some of the stems. Pipe beads of blue icing in the centres.

6 Spoon most of the yellow icing into a fresh piping bag fitted with a clean petal nozzle and pipe yellow flowers on the remaining stems. Pipe beads of blue icing in the centres.

7 ▲ Decorate the side of the cake. Pipe stems with leaves evenly spaced all around the side with the green icing, and pipe beads of the blue icing to make flowers at the end of each stem. Spoon the reserved yellow icing into a fresh piping bag fitted with a clean No 3 writing nozzle and pipe small beads in the centre of the blue flowers.

8 Pipe beads of green icing round the top and bottom edges of the cake.

Valentine's Heart Cake

Cakes decorated with hearts can be very adaptable. Although this one was designed with Valentine's Day in mind, it could also be used to celebrate a birthday for someone special, an anniversary, or be made as two tiers for a wedding cake.

INGREDIENTS
Serves 30
20 cm/8 inch square Light Fruit Cake
3 tbsp apricot jam, warmed
and sieved
900 g/2 lb marzipan
1.5 kg/3 lb/2 x quantity Royal Icing
115 g/4 oz/⅓ quantity Sugarpaste
Icing
red food colouring

MATERIALS AND EQUIPMENT
1 x 25 cm/10 inch square
cake board
5 cm/2 inch heart-shaped cutter
2.5 cm/1 inch heart-shaped cutter
4 greaseproof paper piping bags
No 1 and No 2 writing and No 42
star nozzles
heart-patterned ribbon

STORING
*The finished cake can be stored
for up to four weeks in an
airtight container.*

1 Brush the cake with the apricot jam.
Roll out the marzipan on a surface
lightly dusted with icing sugar and
cover the cake. Leave to dry for about
12 hours.

2 Secure the cake to the cake board
with a little of the royal icing. Flat
ice the cake with three or four layers of
smooth icing, allowing each layer to dry
overnight before applying the next. Set
aside a little of the royal icing in an
airtight container for piping.

3 ▲ To make the heart decorations,
colour the sugarpaste icing red.
Roll out the red icing on a work surface
lightly dusted with icing sugar and cut
out 12 hearts with the 5 cm/2 inch
heart-shaped cutter. Place the 2.5 cm/
1 inch heart-shaped cutter in the centre
of each larger heart and cut out a
smaller heart, so you have 12 small
hearts and 12 larger hollow hearts.
Cut out four more smaller hearts from
the red icing so you have 16 total.
Place the hearts on a board covered
with greaseproof paper.

4 ▲ Spoon a little of the reserved
royal icing into a greaseproof paper
piping bag fitted with a No 1 writing
nozzle. Pipe wavy lines around the
edges of four of the small hearts. Leave
all the hearts to dry for several hours or
overnight.

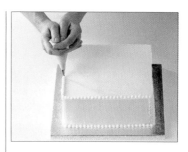

5 ▲ Spoon some more royal icing into
a fresh piping bag fitted with a No
42 nozzle. Pipe swirls around the top
and bottom edges of the cake with some
of the royal icing.

6 ▲ Colour a heaped tablespoon of
the remaining royal icing red and
spoon into a fresh piping bag fitted with
a clean No 1 writing nozzle. Pipe red
dots on top of each white swirl of icing.

7 ▲ Arrange four of the large hearts
on top of the cake, securing with a
little royal icing.

8 Decorate with the ribbon. Spoon the
remaining white royal icing into a
fresh piping bag fitted with a No 2
writing nozzle. Pipe beads of icing
down each side of the cake, above and
below the ribbon. Allow all the piping
to dry for several hours.

9 Arrange the remaining large hearts
on top of the cake, securing with a
little royal icing. Arrange the remaining
small hearts on the sides.

Harvest Blackberry Ring

Gracious blackberry branches twisting their way over the cake, and leaves tinged with reddish-brown, create an autumnal theme.

INGREDIENTS
Serves 20
*1 quantity 18 cm/7 inch round
Light Fruit Cake mix
3 tbsp apricot jam, warmed
and sieved
450 g/1 lb marzipan
900 g/2 lb/2⅔ x quantity
Sugarpaste Icing
tangerine, purple, green and paprika
food colourings*

MATERIALS AND EQUIPMENT
*20 cm/8 inch ring mould
25 cm/10 inch round cake board*

STORING
*The finished cake can be stored
for up to four weeks in an
airtight container.*

1 Preheat the oven to 150°C/300°F/
Gas 2. Grease the cake tin, line with
greaseproof paper and grease the paper.
Spoon in the cake mixture and smooth
the surface with the back of a wet metal
spoon. Bake in the centre of the oven
for 1½–2 hours or until a skewer
inserted in the centre of the cake comes
out clean. Leave the cake to cool in the
mould on a wire rack. When completely
cool, turn out.

2 Brush the cake with the apricot jam.
Measure half the circumference of
the cake with a piece of string. Measure
the height to include the top as well as
the sides of the cake (see step 4 for
guidance). Take three-quarters of the
marzipan and cut in half. Cover the
cake in two halves as follows. Roll out
each piece of marzipan on a work
surface lightly dusted with icing sugar
and trim each using the string
measurements as a guide. Trim and
press the joins together to secure.

3 Measure the height and
circumference of the inside of the
ring with string. Cover the inside by
rolling out the remaining one-quarter of
marzipan. Trim to fit and press the joins
together to secure. Position the cake on
the board. Leave to dry for 12 hours.

4 ▲ Measure half the circumference
of the cake with a piece of string.
Measure the height to include the top as
well as the sides of the cake.

5 ▲ Colour 675 g/1½ lb of the
sugarpaste icing pale tangerine. Cut
off three-quarters of this and cut in half.
Keep the remaining icing well wrapped.
Brush the marzipan lightly with water.
Cover the top and sides of the cake in
two pieces by rolling out each piece of
icing. Trim and press the joins together.

6 Measure the height and
circumference of the inside of the
ring with string. Cover the inside of the
ring by rolling out the remaining one-
quarter of sugarpaste icing, using the
string measurement as a guide. Trim to
fit and press the joins together to secure.

7 ▲ Colour one-quarter of the white
sugarpaste icing purple. To mould
the blackberries, take a little of the
purple icing and form into balls of
different sizes for the bases. Make a
number of smaller balls and stick them
on the outside of the larger ones,
securing with water. Place on a piece of
greaseproof paper and leave to dry
while making the leaves and branches.

8 ▲ Colour two-thirds of the
remaining white sugarpaste icing
green and the rest paprika. Reserve half
of the green icing for the stems, and
knead the remaining green and the
paprika icing lightly together until
marbled. Roll out and cut out leaf
shapes. Make the branches by rolling
the green icing into long thin strands.

9 To assemble, arrange the branches
on the cake, securing them with a
little water and twisting them as
necessary, covering any joins in the
icing where possible. Attach the leaves,
bending them into shape, then arrange
the blackberries on the cake attaching
all with a little water.

*P*ansy Retirement Cake

Sugar-frosted edible flowers make a very effective cake decoration. If pansies are not in season, use other edible flowers such as nasturtiums, roses or tiny daffodils to wish someone a happy retirement. Just co-ordinate the colour of the icing, piping and ribbon with the colour of the flowers.

INGREDIENTS
Serves 20–25
20 cm/8 inch round Light Fruit Cake
3 tbsp apricot jam, warmed
and sieved
675 g/1½ lb marzipan
1.1 kg/2½ lb/1⅔ x quantity
Royal Icing
orange food colouring
1 size 3 egg white, lightly beaten
caster sugar, for frosting
about 7 pansies (orange and purple)

MATERIALS AND EQUIPMENT
25 cm/10 inch round cake board
2 greaseproof paper piping bags
No 19 star and No 1
writing nozzles
2 cm/¾ inch wide purple ribbon
3 mm/⅛ inch wide dark
purple ribbon

STORING
The finished cake can be stored
for up to four weeks in an
airtight container.

1 Brush the cake with the apricot jam. Roll out the marzipan on a work surface lightly dusted with icing sugar and cover the cake. Leave to dry for 12 hours.

2 Secure the cake to the cake board with a little of the royal icing. Colour one-quarter of the royal icing pale orange. Flat ice the cake with three or four layers of smooth icing, allowing each layer to dry overnight before applying the next, using the orange icing for the top and the white for the sides. Set aside a little of both icings in airtight containers, to decorate the cake.

3 ▲ To sugar-frost the pansies, have ready a small bowl with the egg white and a plate with caster sugar. Dry the pansies on kitchen paper. If possible, leave some stem attached. Evenly brush the pansies all over on both sides of the petals with the egg white. Holding the flowers by their stems, sprinkle them evenly with the sugar, then shake off any excess. Place the frosted flowers on a flat board or wire rack covered with greaseproof or kitchen paper and leave to dry in a warm place overnight.

4 ▲ Spoon the reserved white royal icing into a greaseproof paper piping bag fitted with a No 19 star nozzle. Pipe a row of scrolls around the top of the cake.

5 ▲ Reverse the direction of the scrolls and pipe another row directly underneath the first row.

6 ▲ Pipe another row of scrolls around the bottom of the cake. Spoon the reserved orange icing into a fresh piping bag fitted with a No 1 writing nozzle. Pipe around the outline of the top of each scroll.

7 Using the same piping bag, pipe a row of single dots underneath the top row of reverse scrolls and a double row of dots above the bottom row of scrolls. Arrange the sugar-frosted pansies on top of the cake. Decorate with the ribbons, centring the narrow, darker ribbon on top of the wider one.

Birthday Parcel

*Here is a birthday cake that is all wrapped up and ready to eat.
The pattern on the iced present can be changed by
using different shaped cutters.*

INGREDIENTS
Serves 10
15 cm/6 in square Madeira Cake
¾ quantity orange-flavour
Butter Icing
3 tbsp apricot jam, warmed
and sieved
450 g/1 lb/1⅓ x quantity
Sugarpaste Icing
blue, orange and green food colourings

MATERIALS AND EQUIPMENT
15–18 cm/7–8 inch square cake board
small round and triangular
cocktail cutters

STORING
*The finished cake can be kept for up
to one week in an airtight container.*

1 Cut the cake in half horizontally and sandwich together with the butter icing. Brush the cake with apricot jam. Colour three-quarters of the sugarpaste icing blue. Divide the remaining sugarpaste icing in half and colour one-half orange and the other half green. Wrap the orange and green sugarpaste separately in plastic wrap and set aside. Roll out the blue icing on a work surface lightly dusted with icing sugar and use it to cover the cake. Position on the cake board.

2 While the sugarpaste covering is still soft, cut out circles and triangles from the blue icing with the cocktail cutters, lifting out the shapes to expose the cake beneath.

3 ▲ Roll out the orange and green icings and use the same cutters to cut out circles and triangles. Replace the exposed holes in the blue icing with the orange and green shapes, easing in to fit. Gather together the orange and green trimmings.

4 ▲ Roll out the orange trimmings and cut three strips about 2 cm/ ¾ inch wide and long enough to go over each corner of the cake. Roll out the green trimmings and cut three very thin strips the same length as the orange ones. Place the orange and green strips next to each other to give three striped ribbons, and secure the pieces together with a little water.

5 Place one striped ribbon over one corner of the cake, securing with a little water. Place a second strip over the opposite corner.

6 ▲ Cut the remaining ribbon in half. Bend each half to make loops and attach both to one corner of the cake with water to form a loose bow.

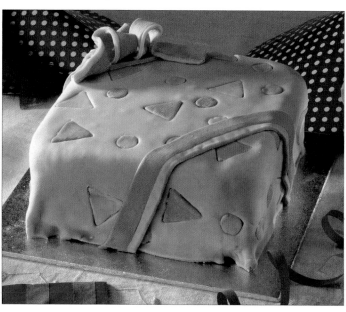

*E*aster Egg Nest Cake

Celebrate Easter with a fresh-tasting lemon sponge, colourfully adorned with marzipan nests and chocolate eggs.

INGREDIENTS
Serves 10
1 quantity lemon-flavour Quick-Mix Sponge Cake mix
350 g/12 oz/1 quantity lemon-flavour Butter Icing
225 g/8 oz marzipan
pink, green and purple food colourings
foil-wrapped chocolate eggs

MATERIALS AND EQUIPMENT
20 cm/8 inch ring mould
25 cm/10 inch cake board

STORING
This cake can be kept for up to three days in an airtight container in the refrigerator.

1 Preheat the oven to 160°C/325°F/Gas 3. Grease and flour the ring mould. Spoon the cake mixture into the mould and smooth the surface. Bake in the centre of the oven for about 25 minutes, or until firm to the touch. Turn out on to a wire rack and leave to cool completely.

2 ▲ Cut the cake in half horizontally and sandwich together with about one-third of the butter icing. Position the cake on the cake board. Spread the remaining icing over the outside of the cake to cover completely.

3 Smooth the top of the cake with a palette knife and swirl the icing around the side of the cake.

4 ▲ To make the marzipan plaits, divide the marzipan into three portions and colour it pink, green and purple. Cut each portion in half. Using one-half of each of the colours, roll each one out with your fingers on a work surface lightly dusted with icing sugar to make a thin sausage shape long enough to go around the bottom edge of the cake. Pinch the ends together at the top, then twist the individual strands into a rope. Pinch the other ends to seal neatly.

5 ▲ Place the rope on the cake board around the bottom edge of the cake.

6 To make the nests, take the remaining portions of coloured marzipan and divide each colour into five. Roll each piece into a rope about 16 cm/6½ inches long. Take a rope of each colour, pinch the ends together, twist to form a multi-coloured rope and pinch the other ends. Form the rope into a circle and repeat to make the remaining four nests.

7 ▲ Arrange the nests so they are evenly spaced on the top of the cake and place several chocolate eggs in the middle of each.

*B*luebird Bon Voyage Cake

This cake is sure to see someone off on an exciting journey in a very special way.

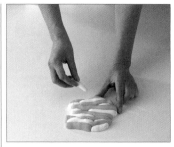

INGREDIENTS
Serves 12–15
450 g/1 lb/²⁄₃ quantity Royal Icing
blue food colouring
800 g/1¾ lb/2½ x quantity
Sugarpaste Icing
20 cm/8 inch round Madeira Cake
1 quantity Butter Icing
3 tbsp apricot jam, warmed
and sieved
silver balls

MATERIALS AND EQUIPMENT
25 cm/10 inch round cake board
greaseproof paper piping bags
No 1 writing nozzle
thin pale blue ribbon

STORING
The finished cake can be kept for up to one week in an airtight container.

1 Make up the royal icing, keeping about two-thirds softer for filling in, and the rest stiffer for the outlines and further piping. Colour the softer icing blue. Cover the icings and leave overnight. Stir before using.

2 ▲ On greaseproof paper, draw the birds several times in two sizes. Tape the paper to a baking sheet, then secure a piece of baking parchment over the top.

3 ▲ Fit a paper piping bag with a No 1 writing nozzle and spoon in some of the stiffer icing for piping the outlines. Pipe over the outlines of the birds with a continuous thread of icing.

4 ▲ Half-fill a fresh paper piping bag with the blue icing. Cut the pointed end off the bag in a straight line. Do not make the opening too large or the icing will flow too quickly. Pipe the icing into the outlines to fill, working from the outlines into the centre. Do not touch the outlines or they may break. To prevent air bubbles, keep the end of the bag in the icing. The icing should look overfilled and rounded, as it will shrink slightly as it dries.

5 Working quickly, brush through the icing to fill in any gaps and to ensure it goes right to the outlines. If any air bubbles appear, smooth them out or burst with a pin. Leave the run-outs on the paper for two days to dry.

6 ▲ Colour two-thirds of the sugarpaste icing blue and leave the rest white. Form the icing into small rolls and place them together on a work surface lightly dusted with icing sugar, alternating the colours. Form into a round and lightly knead together until the icing is marbled. Do not over-knead or you will lose the effect. Cut off about one-quarter of the sugarpaste icing, wrap in clear film and set aside.

7 Cut the cake horizontally into three even layers and sandwich together with the butter icing. Brush with the apricot jam. Roll out the marbled sugarpaste icing and use it to cover the cake. Roll out the reserved sugarpaste icing to a 25 cm/10 inch circle and use it to cover the cake board.

8 ▲ Position the cake to one edge of the board. Fit a piping bag with the writing nozzle and half-fill with the remaining stiffer royal icing. Pipe a wavy line all around the edge of the cake board. Working quickly before the icing dries, position the silver balls so they are evenly spaced in the icing.

9 Remove the birds from the greaseproof paper using a palette knife and secure them to the cake with a little royal icing. Pipe a bead of white icing on each for the eye and place a silver ball in the centre. Drape the ribbon between the birds' beaks, securing with icing.

*F*udge-frosted Starry Roll

Whether it's a birthday or another occasion you are wanting to celebrate, this sumptuous looking cake is sure to please.

INGREDIENTS
Serves 8
1 quantity *Swiss Roll mix*
½ quantity *chocolate-flavour Butter Icing*
50 g/2 oz *white chocolate*
50 g/2 oz *plain chocolate*
1½ x quantity *Fudge Frosting*

MATERIALS AND EQUIPMENT
23 x 33 cm/9 x 13 inch Swiss roll tin
small star cutter
several greaseproof paper piping bags
No 19 star nozzle

STORING
This cake can be kept for up to two days in an airtight container in the refrigerator.

1 Preheat the oven to 180°C/350°F/ Gas 4. Grease the tin, line the base with greaseproof paper and grease the paper. Spoon in the cake mixture and gently smooth the surface. Bake for about 12–15 minutes, or until springy to the touch.

2 Turn out on to a sheet of greaseproof paper lightly sprinkled with caster sugar, peel off the lining paper and roll up the Swiss roll, leaving the lining paper inside. When cold, unroll carefully, remove the paper and spread the cake with the butter icing. Re-roll and set aside on a sheet of greaseproof paper on a wire rack.

3 ▲ To make the chocolate decorations, cover a board with baking parchment and tape down at each corner. Melt the white chocolate, then pour on to the baking parchment. Spread the chocolate evenly with a palette knife and allow to stand until the surface is firm enough to cut, but not so hard that it will break. It should no longer feel sticky when touched with your finger. Press a small star cutter firmly through the chocolate and lift off the paper with a palette knife. Set aside.

4 ▲ Melt the plain chocolate and allow to cool slightly. Cover a rolling pin with baking parchment and attach it with tape. Fill a paper piping bag with the chocolate and cut a small piece off the pointed end in a straight line. Pipe lines of chocolate backwards and forwards over the baking parchment, to the size you choose. Make at least nine curls so you have extra in case of breakages. Leave the chocolate lace curls to set in a cool place, then carefully peel off the paper.

5 ▲ Make the fudge frosting. When cool enough to spread, cover the Swiss roll with about two-thirds of it, making swirls with a palette knife.

6 ▲ Fit a fresh paper piping bag with the No 19 star nozzle and spoon in the remaining frosting. Pipe diagonal lines, like a twisted rope, on either side of the roll and across both ends.

7 ▲ Position the lace curls in the icing, and arrange the stars. Transfer the cake to a serving plate and decorate with more stars.

M arbled Cracker Cake

Here is a Christmas cake decorated in an untraditional way.
The cake can be made well ahead of Christmas and then decorated nearer the time.

INGREDIENTS
Serves 20–25
20 cm/8 inch round Rich Fruit Cake
3 tbsp apricot jam, warmed
and sieved
675 g/1½ lb marzipan
800 g/1¾ lb/2⅓ x quantity
Sugarpaste Icing
red and green food colourings
edible gold balls

MATERIALS AND EQUIPMENT
wooden cocktail sticks
25 cm/10 inch round cake board
red, green and gold thin gift
wrapping ribbon
3 red and 3 green ribbon bows

STORING
The finished cake can be kept
for up to three months in an
airtight container.

1 Brush the cake with the jam. Roll out the marzipan on a work surface lightly dusted with icing sugar and cover the cake. Leave to dry for 12 hours.

2 ▲ Take 500 g/1¼ lb of the sugarpaste icing and form a smooth roll. Put some red food colouring on the end of a cocktail stick and dab a few drops on to the icing. Repeat with the green. Knead just a few times. Roll out the sugarpaste, on a work surface lightly dusted with icing sugar, until marbled.

3 Brush the marzipan with a little water and cover with the icing. Position the cake on the cake board.

4 ▲ Colour half of the remaining sugarpaste icing red and the rest green. Roll about half of the red icing into five 5 x 1 cm/2 x ½ inch rectangles for the crackers. Roll half of the green icing into a 13 x 1 cm/5 x ½ inch roll and cut off ten 1 cm/½ inch lengths. These are the ends of the crackers. Attach two green ends to each red cracker with a little water. Gather together any icing trimmings. Roll out a small piece of green icing thinly and cut into two 13 x 1 cm/5 x ½ inch strips. Cut each strip into five diamonds. Attach two green diamonds to each cracker, then press a gold ball in the centre. Leave to dry on greaseproof paper for several hours or overnight.

5 ▲ Meanwhile, roll out the remaining red and green icings, including any trimmings, into 1 cm/ ½ inch wide strips. Cut each strip into diamonds – you will need about 24 diamonds in each colour.

6 ▲ Attach alternate red and green diamonds around the top and base of the cake, securing with water.

7 ▲ Cut the ribbons into about 10 cm/4 inch lengths. Run the blade of a pair of scissors or a sharp knife down the length of them to curl.

8 Arrange the crackers in a pile on top of the cake and decorate with the curled ribbons. Attach the bows in alternate colours with a little softened sugarpaste icing, evenly spaced between the diamonds around the top edge of the cake.

*T*ip

Add the colour to the icing sparingly at first because the colour becomes more intense as the icing stands. It is advisable to leave the icing for about 10 minutes to see if it is the shade you need.

*D*ouble Heart Engagement Cake

For a celebratory engagement party, these sumptuous cakes make the perfect centrepiece.

INGREDIENTS
Serves 20
2 x quantity chocolate-flavour
Quick-Mix Sponge Cake mix
350 g/12 oz/12 squares
plain chocolate
2 x quantity coffee-flavour
Butter Icing
icing sugar, for sifting
fresh raspberries, to decorate

MATERIALS AND EQUIPMENT
2 x 20 cm/8 inch heart-shaped
cake tins
2 x 23 cm/9 inch heart-shaped
cake boards

STORING
The finished cake can be kept for up to three days in an airtight container in the refrigerator.

1 Preheat the oven to 160°C/325°F/ Gas 3. Grease the tins, line the bases with greaseproof paper and grease the paper. Divide the cake mixture evenly between the tins and smooth the surfaces. Bake in the centre of the oven for 25–30 minutes or until firm to the touch. Turn out on to a wire rack, peel off the lining paper and leave to cool completely.

2 Meanwhile, melt the chocolate in a heatproof bowl over a saucepan of hot water (you may find it easier to work with half the chocolate at a time). Pour the melted chocolate on to a firm, smooth surface such as a marble or plastic laminate set on a slightly damp cloth to prevent slipping. Spread the chocolate out evenly with a large palette knife. Leave the chocolate to cool slightly. It should feel just set, but not hard.

3 ▲ To make the chocolate curls, hold a large sharp knife at a 45° angle to the chocolate and push it along the chocolate in short sawing movements from right to left and left to right. Remove the curls by sliding the point of the knife underneath each one and lifting off. Leave to firm on baking parchment. Repeat with remaining chocolate.

4 ▲ Cut each cake in half horizontally. Use about one-third of the butter icing to fill both cakes, then sandwich them together.

5 Use the remaining icing to coat the tops and sides of the cakes.

6 ▲ Place the cakes on the cake boards. Generously cover the tops and sides of the cakes with the chocolate curls, pressing them gently into the butter icing.

7 Sift a little icing sugar over the top of each cake and decorate with raspberries. Chill until ready to serve.

Chocolate-iced Anniversary Cake

This cake is special enough to celebrate any wedding anniversary. Tropical fruits and a glossy chocolate icing make it very appealing for all ages.

INGREDIENTS
Serves 12–15
20 cm/8 inch round Madeira Cake
1½ x quantity chocolate-flavour
Butter Icing
1 quantity Satin Chocolate Icing
chocolate buttons
selection of fresh fruits, such as
kiwi, nectarine or
peach, apricot, physalis

MATERIALS AND EQUIPMENT
greaseproof paper piping bag
No 22 star nozzle
thin gold ribbon, about 5 mm/
¼ in wide
florist's wire

STORING
This cake can be kept for up to five days in the refrigerator.

1 Cut the cake into three horizontal layers and sandwich together with about three-quarters of the chocolate butter icing. Place the cake on a wire rack with a baking sheet underneath.

2 ▲ Make the satin chocolate icing and immediately pour over the cake to coat completely. Working quickly, ease the icing gently over the surface of the cake, using a palette knife if necessary. Allow to set.

3 ▲ Transfer the cake to a serving plate. Fit a paper piping bag with the star nozzle and spoon in the remaining chocolate butter icing. Pipe scrolls around the top edge of the cake.

4 Cut several chocolate buttons into quarters and use to decorate the butter icing.

5 ▲ Prepare the fruit for the top of the cake. Peel and slice the kiwi and cut into quarters, and slice the nectarine or peach, apricot and Cape gooseberries.

6 Arrange the fruit on top of the cake. For each ribbon decoration, make two small loops using the thin gold ribbon. Twist a piece of florist's wire around the ends of the ribbon to secure the loops. Trim the ends of the ribbon. Cut the wire to the length you want and use it to put the loops in position on the cake. Make about seven ribbon decorations. Remove the ribbons and wire before serving.

*L*ucky Horseshoe

This horseshoe-shaped cake, made to wish 'good luck', is made from a round cake and the horseshoe shape is then cut out.

INGREDIENTS
Serves 30–35
25 cm/10 inch Rich Fruit Cake
4 tbsp apricot jam, warmed and sieved
800 g/1¾ lb marzipan
1 kg/2¼ lb/3 x quantity Sugarpaste Icing
peach and blue food colourings
silver balls
115 g/4 oz/⅙ quantity Royal Icing

MATERIALS AND EQUIPMENT
28–30 cm/11–12 inch round cake board
crimping tool
large blossom cutter
small blossom cutter
pale blue ribbon, 3 mm/⅛ in wide

STORING
The cake can be kept for up to three months in an airtight container.

1 Draw a horseshoe shape on a sheet of greaseproof paper. Cut this shape out of the cake, using the template as a guide. Brush the cake with the apricot jam. Roll out 350 g/12 oz of the marzipan to a 25 cm/10 inch circle on a work surface lightly dusted with icing sugar. Using the template as a guide, cut out the shape and cover the top of the cake with the marzipan. Reserve the trimmings for the inside of the ring.

2 Measure the circumference of the cake as far as the openings of the horseshoe and the height of the side with string. Take the remaining marzipan and roll out for the side, using the string measurement as a guide. Use to cover the side. Using the same method and the reserved trimmings, cover the inside of the horseshoe. Position the cake on the board and leave to dry for 12 hours.

3 ▲ Colour 800 g/1¾ lb of the sugarpaste icing peach. Brush the marzipan lightly with water and cover the cake with the sugarpaste icing in the same way as described for the marzipan, covering first the top, then the side, then the inside of the horseshoe.

4 Using a crimping tool dipped in cornflour, carefully crimp the top edge of the cake.

5 Draw and measure the design for the ribbon insertion on the horseshoe template. Cut 13 pieces of pale blue ribbon fractionally longer than the size of each slit.

6 ▲ Place the template on the cake, securing with pins if necessary, and cut through the drawn lines into the icing with a scalpel to make slits for the ribbon. Remove the template.

7 ▲ With the aid of a pointed tool, insert one end of the ribbon into the first slit and the other end into the second slit. Leave a space and repeat, filling all the slits with the pieces of ribbon. Leave to dry for 12 hours.

8 ▲ Draw a small horseshoe shape on a piece of card and cut out. Take the remaining sugarpaste icing and colour one-half pale blue and leave the other half white. Roll out the blue icing on a work surface lightly dusted with icing sugar. Using the card template as a guide, cut out nine shapes with a sharp knife. Mark small lines around the centre of each horseshoe with the knife. Cut out 12 large and 15 small blossoms with the blossom cutters, then press a silver ball into the centres of the larger blossoms. Leave to dry on greaseproof paper. Repeat with the white icing.

9 Decorate the cake with the ribbon. Arrange the horseshoes and blossoms on the cake and board, securing with a little royal icing.

*T*ip

Save the discarded section of the round cake to use in the Truffle Mix, if wished. Horseshoe-shaped tins can be purchased or hired from cake decorating specialists.

Golden Wedding Heart Cake

*Creamy gold colours, delicate frills and dainty iced blossoms
give this cake a special celebratory appeal.*

INGREDIENTS
Serves 30
23 cm/9 inch round Rich Fruit Cake
4 tbsp apricot jam, warmed
and sieved
900 g/2 lb marzipan
900 g/2 lb/2⅔ x quantity
Sugarpaste Icing
cream food colouring
115 g/4 oz/⅙ quantity Royal Icing

MATERIALS AND EQUIPMENT
28 cm/11 inch round cake board
crimping tool
small heart-shaped plunger tool
7.5 cm/3 inch plain cutter
dual large and small blossom cutter
stamens
frill cutter
foil-wrapped chocolate hearts

STORING
*The finished cake can be kept
for up to three months in an
airtight container.*

1 Brush the cake with apricot jam.
Roll out the marzipan on a work
surface lightly dusted with icing sugar
and use it to cover the cake. Leave to
dry for 12 hours.

2 Colour 675 g/1½ lb of the
sugarpaste icing very pale cream.
Roll out the icing on a work surface
lightly dusted with icing sugar. Brush
the marzipan with a little water and
cover the cake with the sugarpaste
icing. Position the cake on the cake
board. Using a crimping tool dipped in
cornflour, carefully crimp the top edge
of the cake.

3 ▲ Divide the circumference of the
top of the cake into eight equal
sections, and stick pins in as markers.
Use these as a guide to crimp evenly
spaced slanting lines going from the top
to the bottom edges of the cake. Using
the plunger tool, emboss the bottom
edge of the cake. Place the plain cutter
lightly in the centre of the cake and use
as a guide to emboss more hearts in a
circle around the cutter. Leave the cake
to dry for several hours.

4 ▲ Take the remaining sugarpaste
icing and colour one-half cream and
the other half pale cream. Retain half of
each colour, and wrap the remainder in
clear film. Roll out each colour evenly
and thinly. Dip the end of the blossom
cutter in cornflour and cut out the
flower shapes. Make a pin hole in the
centre of each larger flower as you
make it. Leave to dry on a foam pad.
When dry, pipe a little royal icing on to
a stamen and thread it through the hole
of each larger flower. This will hold it
in position. Allow to dry.

5 ▲ To make the frills, roll out the
two shades of reserved sugarpaste
icing thinly. Using the frill cutter, cut
out two rings from each colour.

6 ▲ Position the end of a wooden
cocktail stick over 5 mm/¼ inch of
the outer edge of the ring. Roll the stick
firmly back and forth around the edge
with your finger until the edge becomes
thinner and begins to frill. Continue
until the ring is completely frilled.
Repeat with remaining rings. Using a
sharp knife, cut each ring in half to
make two frills. You should have four
frills in each shade.

7 ▲ Using a little water, attach the
frills in alternate shades next to the
crimped lines running down the side of
the cake. Crimp the edges of the deeper
coloured frills.

8 Arrange the blossom flowers on the
top and side of the cake, securing
with a little royal icing. Before serving,
place the chocolate hearts in the centre
of the cake.

Christmas Tree Cake

No piping is involved in this bright and colourful Christmas tree cake, making it a good choice for all the family to help decorate.

INGREDIENTS
Serves 20 – 25
20 cm/8 inch round Rich Fruit Cake
3 tbsp apricot jam, warmed and sieved
900 g/2 lb marzipan
green, red, yellow and purple food colourings
225 g/8 oz/¹⁄₃ quantity Royal Icing
silver balls

MATERIALS AND EQUIPMENT
25 cm/10 inch round cake board

STORING
The finished cake can be kept for up to three months in an airtight container.

1 Brush the cake with the apricot jam. Colour 675 g/1½ lb of the marzipan green. Roll out the green marzipan on a work surface lightly dusted with icing sugar and use it to cover the cake. Leave to dry for 12 hours.

2 ▲ Make the royal icing. Secure the cake to the cake board with a little of the icing. Spread the icing evenly on the side of the cake to cover just half way up. Starting at the bottom of the cake, press the flat side of a palette knife into the icing, then pull away sharply to form a peak. Repeat until the iced area is covered with peaks.

3 ▲ Draw three Christmas tree shapes in different sizes on to a piece of card and cut out. Take half of the remaining marzipan and colour it a slightly deeper shade of green than the top. Using the card templates as a guide, cut out three Christmas tree shapes. Arrange the trees on top of the cake.

4 ▲ Divide the remaining marzipan into three portions and colour it red, yellow and purple. Use a little of the marzipan to make five 9 cm/3 inch rolls from each colour. Loop the coloured lengths alternately around the top edge of the cake, pressing on to the top to secure firmly.

5 ▲ Make small balls from red marzipan and press on to the end of each loop.

6 ▲ Use the remaining marzipan to make the tree decorations. Roll the red marzipan into a thin rope and cut into eight 2.5 cm/1 inch lengths for the candles. Shape eight flames from the yellow icing and stick on the end of each candle. Mould 11 small balls from the purple icing and press a silver ball into the centre of each.

7 Arrange the candles and balls on the trees, securing them with a little water if necessary.

Daisy Christening Cake

A ring of moulded daisies sets off this pretty pink christening cake. It can be made in easy stages, giving time for the various icings to dry before adding the next layer.

INGREDIENTS
Serves 20–25
20 cm/8 inch round Rich Fruit Cake
3 tbsp apricot jam, warmed
and sieved
675 g/1½ lb marzipan
900 g/2 lb/1⅓ x quantity Royal Icing
115 g/4 oz/⅓ quantity
Sugarpaste Icing
pink and yellow food colourings

MATERIALS AND EQUIPMENT
25 cm/10 inch round cake board
5 cm/2 inch fluted cutter
wooden cocktail stick
2 greaseproof paper piping bags
No 42 nozzle
pink and white ribbon

STORING
The finished cake can be kept for up to three months in an airtight container.

1 Brush the cake with the apricot jam. Roll out the marzipan on a work surface lightly dusted with icing sugar and use to cover the cake. Leave to dry for 12 hours.

2 Secure the cake to the cake board with a little of the icing. Colour three-quarters of the icing pink. Flat ice the cake with three or four layers of smooth icing, using the white icing for the top and the pink for the sides. Allow each layer to dry overnight before applying the next. Set aside a little of both icings in airtight containers, to decorate the cake.

3 Meanwhile, make the daisies. You will need about 28. For each daisy cut off a small piece of sugarpaste icing. Dust your fingers with a little cornflour to prevent sticking.

4 ▲ Shape the icing with your fingers to look like a golf tee, with a stem and a thin, flat, round top.

5 ▲ Using scissors, make small cuts all the way around the edge of the daisy. Carefully curl the cut edges slightly in different directions. Place the daisies on a sheet of greaseproof paper to dry.

6 ▲ When dry, trim the stems and paint the edges with pink and the centres with yellow food colouring.

7 ▲ To make the plaque, roll out the remaining sugarpaste icing on a work surface lightly dusted with icing sugar and cut out a circle with the fluted cutter. Position the end of a wooden cocktail stick over 5 mm/¼ inch of the outer edge of the circle. Roll the stick firmly back and forth around the edge with your finger until the edge becomes thinner and begins to frill. Continue until the edge of the plaque is completely frilled. Place on a sheet of greaseproof paper to dry, then paint the name in the centre of the plaque and the edges with pink food colouring.

8 ▲ Fit a paper piping bag with the nozzle and pipe a twisted rope around the top and bottom edges of the cake with the remaining white royal icing. Wash the nozzle, fit it in a fresh paper piping bag and pipe a row of stars around the top of the cake with the remaining pink icing.

9 Secure the plaque to the centre of the cake with a little royal icing. Arrange the daisies on the cake, also securing with the icing, and decorate with the ribbons.

*B*irthday Bowl of Strawberries

All kinds of fun designs can be painted on cakes with edible food colourings.
With this one the strawberry theme is carried on into the moulded
decorations too, providing a fresh, summery birthday cake.

INGREDIENTS
Serves 20
1 quantity Butter Icing
20 cm/8 inch petal-shaped Madeira
Cake (make using quantities for
a 20 cm/8 inch round cake)
3 tbsp apricot jam, warmed
and sieved
675 g/1½ lb/2 x quantity
Sugarpaste Icing
pink, red, yellow, green and claret
food colourings
yellow powdered food colouring

MATERIALS AND EQUIPMENT
25 cm/10 inch petal-shaped
cake board
paint palette or small saucers
thin red and green ribbons

STORING
The finished cake can be kept
for up to one week in an
airtight container.

1 Colour the butter icing pink. Cut the cake into three horizontal layers and sandwich together with the butter icing. Brush the cake with apricot jam. Roll out 500 g/1¼ lb of the sugarpaste icing on a work surface lightly dusted with icing sugar and use to cover the cake. Position on the cake board and leave to dry for 12 hours.

2 ▲ To make the strawberries, colour three-quarters of the remaining sugarpaste icing red, and equal portions of the rest yellow and green. Dust your fingers with cornflour to prevent sticking, and mould the red icing into strawberry shapes. Make tiny oval shapes from the yellow icing to represent seeds and lightly press on to the strawberries. Shape the green icing into small flat circles slightly bigger than the tops of the strawberries. Using scissors, make small cuts all the way round the circles and carefully curl the cut edges slightly. Attach to the tops of the strawberries, securing with a little water. Leave to dry on greaseproof paper.

3 ▲ Put the red, green, yellow and claret food colourings in a palette and water them down slightly. Draw or paint on an outline of the vase with the claret colour, then fill in the pattern.

4 ▲ Use a little powdered yellow food colouring to add highlights.

5 ▲ Finish painting the design, filling in the strawberries in the bowl and around the edge of the cake.

6 ▲ Decorate the cake with the ribbons. Secure two strawberries to the top of the cake, and arrange the others around the bottom edge.

Holly Leaf Log

Christmas cakes can be made in all shapes and sizes.
This log-shaped cake is for chocolate and coffee lovers.

INGREDIENTS
Serves 8
1 quantity Swiss Roll
½ quantity coffee-flavour Butter Icing
75 g/3 oz/3 squares plain chocolate
1½ x quantity Fudge Frosting

MATERIALS AND EQUIPMENT
Swiss roll tin
holly leaf cutter
2 greaseproof paper piping bags
No 1 writing and No 30 star nozzles

STORING
This cake can be kept for two days
in the fridge in an airtight container.

1 Make and bake the Swiss roll. Turn out on to a sheet of greaseproof paper lightly sprinkled with caster sugar and roll up leaving the lining paper inside. Leave to cool completely on a wire rack.

2 ▲ Unroll the cake carefully and remove the paper. Reserve a spoonful of the butter icing for piping on the holly leaves, and spread the remainder over the cake. Re-roll the cake, place on a sheet of greaseproof paper on a wire rack and set aside.

3 To make the chocolate decorations, cover a baking sheet with baking parchment and tape it down at each corner. Melt the chocolate in a heatproof bowl over a pan of hot water, then pour on to the baking parchment.

4 Spread out the chocolate evenly with a palette knife, and allow to cool until the surface is firm enough to cut, but not so hard that it will break. The chocolate should no longer feel sticky when touched with your finger.

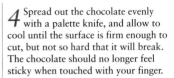

5 ▲ Press a holly leaf cutter firmly through the chocolate and lift off the leaves with a small palette knife. Spoon the reserved butter icing into a greaseproof paper piping bag fitted with the No 1 writing nozzle. Use to pipe decorations on the chocolate leaves.

6 ▲ Make the fudge frosting and, when cool enough to spread, quickly cover the Swiss roll with about two-thirds of the frosting. Working quickly before the frosting becomes too stiff, make swirls over the surface with a palette knife.

7 ▲ Spoon the remaining frosting into a fresh piping bag fitted with the No 30 star nozzle. Pipe several lines of scrolls down the length of the cake. Transfer to a serving plate and arrange the chocolate leaves on the cake, pressing lightly to secure.

*S*tarry New Year Cake

Although it is not so traditional to welcome in the New Year with a cake as it is at Christmas, why not start a new tradition?

INGREDIENTS
Serves 15–20
23 cm/9 inch round Madeira Cake
2 x quantity Butter Icing
800 g/1¾ lb/2⅓ x quantity Sugarpaste Icing
grape violet and mulberry food colourings
gold, lilac shimmer and primrose sparkle powdered food colourings

MATERIALS AND EQUIPMENT
star-shaped cutter
florist's wire
28 cm/11 inch round cake board
purple ribbon with gold stars

STORING
The finished cake can be kept for up to one week in an airtight container.

1 Cut the cake horizontally into three layers. Sandwich the layers together with three-quarters of the butter icing. Spread the remaining butter icing in a thin layer over the top and sides.

2 Colour 500 g/1¼ lb of the sugarpaste icing purple with the grape violet and a touch of the mulberry food colourings. Roll out on a work surface lightly dusted with icing sugar and cover the cake. Leave to dry overnight.

3 ▲ Place the cake on a sheet of greaseproof paper to protect the work surface. Water down a little of the gold and lilac shimmer powdered food colourings, then load up the end of a paintbrush with one of the colours. Position the brush over the area you want to colour, then flick your wrist in the direction of the cake, so the colour falls on to it in small beads. Repeat with the other colour until the whole cake is covered. Leave to dry.

4 To make the stars, divide the remaining sugarpaste icing into three portions. Colour one portion purple, the same as the coated cake, one portion with the lilac shimmer and one portion with the primrose sparkle. Roll out each colour separately to about 3 mm/⅛ inch thick. Cut out stars with the star-shaped cutter and place on a piece of greaseproof paper. You will need 30 stars total. Highlight the stars with the dry powdered colours, brushing gold on the purple stars, primrose on the yellow and lilac on the lilac stars. Using the watered-down gold and lilac colours, flick them on to each star as before.

5 ▲ While the icing is still soft, cut short lengths of florist's wire and carefully push them through the middle of 15 of the stars, but not all the way through. Leave to dry overnight.

6 ▲ Position the cake on the cake board or plate. Arrange three unwired stars in each colour in a diagonal line on the top edge of the cake, securing with a little water. Repeat to make four more groupings of the stars. Stick the wired stars at angles all over the top of the cake as you arrange the flat ones.

7 Decorate the base of the cake with the ribbon.

Trailing Orchid Wedding Cake

A special celebration such as a wedding deserves a very special cake.

INGREDIENTS
Serves 100
30 cm/12 inch round Madeira Cake mix
25 cm/10 inch round Madeira Cake mix
50 g/2 oz/2 squares plain chocolate
50 g/2 oz/2 squares white chocolate
7½ x quantity Butter Icing
1½ x quantity chocolate-flavour Butter Icing

MATERIALS AND EQUIPMENT
30 cm/12 inch oval cake tin
25 cm/10 inch oval cake tin
about 22 rose leaves
plain scraper
several greaseproof paper piping bags
No 4 writing and basket-weave nozzles
35 cm/14 inch oval thick cake board
25 cm/10 inch oval thin cake board
orchids

STORING
Decorate the cake the day before the wedding, adding the leaves and flowers on the day.

1 Grease the oval cake tins, line with a double thickness of greaseproof paper and grease the paper. Make the cakes one at a time and bake, following the baking times for the 30 cm/12 inch and 25 cm/10 inch round Madeira cakes. Leave to cool slightly in the tin, then turn out on to a wire rack, peel off the lining paper and leave to cool.

2 To make the chocolate leaves, wash and dry the rose leaves well on kitchen paper. Melt the chocolates in two separate heatproof bowls over pans of hot water.

3 ▲ Brush the underside of each leaf, some with plain, some with the white chocolate. Do not go over to the other side of the leaf. Place the leaves chocolate-side up on baking parchment, and leave to set in a cool place. Peel the leaf from the chocolate. Handle the chocolate as little as possible as the warmth of your hands will melt it. If the chocolate seems too thin, re-coat.

4 Make the butter icings in batches, whisking until smooth. Level off the tops of the cakes if they have domed. Cut each cake in half horizontally, then sandwich each one back together with some of the plain butter icing.

5 Invert each cake on to a board covered with greaseproof paper. Spread some of the plain butter icing over the sides and smooth with the scraper.

6 ▲ Spread the icing over the top of each cake. To make the surface really smooth, spread with a long metal palette knife which has been dipped into hot water.

7 ▲ To pipe the basket-weave design on each cake, spoon some of the chocolate-flavour butter icing into a greaseproof paper piping bag fitted with a No 4 writing nozzle. (You will need to work in batches with several piping bags.) Pipe a vertical line on the side of the cake from the base to the top of the cake. Pipe several more lines.

8 Spoon some of the plain butter icing into a fresh piping bag fitted with a basket-weave nozzle. (You will need to work in batches with several piping bags.) Across the second vertical line of chocolate icing, pipe 2 cm/¾ inch horizontal lines of basic butter icing, going across the vertical line at 1 cm/½ inch intervals. You will need about three horizontal lines across each vertical for the smaller cake and three to four for the larger one. Fill in the spaces between the horizontal lines with an alternating row of horizontal lines over the third chocolate vertical. Repeat until the sides of each cake have been covered with the design.

9 ▲ Transfer the larger cake to the thick cake board and the smaller cake to the thin one (you should not be able to see the thin board). Keeping the smaller cake on the thin board, position it on top of the larger cake, to one end. Using a piping bag fitted with a No 4 writing nozzle, pipe beads of chocolate butter icing round the top and bottom edges of each cake. Keep in a cool place overnight. On the day, arrange the chocolate leaves and orchids on the tops of each cake. Keep in a cool place until required.

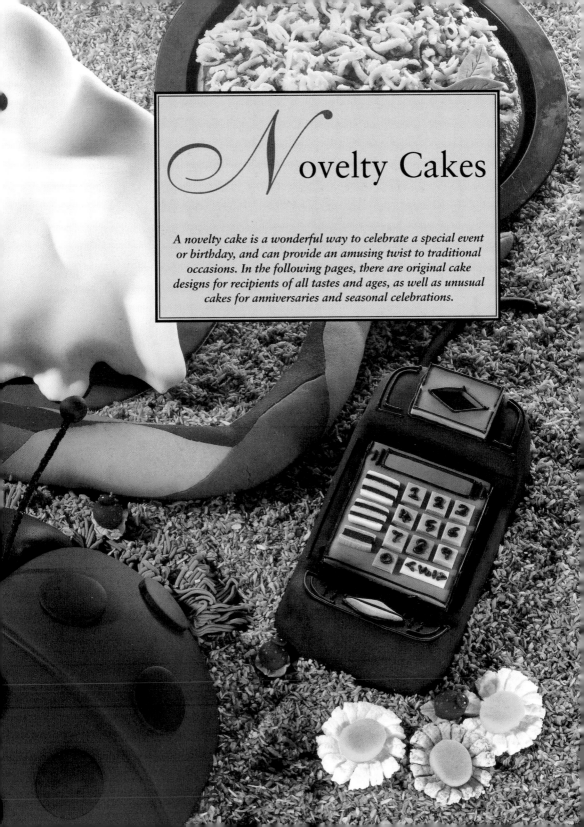

Novelty Cakes

A novelty cake is a wonderful way to celebrate a special event or birthday, and can provide an amusing twist to traditional occasions. In the following pages, there are original cake designs for recipients of all tastes and ages, as well as unusual cakes for anniversaries and seasonal celebrations.

Mobile Phone Cake

Mobile telephones keep getting smaller, but fortunately this delicious cake is a good size!

INGREDIENTS
Serves 8–10
1 quantity Quick-Mix Sponge
Cake mix
2 tbsp apricot jam, warmed
and sieved
350 g/12 oz/1 quantity
Sugarpaste Icing
black food colouring
10 small square sweets
1–2 striped liquorice sweets
2–3 tbsp icing sugar
½–1 tsp water

MATERIALS AND EQUIPMENT
900 g/2 lb loaf tin
23 x 18 cm/9 x 7 in cake board
diamond-shaped biscuit cutter
piping bag fitted with a small
plain nozzle

STORING
*The finished cake can be kept in
a cool, dry place for three to
four days.*

Tip

The dial pad is made from small sweets. However, you could increase the quantity of sugarpaste icing slightly, colour it as wished, then cut it to shape.

1 Preheat the oven to 180°C/350°F/
Gas 4. Grease the tin, line with greaseproof paper and grease the paper. Spoon the cake mixture into the prepared tin and smooth the surface. Bake in the centre of the oven for 40–50 minutes, or until a skewer inserted into the centre of the cake comes out clean. Leave the cake in the tin for 5 minutes, then turn out on to a wire rack, peel off the lining paper and leave to cool.

2 ▲ Turn the cake upside-down and starting about 2.5 cm/1 in along the cake, slice into it, across and at an angle, about 1 cm/½ in deep. Cut out this wedge, then slice horizontally along the length of the cake, stopping about 2.5 cm/1 in away from the end. Withdraw the knife and re-insert it at the end of the cake and slice vertically into the cake to meet up with the horizontal cut. Remove the inner piece of cake and discard.

3 ▲ Place the cake on the cake board and brush the cake evenly with the apricot jam. Colour three-quarters of the sugarpaste icing black. On a work surface lightly dusted with icing sugar, roll out to a 5 mm/¼ in thickness and use to cover the cake. Trim away any excess sugarpaste and reserve, wrapped in clear film.

4 ▲ Colour the remaining sugarpaste icing grey with a little black food colouring. On a work surface lightly dusted with icing sugar, roll out to a 5 mm/¼ in thickness. Cut out an oblong to fit the centre of the cake, leaving a 1 cm/½ in border. Cut out another piece about 2.5 cm/1 in square and stamp out the centre of the square using the diamond-shaped biscuit cutter. Stick all the pieces on the phone with a little water, placing the diamond at the bottom of the phone and the square at the top.

5 ▲ Position the sweets and a strip of kitchen foil for the dial pad. To make the glacé icing, mix the icing sugar with the water and black food colouring to a piping consistency. Fill the piping bag and pipe border lines around the edges of the phone and the grey pieces. Pipe the numbers on the keys.

6 Knead the reserved black sugarpaste icing and, with your hands, roll into a sausage shape for the aerial. Indent the top with a knife and position at the top of the phone to one side. Secure with a little water.

Terracotta Flowerpot

Ideal for celebrating a gardener's birthday or Mother's Day, this cake is baked in a pudding basin for the flowerpot shape and filled with a colourful arrangement of icing flowers and foliage.

INGREDIENTS
Serves 15
3-egg quantity Madeira Cake mix
175 g/6 oz jam
175 g/6 oz/½ quantity Butter Icing
2 tbsp apricot jam, warmed and sieved
550 g/1¼ lb/1⅔ x quantity
Sugarpaste Icing
125 g/4 oz/⅙ quantity Royal Icing
dark orange, black, red, silver,
green, purple and yellow food
colourings
2 chocolate-flake bars,
coarsely crushed

MATERIALS AND EQUIPMENT
1.1 l/2 pt pudding basin
string
paintbrush
thin green wire
23 cm/9 in round cake board

STORING
The finished cake can be kept in an airtight container for up to three days.

1 Preheat the oven to 160°C/325°F/ Gas 3. Grease the basin, line the base with greaseproof paper and grease the paper. Spoon the cake mixture into the prepared basin and smooth the surface. Bake in the centre of the oven for 1¼ hours, or until a skewer inserted into the centre of the cake comes out clean. Cover with kitchen foil for the last 10 minutes if the top begins to brown. Turn the cake out on to a wire rack, peel off the lining paper and leave to cool.

2 Trim the top of the cake flat if it has domed. Cut the cake horizontally into three and fill with the jam and butter icing.

3 Cut out a shallow circle from the top of the cake, leaving a 1 cm/½ in rim around the edge.

4 ▲ Brush the outside of the cake and the rim with the apricot jam. Colour two-thirds of the sugarpaste icing dark orange. Measure the circumference of the cake at its widest part and the height, including a turnover for the rim, with string. On a work surface lightly dusted with icing sugar, roll out the icing to these measurements and use to cover the cake. Reserve any trimmings, wrapped in clear film. Leave the cake to dry for 12 hours.

5 ▲ Using the reserved trimmings, shape the decorations and handles for the flowerpot. Leave to dry on greaseproof paper. Sprinkle the crushed chocolate into the top of the flowerpot for soil.

6 Colour a small piece of the remaining sugarpaste icing a very pale orange, roll out into an oblong and fold over to make a seed bag. Colour a little of the icing black and make the seeds. Colour two more small pieces of icing red and silver and shape the trowel. Leave to dry on greaseproof paper.

7 ▲ Colour the remaining sugarpaste icing green, purple and a very small amount yellow. Mould individual flower petals with the purple icing and stick them together in flower shapes with royal icing. Roll out the yellow icing and cut out the flower centres with a small knife. Position in the centre of each flower with a small ball of yellow icing, securing with royal icing. Leave to dry on greaseproof paper.

8 ▲ Shape the leaves with the green icing using your fingers and mark the veins with a knife. Insert short pieces of wire up some of the stems so you can arrange them in the flowerpot. Leave to dry over the handle of a wooden spoon. Roll out any remaining green icing and snip to represent grass. Paint a design on the seed packet with food colourings.

9 Attach the dark-orange decorations to the flowerpot with royal icing. Arrange the leaves and flowers in the pot. Place the cake on the cake board and position the trowel, seed packet and grass around the outside. Remove the wire from the leaves before serving.

*L*adybird Cake

*Create a little animal magic and make this cake
for a nature lover or gardener.*

INGREDIENTS
Serves 10–12
*1½ x quantity lemon-flavoured
Quick-Mix Sponge Cake mix
175 g/6 oz/½ quantity lemon-
flavoured Butter Icing
2 tbsp apricot jam, warmed
and sieved
4 tbsp lemon curd, warmed
1 kg/2¼ lb/3 x quantity
Sugarpaste Icing
red, black and green food
colourings
5 marshmallows
50 g/2 oz yellow marzipan
edible ladybird icing decorations
(optional)*

MATERIALS AND EQUIPMENT
*1.1 L/2 pt ovenproof mixing bowl
28 cm/11 in round cake board
4 cm/1½ in and 5 cm/2 in plain
round biscuit cutters
garlic press
2 pipe cleaners*

STORING
*The finished cake can be kept in
a cool, dry place for three to
four days.*

1 Preheat the oven to 180°C/350°F/
Gas 4. Grease the bowl, line the
base with greaseproof paper and grease
the paper. Spoon the cake mixture into
the prepared bowl and smooth the
surface. Bake in the centre of the oven
for 55–60 minutes, or until a skewer
inserted into the centre of the cake
comes out clean. Leave the cake in the
basin for 5 minutes, then turn out on to
a wire rack, peel off the lining paper
and leave to cool.

2 ▲ Cut the cake in half horizontally
and sandwich together with the
butter icing. Cut off about one-third of
the cake and brush both pieces of cake
with the lemon curd.

3 ▲ Colour a little less than half of
the sugarpaste icing red. On a work
surface lightly dusted with icing sugar,
roll out to about a 5 mm/¼ in thickness
and use to cover the large piece of cake.
Using a wooden skewer or the back of a
knife, make an indentation down the
centre of the cake for the wing casings.

4 Colour just over half of the
remaining sugarpaste icing black.
Roll out three-quarters of the icing and
use to cover the small piece of cake.
Place the cakes on the cake board and
assemble the ladybird's head and body,
gently pressing them together to secure.

5 Roll out a little of the white
sugarpaste icing and cut out two
circles for the eyes, using the 5 cm/2 in
round biscuit cutter. Stick in position
with a little water.

6 ▲ Roll out the reserved black
sugarpaste icing and cut out eight
circles, using the 4 cm/1½ in round
biscuit cutter. Stick one on each eye
and stick the rest on to the body with
a little water. Reserve the trimmings.

7 Colour the remaining sugarpaste
icing green. To make the grass,
break off small pieces and squeeze
through the garlic press. Trim off with a
knife. Brush the cake board with a little
water and position the grass.

8 ▲ To make the marshmallow
flowers, roll the marzipan into a
2 cm/¾ in long sausage shape and cut
into slices. Set aside. On a work surface
lightly dusted with icing sugar, flatten
each marshmallow with a rolling pin.
Snip around the marshmallows to make
petals. Press a marzipan circle into the
centre of each flower.

9 To make the antennae, paint the pipe
cleaners with black food colouring
and press a small ball of the reserved
black sugarpaste icing on to the end of
each one. Bend each pipe cleaner slightly
and insert into the cake between the head
and the body. Arrange the ladybird
decorations around the cake, if using.

Easter Cake

This delicious, spicy Easter fruit cake is covered with ribbons and miniature eggs made from chocolate modelling paste.

INGREDIENTS
Serves 16
125 g/4 oz/½ cup soft margarine
125 g/4 oz/½ cup light brown sugar
3 eggs
175 g/6 oz/1½ cups plain flour
2 tsp ground mixed spice
400 g/14 oz/3½ cups mixed dried fruit
50 g/2 oz/¼ cup glacé cherries, chopped
50 g/2 oz/¼ cup hazelnuts
3 tbsp apricot jam, warmed and sieved
450 g/1 lb marzipan
brown food colouring

For the Chocolate Moulding Icing
125 g/4 oz plain or milk chocolate
2 tbsp liquid glucose
1 egg white
450 g/1 lb/3½ cups icing sugar

For the Chocolate Modelling Paste
50 g/2 oz plain chocolate
50 g/2 oz white chocolate
2 tbsp liquid glucose
pink food colouring

MATERIALS AND EQUIPMENT
1.5 l/2½ pt pudding basin
25 cm/10 in round gold cake board
clean piece of sponge
several squares of gold foil

STORING
The finished cake can be kept for up to four weeks.

1 Preheat the oven to 150°C/300°F/ Gas 2. Grease the basin, line the base with greaseproof paper and grease the paper. Cream together the margarine and brown sugar and gradually add the eggs. Sift the remaining flour and the spice into the bowl and stir in the fruit and nuts.

2 Spoon the cake mixture into the prepared basin and smooth the surface. Bake in the centre of the oven for 1½ hours, or until a skewer inserted into the centre of the cake comes out clean. Turn the cake out on to a wire rack, peel off the lining paper and then leave to cool.

3 To make the chocolate moulding icing, break up the chocolate and place in a bowl with the glucose over a pan of hot water. Leave until melted, cool slightly then add the egg white. Gradually add the icing sugar, beating well after each addition, until too stiff to stir. Turn out on to a work surface lightly dusted with icing sugar and knead in the remaining sugar until stiff.

4 To make the modelling paste, melt the plain and white chocolate in separate bowls. Add half the glucose to the plain chocolate and mix to a stiff paste. Add some pink food colouring and the remaining glucose to the white chocolate and mix to a stiff paste. Wrap the pastes separately in clear film and chill until firm.

5 ▲ Cut a triangular wedge out of the cake. Place the cake on the board and brush with the apricot jam. On a work surface lightly dusted with icing sugar, roll out the marzipan and use to cover the cake, tucking the marzipan into the cut front section. Reserve the trimmings, wrapped in clear film.

6 On a work surface lightly dusted with cornflour, roll out the chocolate moulding icing and use to cover the cake. Cut two thin strips from the marzipan trimmings and stick on the inside edges of the cut-out wedge with a little water.

7 ▲ Thin the brown food colouring with water. Dip the sponge in the colour and pat over the surface of the icing. Leave to dry.

8 ▲ Lightly knead two-thirds of each of the modelling pastes and shape into 18 small eggs. Cover some of the eggs with gold foil and position them all inside the cut-out wedge. To make the bow, roll out the remaining modelling paste and cut two strips 2 cm/¾ in wide and 25 cm/10 in long from the dark paste and two strips 5 mm/¼ in wide and 20 cm/8 in long from the pink paste. Stick the pink strips to the dark ones with a little water. From these strips, cut two 13 cm/5 in lengths, press the ends together to form loops and secure to the cake. Secure two 8 cm/3 in length for ribbons ends and cover the centre of the bow with another small strip. Place a piece of crumpled kitchen foil under each strip until hardened.

Pizza Cake

Quick, easy and impressive – this deliciously sweet cake is a definite winner for pizza fanatics everywhere. Serve in small wedges.

Ingredients
Serves 8–10
1 quantity Quick-Mix Sponge Cake mix
350 g/12 oz/1 quantity Butter Icing
175 g/6 oz yellow marzipan
1 tbsp desiccated coconut
red and green food colouring
icing sugar
25 g/1 oz sugarpaste icing

MATERIALS AND EQUIPMENT
23 cm/9 in shallow round cake tin
25 cm/10 in pizza plate
cheese grater

STORING
The finished cake can be kept in the refrigerator for up to one week.

Tip
This recipe can be adapted easily for peperoni pizza fanatics. You will need an extra 175 g/6 oz/½ quantity of sugarpaste icing. Colour with brown food colouring, then roll out to a thick sausage shape with your hands. Slice thinly and add to the pizza cake as an extra topping ingredient.

1 Preheat the oven to 180°C/350°F/ Gas 4. Grease the tin, line the base with greaseproof paper and grease the paper. Spoon the cake mixture into the prepared tin and smooth the surface. Bake in the centre of the oven for 40–50 minutes, or until a skewer inserted into the centre of the cake comes out clean. Leave the cake in the tin for 5 minutes, then turn out on to a wire rack, peel off the lining paper and leave to cool.

2 ▲ Colour the butter icing red. Place the cake on the pizza plate and spread evenly with the butter icing to represent the tomato topping. Leave a 1 cm/½ in border around the edge of the cake.

3 ▲ Knead the marzipan for a few minutes to soften it slightly, then grate it. Sprinkle over the red butter icing to represent cheese.

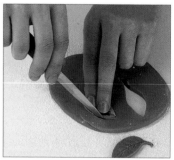

4 ▲ Colour the sugarpaste icing green. On a work surface lightly dusted with icing sugar, roll out to about a 5 mm/¼ in thickness. Cut out two leaf shapes freehand or cut around a real leaf. Mark the veins with a knife and add to the pizza cake for the garnish.

5 ▲ Place the desiccated coconut in a small bowl and colour with green food colouring. Scatter over the pizza cake to represent chopped herbs.

Christening Sampler

Instead of embroidering a sampler to welcome a new-born baby, why not make a sampler cake to celebrate?

INGREDIENTS
Serves 30
20 cm/8 in square Rich Fruit Cake
3 tbsp apricot jam, warmed and sieved
450 g/1 lb marzipan
675 g/1½ lb/2 x quantity Sugarpaste Icing
brown, blue, pink, yellow, orange, green, cream and purple food colourings

MATERIALS AND EQUIPMENT
25 cm/10 in square cake board
paintbrush
small heart-shaped biscuit cutter

STORING
The finished cake can be kept in an airtight container for up to three weeks.

Tip

Using the same techniques described here, you can change the overall design by modelling different figures and choosing different colours. You could also make a larger name plaque and pipe the baby's christian name on to it.

1 Brush the cake with the apricot jam. On a work surface lightly dusted with icing sugar, roll out the marzipan and use to cover the cake. Leave to dry for 12 hours.

2 Take two-thirds of the sugarpaste icing and cut off one-third of this. Roll out the smaller portion to the size of the top of the cake. Brush the top of the cake with a little water and cover with the icing.

3 ▲ Colour the larger portion of sugarpaste icing brown and divide into four equal amounts. Roll out each to the width of the cake side and about 1 cm/½ in longer than the height. Brush each cake side with a little water, then press the brown icing into place, folding over the extra at the top to represent a picture frame. Cut off each corner at an angle to make a mitred join. Reserve any trimmings. Place the cake on the cake board.

4 ▲ Paint the sides with brown food colouring thinned with a little water to represent wood grain.

5 ▲ Take the remaining sugarpaste icing and colour small amounts yellow, orange, brown, purple, cream, and two shades each of blue, green and pink. Leave a little white. Use these colours to shape the ducks, teddy bear, bulrushes, water, apple-blossom branch and leaves. Roll out a small piece of pink icing and cut out a heart with the small heart-shaped biscuit cutter. Roll out a small piece of white icing and cut out the baby's initial. For the border, roll out strips of light blue and yellow icing and cut into oblongs and squares. Make small balls and squares from the purple icing.

For the apple blossom, gently work together the two pinks and the white sugarpaste to give a marbled effect. Shape the flowers and add a small white ball in the centre of each. Leave all the shapes to dry on greaseproof paper. Then stick all the decorations on to the cake with a little water.

6 ▲ With any leftover coloured icing, roll out long strips of icing with your hands to make the embroidery threads. Form them into loops and use small strips of brown icing to hold the threads together. Arrange around the base of the cake.

Rainbow Snake Cake

This wild cake doesn't need any cooking and its heavy texture and sweet flavour make it an excellent party cake. For a large party, double the ingredients to make an extra-big snake.

INGREDIENTS
Serves 10–15
*675 g/1½ lb white marzipan
red, yellow, orange, purple and
green food colouring
1 quantity Truffle Cake mix
2 round red sweets
125 g/4 oz/2 cups desiccated
coconut
jelly snake sweets (optional)*

MATERIALS AND EQUIPMENT
*5 cocktail sticks
25 cm/10 in round cake board
small piece of thin red card, cut into
a tongue shape
small star-shaped biscuit cutter*

STORING
*The finished cake can be kept in
an airtight container for up to
four days.*

1 ▲ Divide the marzipan into five equal portions and colour one portion red, one portion yellow, one orange, one purple and one green. Remove a tiny ball of icing from the green portion and reserve, wrapped in clear film.

2 ▲ On a work surface lightly dusted with icing sugar, roll out each piece of marzipan into a sausage shape with your hands. They should be about 1 cm/½ in in diameter. Line up the sausage shapes next to one another and twist together the two outside sausages on either side. Firmly push the twists up against the middle sausage.

3 ▲ Roll out the marzipan, making short, sharp downward movements with the rolling pin. Starting at one end, roll out the marzipan a little at a time until about 15 cm/6 in wide. Keep the width even all along the snake. Carefully slide a heavy, sharp knife underneath the marzipan and flip the marzipan over.

4 ▲ Spoon the truffle mix evenly down the centre of the marzipan and mould into a sausage shape. Starting at one end, gather up the sides of the marzipan around the cake mixture and pinch the sides together firmly to seal. Shape the head and the tail.

5 ▲ Carefully coil the snake on to the cake board. Make a small incision for the mouth and insert the red card tongue. Roll out the reserved green marzipan and cut out two eyes using the small star biscuit cutter. Stick the eyes to the head with a little water and press the red sweets on top.

6 Place the desiccated coconut in a bowl and add a few drops of green food colouring and a little water. Stir until the coconut is flecked with green. Scatter around the snake on the cake board for grass.

$\mathcal{M}$arket Stall

An open-air market stall is the theme for this cake, bursting with colourful produce. Vary this design if you like, adding as wide a variety of fruit and vegetables as you can think of.

INGREDIENTS
Serves 30
30 cm/8 in square Rich Fruit Cake
3 tbsp apricot jam, warmed
and sieved
900 g/2 lb marzipan
450 g/1 lb/1⅓ x quantity
Sugarpaste Icing
125 g/4 oz/⅛ quantity Royal Icing
brown, green, red, orange, yellow,
peach, purple, pink and black
food colourings

MATERIALS AND EQUIPMENT
25 cm/10 in square cake board
piping bag fitted with a small
plain nozzle
paintbrush

STORING
The finished cake can be kept in an airtight container for up to three weeks.

1 Slice 4 cm/1½ in off one side of the cake. Brush the cake pieces with the apricot jam. Take half of the marzipan and cut off one-quarter. On a work surface lightly dusted with icing sugar, roll out the small piece of marzipan and use to cover one long side, the top and the two short sides of the cake slice. Roll out the larger piece of marzipan and use to cover the large piece of cake. Leave to dry for 12 hours.

2 ▲ Colour half of the sugarpaste icing brown and other half green. Using three-quarters of the brown icing, cover three sides of the large cake (not the cut side), brushing the marzipan first with a little water. With the remaining brown icing, cover the marzipanned sides of the cake slice in the same way. With the brown trimmings, roll out and cut narrow dividers to fit the top of the cake. Leave to dry on greaseproof paper for several hours.

3 ▲ Place the large piece of cake on the cake board, with the cake slice in front to form a step. Stick the cakes together and to the cake board with a little royal icing.

4 ▲ Measure the length and width of the cake, including the step. Roll out the green sugarpaste icing to about 4 cm/1½ in wider and longer than the measured length. Brush the marzipan tops with a little water and cover the cakes loosely with the green icing. Allow the icing to fall naturally into folds over the edges of the cake. Leave to dry for several hours.

5 ▲ Take the remaining marzipan, reserve a little for the stall-holder, and colour the rest red, orange, yellow, green, brown, peach and purple. Use these colours to shape the fruits and vegetables. Add markings with a paintbrush and food colouring to the melons, peaches and potatoes. For the front of the stall, shape baskets and a potato sack out of different shades of brown. For the stall-holder, colour the reserved marzipan pink, purple, black and flesh-coloured and shape the head, body and arms separately. Stick the figure together with a little royal icing. Make the hands, the facial features and hair, and press on with a little water. Place a melon in the stall-holder's arms. Leave all the marzipan shapes to dry on greaseproof paper for several hours.

6 Assemble on the cake just before serving, attaching the dividers, baskets and the stall-holder to the cake with royal icing.

*G*hostly Spectre

This fun Hallowe'en cake is really simple to make, yet very effective.
Use an 18 cm/7 in square cake of your choice, such as a citrus or chocolate-
flavoured Madeira or a light fruit cake.

INGREDIENTS
Serves 14
2 x quantity orange-flavoured
Quick-Mix Sponge Cake mix
900 g/2 lb/2⅔ x quantity
Sugarpaste Icing
black food colouring
350 g/12 oz/1 quantity Butter Icing

MATERIALS AND EQUIPMENT
18 cm/7 in square cake tin
300 ml/½ pt pudding basin
23 cm/9 in round cake board
paintbrush

STORING
The finished cake can be kept in a cool, dry place for up to four days.

1 Preheat the oven to 150°C/300°F/ Gas 2. Grease the tin and the pudding basin, line the bases with greaseproof paper and grease the paper. Half-fill the basin with the cake mixture and turn the remainder into the tin. Smooth the surfaces and bake in the centre of the oven for 25 minutes for the basin and 1½ hours for the tin, or until a skewer inserted into the centre of the cakes comes out clean. Leave to cool for 5 minutes, then turn out on to a wire rack, peel off the lining paper and leave to cool.

2 Knead a little black food colouring into about one-eighth of the sugarpaste icing. On a work surface lightly dusted with icing sugar, roll out and use to cover the cake board.

3 ▲ Cut two small corners off the large cake and two larger wedges off the other two corners. Stand the large cake on the cake board and secure with a little butter icing. Halve the large cake trimmings and wedge around the base of the cake.

4 ▲ Secure the small cake to the top of the large cake with a little of the butter icing for the head. Secure the small cake trimmings on either side of the head with butter icing for the shoulders. Use the remaining butter icing to cover the cake completely.

5 ▲ On a work surface lightly dusted with icing sugar, roll out the remaining sugarpaste icing to an oval shape about 51 cm/20 in long and 30 cm/12 in wide. Position over the cake, letting the icing fall into folds around the sides. Gently smooth the icing over the top half of the cake.

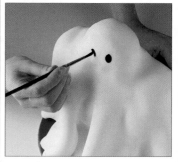

6 ▲ Using black food colouring, paint two oval eyes on to the head.

Artist's Box and Palette

Making cakes is an art in itself, and this cake proves it. It is the perfect celebration cake for artists of all ages.

INGREDIENTS
Serves 30
20 cm/8 in square Rich Fruit Cake
3 tbsp apricot jam, warmed
and sieved
450 g/1 lb marzipan
800 g/1¾ lb/2⅓ x quantity
Sugarpaste Icing
125 g/4 oz/⅙ quantity Royal Icing
brown, yellow, blue, black, silver,
orange, green and purple
food colourings

MATERIALS AND EQUIPMENT
stiff paper for template
25 cm/10 in square cake board
paintbrush

STORING
The finished cake can be kept in
an airtight container for up to
three weeks.

1 Brush the cake with the apricot jam. On a work surface lightly dusted with icing sugar, roll out the marzipan and use to cover the cake. Leave to dry for 12 hours.

2 Make a template out of stiff paper in the shape of an artist's palette that will fit the top of the cake. Colour just less than one-quarter of the sugarpaste icing a pale brown. On a work surface lightly dusted with icing sugar, roll out to the size of the template and cut out the palette shape.

3 Colour about two-thirds of the remaining sugarpaste icing brown. Roll out, brush the marzipanned cake with a little water and cover the cake with the icing. Place the cake on the cake board and leave to dry for several hours.

4 ▲ With the remaining sugarpaste icing, leave half white and divide the remainder into seven equal portions. Colour these yellow, blue, black, silver, orange, green and purple. Shape the box handle with black icing and the box clips and paintbrush ferrules with silver icing. Shape the paintbrush bristles with orange icing and mark the hairs of the bristles with a knife. Shape the paintbrush handles in various colours and attach the handles, ferrules and bristles with a little royal icing. Leave all the pieces to dry on greaseproof paper for several hours.

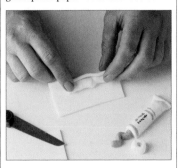

5 ▲ Make two paint tubes from some of the white icing. Roll out an oblong shape for each one and then wrap these around 'sausages' of icing, sealing the edges with a little water. Paint lettering and coloured bands on the tubes with food colouring.

6 ▲ Shape the squeezed-out paint in various colours and attach one to each of the paint tubes with a little royal icing. Leave all the pieces to dry on greaseproof paper for several hours.

7 Using the remaining white icing, roll out two small rectangles for sheets of paper and brush on patterns with watered-down food colouring. Leave the sheets to dry on greaseproof paper for several hours.

8 ▲ Paint wood markings on to the cake box with watered-down brown food colouring and leave to dry. To assemble the cake, attach the handles and clips to the front side of the box and the palette to the top of the cake with a little royal icing. Position the paintbrushes, tubes, squeezed-out paint and the sheets of paper on the cake and around the cake board.

Indian Elephant

Make this cake to celebrate a birthday, to wish someone 'Bon Voyage' or for a festive occasion. Be as colourful as you like with the decorations.

INGREDIENTS
Serves 30
30 cm/12 in square Madeira Cake
675 g/1½ lb/2 x quantity
Butter Icing
225 g/8 oz marzipan
black, green, yellow and pink
food colourings
chocolate coins, silver balls,
coloured and white chocolate
buttons and two sweets
125 g/4 oz/2 cups desiccated
coconut
2 tbsp apricot jam, warmed
and sieved

MATERIALS AND EQUIPMENT
stiff paper for template
36 cm/14 in square cake board

STORING
The finished cake can be kept in
an airtight container for up to
three days.

1 ▲ Make a template from stiff paper in the shape of an elephant. Trace off the design from the photograph of the finished cake and enlarge by 150%, if wished. Place the template on top of the cake and cut out the shape with a sharp knife. Position the cake on the cake board.

2 ▲ Colour the butter icing pale grey using the black food colouring. Cover the top and sides of the cake with the icing and swirl with a palette knife.

3 ▲ Using a cocktail stick and black food colouring, swirl black highlights into the icing.

4 ▲ On a work surface lightly dusted with icing sugar, roll out half of the marzipan and cut out shapes for the elephant's tusk, headpiece and blanket. Place them in position on the cake. Colour the remaining marzipan green, yellow and pink. Roll out thinly and cut out patterns for the blanket, headpiece, trunk and tail. Roll small balls of yellow and pink marzipan to make the ankle bracelets.

5 ▲ Place all the decorations, including the silver balls, chocolate coins and coloured chocolate buttons, in position. Cut the white chocolate buttons in half and use for the toenails and the sweets for the eye.

6 Mix a little green food colouring into the coconut. Brush the cake board with a little apricot jam and sprinkle with the coconut for grass.

The Beautiful Present Cake

For a best friend, mother, grandmother, aunt or sister, this beautiful cake can mark any special occasion.

INGREDIENTS
Serves 15–20
2 x quantity Quick-Mix Sponge Cake mix
350 g/12 oz/1 quantity Butter Icing
4 tbsp apricot jam, warmed and sieved
575 g/1¼ lb marzipan
900 g/2 lb/2⅔ x quantity Sugarpaste Icing
purple and pink food colourings

MATERIALS AND EQUIPMENT
23 cm/9 in square cake tin
25 cm/10 in square cake board
heart-shaped biscuit cutter
small round fluted cutter
pink food-colouring pen

STORING
The finished cake can be kept in a cool, dry place for up to three or four days.

1 Preheat the oven to 180°C/350°F/ Gas 4. Grease the tin, line the base and sides with greaseproof paper and grease the paper. Spoon the cake mixture into the prepared tin and smooth the surface. Bake in the centre of the oven for 1¼ –1½ hours, or until a skewer inserted into the centre of the cake comes out clean. Leave the cake in the tin for 5 minutes, then turn out on to a wire rack, peel off the lining paper and leave to cool.

2 Cut the cake in half horizontally and spread with the butter icing. Sandwich the cake together and place in the centre of the cake board. Brush the cake with the apricot jam. On a work surface lightly dusted with icing sugar, roll out the marzipan to about a 5 mm/¼ in thickness and use to cover the cake.

3 Colour about five-eighths of the sugarpaste icing purple. On a work surface lightly dusted with icing sugar, roll out and use to cover the cake.

4 ▲ Using the heart-shaped cutter, stamp out hearts from the sugarpaste icing to make an even pattern. Remove the hearts with a small, sharp knife, taking care not to damage the surrounding sugarpaste. Knead the hearts together and reserve, wrapped in clear film.

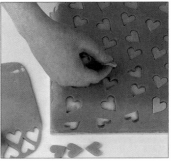

5 ▲ Colour the remaining sugarpaste icing pink and roll out to a 5 mm/ ¼ in thickness. Using the heart-shaped cutter, cut out as many hearts as you need to fill the spaces left by the purple ones, re-rolling the pink sugarpaste as necessary. Reserve the trimmings, wrapped in clear film. Carefully insert the pink hearts into the spaces.

6 Roll out the reserved pink sugarpaste and cut into three strips about 2 cm/¾ in wide and 30 cm/12 in long. Lay one strip across the centre of the cake and another at right angles across the centre, brushing the strips with a little water to secure. Reserve the trimmings.

7 ▲ Divide the remaining strip of pink sugarpaste into quarters and arrange in the centre of the cake to make a bow. Secure with a little water and reserve the trimmings.

8 ▲ Roll out the remaining purple and pink sugarpaste and cut out two rounds from each colour using the small round fluted cutter. With a cocktail stick, carefully roll out the edges of the rounds to make frilled petals. Use a little of the purple sugarpaste to make two tiny balls for the flower centres. Assemble the flowers, securing with a little water and position on the cake. Knead the pink and purple trimmings together, roll out and cut out a name tag. Write a message or a name using the food-colouring pen and position on the cake.

Valentine's Box of Chocolates

This special cake would also make a wonderful gift for Mother's Day. Choose your favourite chocolates to go inside.

INGREDIENTS
Serves 10–12
1½ x quantity chocolate-flavour
Quick-Mix Sponge Cake mix
275 g/10 oz yellow marzipan
8 tbsp apricot jam, warmed
and sieved
900 g/2 lb/2⅔ x quantity
Sugarpaste Icing
red food colouring
225 g/8 oz/about 16–20 hand-
made chocolates

MATERIALS AND EQUIPMENT
heart-shaped cake tin
23 cm/9 inch square piece of
stiff card
23 cm/9 inch square cake board
piece of string
small heart-shaped cutter
length of ribbon and a pin
petits fours cases

STORING
The finished cake can be kept in a cool, dry place for up to three days.

1 Preheat the oven to 180°C/350°F/ Gas 4. Grease the tin, line the base with greaseproof paper and grease the paper. Spoon the cake mixture into the tin and smooth the surface. Bake in the centre of the oven for 45–50 minutes, or until a skewer inserted into the centre of the cake comes out clean. Leave the cake in the tin for about 5 minutes, then turn out on to a wire rack, peel off the lining paper and leave to cool completely.

2 ▲ Place the cake on the piece of card and draw around it with a sharp pencil. Cut the heart shape out of the card and set aside. This will be used as the support for the box lid.

3 ▲ Using a large, sharp knife, cut through the cake horizontally just below where the cake starts to dome. Carefully lift the top section on to the heart-shaped card and place the bottom section on the cake board.

4 Use the piece of string to measure around the outside of the bottom section of cake.

5 ▲ On a work surface lightly dusted with icing sugar, roll out the marzipan into a long sausage shape to the same length as the string. Place the marzipan sausage on the cake around the outside edge. Brush both sections of the cake evenly with apricot jam.

6 Colour the sugarpaste icing red and cut off about one-third. Cut another portion from the larger piece, about 50 g/2 oz in weight. Wrap these two portions separately in clear film and set aside. On a work surface lightly dusted with icing sugar, roll out the icing to a 35 cm/14 inch square and use it to cover the bottom section of cake.

7 ▲ Stand the lid on a raised surface, such as a glass or bowl. Roll out the reserved one-third of sugarpaste icing to a 30 cm/12 inch square and cover the lid section of the cake. Roll out the remaining piece of icing and stamp out small hearts with the cutter. Stick them around the edge of the lid with a little water. Tie the ribbon in a bow and secure on top of the lid with the pin. Carefully lift the top section on to the heart-shaped card and place the bottom section on the cake board.

8 Place the chocolates in the *petits fours* cases and arrange in the bottom section of the cake. Position the lid, placing it slightly off centre, to reveal the chocolates inside. Remove the ribbon and pin before serving.

The Beehive

The perfect cake for an outdoors spring or summer party.
Take the bees along separately on their wires and
insert them into the cake at the picnic.

INGREDIENTS
Serves 8–10
1 quantity Quick-Mix Sponge
Cake mix
900 g/2 lb yellow marzipan
5 tbsp apricot jam, warmed
and sieved
black food colouring
25 g/1 oz sugarpaste icing

MATERIALS AND EQUIPMENT
900 g/2 lb pudding basin
23 cm/9 inch fluted or round
cake board
20 cm/8 inch square of rice paper
florist's wire covered in florist's tape

STORING
The finished cake can be kept in a
cool, dry place for up to two days.

1 Preheat the oven to 180°C/350°F/
Gas 4. Grease and flour the pudding
basin. Spoon in the cake mixture and
smooth the surface. Bake in the centre
of the oven for 40–45 minutes or until
a skewer inserted into the centre of the
cake comes out clean. Leave the cake in
the basin for about 5 minutes, then turn
out on to a wire rack and leave to cool
completely.

2 Cut off about 175 g/6 oz of
marzipan and set aside, wrapped in
clear film. Knead the remainder on a
work surface lightly dusted with icing
sugar, then roll it out into a long, thin
sausage shape. If it breaks when it gets
too long, make more than one sausage.
Place the cake, dome side up, on the
cake board and brush evenly with
apricot jam.

3 ▲ Starting at the back of the base,
coil the marzipan sausage around
the cake, keeping it neat and tight all
the way to the top. Any joins that have
to be made should be placed at the back
of the cake.

4 ▲ Using a small, sharp knife, cut an
arched doorway at the front of the
cake. Remove the cut-out section and
cut away some of the inside cake to
make a hollow. Brush the crumbs away
from the doorway.

5 ▲ To make six bees, divide the
reserved marzipan in half and
colour one portion black. Set aside a
cherry-sized ball of black marzipan,
and wrap in clear film. Divide both the
black and the yellow marzipan into
12 small balls. To make a bee, pinch
together two balls of each colour,
alternately placed. Stick them together
with a little water, if necessary. Cut the
rice paper into six pairs of rounded
wings, then stick them to the bees with
a tiny drop of water.

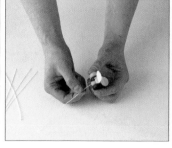

6 ▲ Use the reserved black marzipan
and sugarpaste icing to make the
facial features. Then cut the florist's
wire into various lengths and then use it
to pierce the bees from underneath.
Once secure, press the other end of the
wire into the cake in various places. The
wires must be removed before serving.

$\mathscr{S}$trawberry Cake

*A summer-time cake or for someone who's
simply mad about strawberries!*

INGREDIENTS
Serves 10–12
1 quantity Quick-Mix Sponge
Cake mix
650 g/1 lb 7oz marzipan
green, red and yellow food
colourings
caster sugar, to dredge

MATERIALS AND EQUIPMENT
900 g/2 lb heart-shaped tin
30 cm/12 inch round cake board
icing smoother

STORING
*The finished cake can be kept in a
cool, dry place for up to two days.*

$\mathscr{T}$ip

You can also sandwich the cake
with a half quantity of strawberry-
flavour Butter Icing before brushing
it with apricot jam for extra
flavour! Use a long, serrated knife
and cut the cake horizontally into
two layers.

1 Preheat the oven to 180°C/350°F/
Gas 4. Grease the heart-shaped tin,
line the base with greaseproof paper
and grease the paper. Spoon in the cake
mixture and smooth the surface. Bake
in the centre of the oven for 35–40
minutes or until a skewer inserted into
the centre of the cake comes out clean.

2 Leave in the tin for approximately
5 minutes, then turn out on to a
wire rack, peel off the lining paper and
leave to cool completely.

3 ▲ Cut off about 175 g/6 oz of the
marzipan and colour it green. Brush
the cake board with a little apricot jam,
then roll out the green marzipan on the
work surface lightly dusted with icing
sugar and use to cover the cake board.
Trim the edges. Use an icing smoother
to make the marzipan as flat and as
smooth as possible.

4 ▲ Evenly brush the remaining
apricot jam over the top and sides
of the cake. Position the cake on the
cake board. Cut off about 275 g/10 oz
of the remaining marzipan and colour it
red. Roll it out to about 5 mm/¼ inch
thick and use to cover the cake,
smoothing down the sides and edges.
Trim the edges. Use the handle of a
teaspoon to indent the strawberry
evenly and lightly all over.

5 To make the stalk, cut off another
175 g/6 oz of marzipan and colour
it bright green. Cut it in half and roll
out one portion into a 10 × 15 cm/4 ×
6 inch rectangle. Use a sharp knife to cut
'V' shapes out of the rectangle, leaving
a 2.5 cm/1 inch border across the top,
to form the calyx. Position this on the
cake, curling and moving the sections to
make them look more realistic.

6 ▲ Roll the other half of the green
marzipan in your hands into a
sausage shape about 13 cm/5 inches
long. Bend it slightly, then position it on
the cake to form the stalk.

7 ▲ To make the strawberry seeds,
colour the remaining marzipan
yellow. Pull off tiny pieces about the
size of an apple pip and roll them into
little tear-shaped seeds. Place them in
the indentations all over the strawberry.
Dust the cake and board with sifted
caster sugar.

n Apple Tree

For this unusual centrepiece, choose whichever fruit you prefer. You could make
the apples green instead of red, or have a mixture of red and green apples or golden pears.

INGREDIENTS
Serves 10–12
1 quantity chocolate-flavour Quick-
Mix Sponge Cake mix
1 quantity chocolate-flavour Swiss
Roll, baked and rolled with
¼ quantity chocolate-flavour
Butter Icing
¼ quantity chocolate-flavour
Butter Icing
½ quantity Butter Icing, coloured
green with food colouring
225 g/8 oz marzipan
red and green food colouring
green-coloured desiccated coconut
(see Puppies in Love, step 4)
tiny fresh flowers, to
decorate (optional)

MATERIALS AND EQUIPMENT
450 g/1 lb fluted round cake tin or
pudding basin
15 cm/6 inch round cake board
wooden cocktail stick
2 x 30 cm/12 inch lengths of
florist's wire
florist's tape
greaseproof paper piping bag
leaf nozzle

STORING
The finished cake can be kept in a
cool, dry place for up to a day.

ip

To stand the tree up at a slight angle, you can cut out a template of thick card from around the un-iced cake. Then decorate the cake on the card and prop it up on a small block of wood. Alternatively, decorate the cake flat on a cake board.

1 Preheat the oven to 180°F/350°C/ Gas 4. Grease and flour the tin or pudding basin. Spoon in the cake mixture and smooth the surface. Bake in the centre of the oven for 35–40 minutes or until a skewer inserted into the centre of the cake comes out clean. Leave in the tin for about 5 minutes, then turn out on to a wire rack and leave to cool.

2 ▲ Arrange the Swiss roll on the card template or cake board (see Tip), trimming it, if necessary. Spread the chocolate butter icing over the tree trunk, making swirls. Use about three-quarters of the green butter icing for the top of the tree, making it peak and swirl. Position on top of the tree trunk.

3 ▲ Colour about 25 g/1 oz of the marzipan green. Colour the remainder red, then roll it into cherry-size balls. Roll the green marzipan into tiny sausage shapes to make the stalks and leaves. Use the cocktail stick to make tiny holes in the tops of the apples, then insert the stalks and leaves.

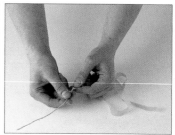

4 ▲ Twist the florist's tape around the florist's wire, then cut it into 7.5 cm/3 inch lengths. Press the lengths of wire through the apples, bending the ends so the apples cannot fall off when hanging. Press the hanging apples into the tree, reserving the extra apples to scatter around the bottom.

5 ▲ Use the remaining green butter icing to fill the piping bag. Practise piping the leaves on a piece of greaseproof paper before piping leaves all over the tree top. Scatter the green desiccated coconut around the base of the tree and pipe a few extra leaves. Add a few tiny fresh flowers for effect, if liked. The wires must be removed from the cake before serving.

Banjo Cake

The perfect cake for the musician in the family. It can be set on a large tray or you could cut out card for a template to support it.

INGREDIENTS

Serves 15–20
2 x quantity Quick-Mix Sponge Cake mix
115 g/4 oz/6 tbsp seedless raspberry jam, warmed
900 g/2 lb/2⅔ x quantity Sugarpaste Icing
lime green food colouring
2 coloured sticks of liquorice
4 round lollipops
4 tbsp coloured vermicelli
piece of flat green liquorice
2 long red liquorice bootlaces
4 long green liquorice bootlaces
sugarpaste stars, or other decoration

MATERIALS AND EQUIPMENT

20 cm/8 inch round cake tin
18 cm/7 inch square cake tin
54 cm/21 inch stiff card
5 cm/2 inch round cutter
ribbon and 2 pins, for the strap

STORING

The finished cake can be made up to two days in advance kept in a cool, dry place.

1 Preheat the oven to 180°C/350°F/ Gas 4. Grease the tins, line the bases with greaseproof paper and grease the paper. Divide the cake mixture between the two tins and smooth the surfaces. Bake for 35–40 minutes, or until firm to the touch. Turn out on to a wire rack, peel off the lining paper and leave to cool completely.

2 ▲ Cut off the dome from the round cake and place bottom side up on the work surface. Cut the dome off the square cake, then cut in half down the middle. Place the cakes together to form the banjo shape, then draw around them on to stiff card. Cut out the shape to make the reinforcing template.

3 ▲ Use the cutter to stamp out a shallow hollow from the centre of the round cake. Place both cakes on the card base and brush with the raspberry jam. Colour the sugarpaste icing with the lime green food colouring and roll out on a work surface lightly dusted with icing sugar to about a 62 x 25 cm/ 25 x 10 inch rectangle. Use to cover the banjo in one piece, easing the icing into the hollow and down the sides. Make finger indentations along the length of the neck of the banjo.

4 Cut off four 1 cm/½ inch pieces from one of the sticks of liquorice and press into the cake at the top end of the neck to resemble stays for the strings. Place the remains of the liquorice stick with the other one at the base of the banjo, next to the hollow. Dip the lollipops in water, then in the coloured vermicelli to coat. Press the lollipops into the sides of the neck end so that they line up with the pieces of liquorice stick forming the stays.

5 Place the two flat pieces of liquorice side by side at the base, securing with a little water. Cut the red liquorice bootlace into about 5 cm/2 inch lengths and position them along the length of the banjo neck, in the indentations. Use a little water to stick them in place, if necessary.

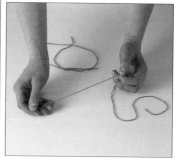

6 ▲ Dip the green liquorice bootlaces in hot water, then stretch and smooth each one until perfectly straight. Wrap one end of the banjo strings around the liquorice sticks at the top of the neck end and bring the other ends down so they meet together on the flat liquorice at the rounded end. Secure the ribbon strap with pins pushed through each end and into the cake. Decorate the banjo with sugarpaste stars and more coloured vermicelli, if wished. The pins *must* be removed from the cake before serving.

A Basket of Flowers

This attractive arrangement of flowers looks very impressive, yet none of the stages are very difficult to do.

INGREDIENTS
Serves 10–12
1½ x quantity orange-flavour
Quick-Mix Sponge Cake mix
2 x quantity orange-flavour
Butter Icing
orange, yellow, pink, red, black and
green food colourings
900 g/2 lb/2⅔ x quantity
Sugarpaste Icing

MATERIALS AND EQUIPMENT
deep 20 cm/8 inch round cake tin
20 cm/8 inch oval cake board
3 greaseproof paper piping bags
small round nozzle
small straight serrated nozzle
selection of small flower and
leaf cutters
30 cm/12 inch piece of strong wire,
bent to a curve with the two ends
about 20 cm/8 inch apart
plasticine

STORING
*The finished cake can be kept in a
cool, dry place for up to three days.*

1 Preheat the oven to 180°C/350°F/ Gas 4. Grease the cake tin, line the base with greaseproof paper and grease the paper. Spoon the cake mixture into the prepared tin and smooth the surface. Bake in the centre of the oven for 45–50 minutes or until a skewer inserted into the centre of the cake comes out clean. Turn out on to a wire rack, peel off the lining paper and leave the cake to cool completely.

2 Place the butter icing in a bowl and beat in a few drops of orange food colouring. Cut the cake in half down the middle and spread the bottom of one half with a little of the butter icing. Sandwich with the other half of the cake, base to base.

3 Cut a thin slice from the bottom of the sandwiched cake. Place a little butter icing on the cake board and position the cake on top, with the large flat surface facing upwards.

4 ▲ Spread more of the butter icing over the cut surface of the cake, covering right up to the edges.

5 Place about 4 tbsp of the butter icing in a small bowl and colour it with a little more orange food colouring to make it a slightly deeper colour. Fit a paper piping bag with the small round nozzle and fill with the deeper orange butter icing. Pipe a decorative border around the top edge of the basket.

6 Fit the clean round nozzle into a fresh paper piping bag and fill with the lighter orange butter icing. Pipe vertical lines about 2.5 cm/1 inch apart all around the sides of the cake. Fit a fresh paper piping bag with the serrated nozzle and fill with more orange butter icing. Starting at the top of the cake pipe short lines alternately crossing over, then stopping at the vertical lines to give a basket-weave effect.

7 Divide the sugarpaste icing into two. Cut one of the portions in half and colour one half pale orange and the other half darker orange. Wrap these separately in clear film and set aside. Divide the other portion of sugarpaste icing into five equal amounts. Colour these yellow, pink, red, black and green.

8 ▲ Roll out the yellow, pink and red portions on a work surface lightly dusted with icing sugar and use the flower cutters to stamp out the flower shapes. Place some of the flowers in an egg carton so they dry curved and place others on a baking sheet so they dry flat. Leave the flowers for at least 2 hours to dry out.

9 Use a little of the orange, yellow and black sugarpaste icings to roll into tiny balls to make the centres of the flowers, sticking them in place with a little water.

10 Roll out the green icing and use a leaf-shaped cutter to stamp out leaves, indenting them with a small sharp knife and curling them slightly to give them more interest. Place them on the baking sheet to dry out.

11 When dry, arrange the flowers and leaves attractively on top of the basket and the cake board.

12 ▲ To make the handle for the basket, roll the two shades of orange sugarpaste icing into balls about the size of small marbles. Thread these alternately on to the curved piece of wire, leaving about 2.5 cm/1 inch of wire exposed at each end. Stand the handle in two pieces of plasticine stuck to the work surface or a baking sheet, supported by a tea towel pushed under the handle to stop it falling over. Leave to dry for at least 2 hours. To finish, gently press the handle into the cake, pushing it in until secure.

Children's Party Cakes

A special cake is the perfect way to celebrate a child's birthday or other important event. Filled with novelty and fun cake ideas – dinosaurs, clowns, caterpillars, puppies and many, many more – for children of all ages, the cakes in this chapter will make every kid's party an instant success.

$\mathcal{E}$ lephant Cake

*Any medium-sized roasting tin will work for
this cake, but one with rounded edges is preferable
as this improves the finished result.*

INGREDIENTS
Serves 10–12
1½ x quantity lemon-flavour Quick-
Mix Sponge Cake mix
1 quantity lemon-flavour Butter
Icing (optional)
8 tbsp apricot jam, warmed
and sieved
900 g/2 lb/2⅔ x quantity
Sugarpaste Icing
pink, blue and grey food colourings

MATERIALS AND EQUIPMENT
30 x 23 cm/12 x 9 inch roasting tin
18 cm/7 inch round cake tin, or
card, to use as a template
40 cm/16 inch round cake board,
with a support for the trunk, or 40
x 25 cm/16 x 10 inch square cake
board (optional)
wooden cocktail stick
medium-size round cutter (optional)
bow made from pretty ribbon
pin

STORING
The finished cake can be kept in a
cool, dry place for up to two days.

1 Preheat the oven to 180°C/350°F/
Gas 4. Grease the roasting tin, line
the base and sides with greaseproof
paper and grease the paper. Spoon in
the cake mixture and smooth the
surface. Bake in the centre of the oven
for 45–50 minutes or until a skewer
inserted into the centre of the cake
comes out clean. Leave in the tin for
about 5 minutes, then turn out on to a
wire rack, peel off the lining paper and
leave to cool completely.

2 ▲ Place the cake, dome side down,
on the work surface and position
the template in the centre on the flat
surface. Use a sharp knife to cut around
the template, holding it steady and firm
as you cut. Lift out the cut-out circle,
keeping the outside piece intact.

3 ▲ Use the template to cut out the
elephant's trunk. Place the template
close to one edge of the short side of the
remaining cake and cut out a crescent
shape. Cut off one end of the crescent
to make the elephant's mouth. Cut off
the other end of the cake, just past the
rounded corners, to make the ear.
Discard the two small, middle sections
of cake. Cut horizontally through the
face, ear, trunk and mouth sections of
the cake, then sandwich them back
together with lemon butter icing, if you
are using it.

4 ▲ Assemble the cake on a board or
directly on the table. Place the ear
piece on one side of the round face,
then place the flat edge of the trunk
section up against the face, opposite the
ear. Place the mouth section in the
space between the trunk and the face.
Brush the whole surface with jam.

5 Cut off about 50 g/2 oz of
sugarpaste icing and set aside,
wrapped in clear film. Cut off another
175 g/6 oz of sugarpaste icing and
colour it pink, and 15 g/½ oz and
colour it blue. Set aside, wrapped in
clear film. Colour the remaining icing
grey, cut off about 75 g/3 oz and set
aside. Dust the work surface with icing
sugar then roll out the larger portion of
grey icing into a 50 × 25 cm/20 × 10
inch rectangle. Use this to cover the
entire cake. Smooth down the sides and
edges, snipping with scissors or cutting
the icing in the places where it overlaps.
Trim the edges.

6 To make the ear piece, roll out the
reserved portion of grey icing into a
20 × 10 cm/8 × 4 inch rectangle, then
roll it in small sections with the cocktail
stick, to give a ruffled effect (see Teddy
Bear Christening cake, step 7). Lay this
section on top of the ear, slightly off
centre. Cut off about 150 g/5 oz of the
pink icing and roll it out to a slightly
smaller rectangle, then repeat the
ruffling process with the cocktail stick.
Lay this piece on top of the grey ruffle.

7 Roll out the reserved blue and white
icings and cut out the eye parts,
using the round cutter, if preferred. Stick
in place with a little water, placing a
small round ball of the remaining pink
icing in the centre. Roll out the
remaining pink icing and cut out a
triangular piece for the mouth. Shape the
remaining white icing into a tusk and
then stick them both in place with a little
water. Finally, position the bow,
securing in place with the pin, which
must be removed before serving the cake.

Clown Cake

Made from a clown-shaped tin, this is a quick and easy cake to make and decorate. Choose your own nozzle shapes for the designs, following the contours of the cake.

INGREDIENTS
Serves 10–15
1½ x quantity Quick-Mix Sponge
Cake mix
115 g/4 oz/⅓ quantity
Sugarpaste Icing
2 x quantity Butter Icing
yellow, red, pink and blue
food colourings
small coloured sweets, for
the features

MATERIALS AND EQUIPMENT
900 g/2 lb clown-shaped cake tin
25 x 30 cm/10 x 12 inch cake board
greaseproof paper piping bags
small star, small plain
and large star nozzles
small party hat

STORING
The finished cake can be stored in an airtight container in a cool, dry place for up to two days.

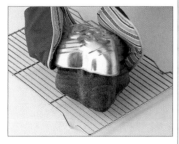

1 ▲ Preheat the oven to 180°C/350°F/ Gas 4. Grease the cake tin generously. Spoon in the cake mixture and smooth the surface. Bake in the centre of the oven for 45–50 minutes or until a skewer inserted into the centre of the cake comes out clean. Leave for 5 minutes before turning out on to a wire rack to cool.

2 ▲ To make a template for the clown's face, hold a piece of greaseproof paper firmly over the face on the cooled tin. Draw around the outline using a pencil and cut around the shape.

3 ▲ On a work surface lightly dusted with icing sugar, roll out the sugarpaste icing to about 5 mm/¼ inch thick, then place the greaseproof paper template on top. Use a small sharp knife to cut around the outline of the template. Place the cut-out sugarpaste on a baking sheet and cover with clear film.

4 To colour the butter icing, place about one-third of the icing in a small mixing bowl and colour it yellow. Place another third in another mixing bowl and colour it red. Divide the remaining butter icing between two small bowls and colour one pink and the other blue.

5 ▲ Place the cake on the cake board. Fit a small star nozzle in a paper piping bag and fill it with the yellow butter icing. Use to pipe along the contours of the hair on the clown's head. Place the cut-out sugarpaste template in position on the cake, then place a small plain nozzle in another piping bag and fill with the red butter icing. Use it to pipe decoratively around the neck and torso area of the clown. Pipe around the mouth, then change the nozzle to a large star shape and pipe in the nose.

6 Place a small star nozzle in another small piping bag and fill with the pink icing. Use to pipe a star border around the edges of the sugarpaste template. Place a large star nozzle in another piping bag and fill with the blue icing. Use to pipe in the buttons and the clown's eyes. Place the sweets in the centres of the eyes, nose and buttons. Position the hat.

Spiders' Web Cake

A spooky cake for any occasion, fancy dress or otherwise. Put as many spiders as you like on the cake, but any leftover ones can be put on the children's plates or arranged to look like they're crawling all over the table.

INGREDIENTS
Serves 6–8
1 quantity lemon-flavour Quick-Mix Sponge Cake mix
1 quantity lemon-flavour Glacé Icing
yellow and black food colourings

For the Spiders
115 g/4 oz/4 squares plain chocolate, broken into pieces
150 ml/¼ pint/⅔ cup double cream
3 tbsp ground almonds
cocoa powder, for dusting
chocolate vermicelli
2–3 liquorice wheels, sweet centres removed
15 g/½ oz Sugarpaste Icing

MATERIALS AND EQUIPMENT
900 g/2 lb fluted dome-shaped tin or pudding basin
20 cm/8 inch cake board
small greaseproof paper piping bag
wooden skewer

STORING
The finished cake can be kept in a cool, dry place for up to two days.

1 Preheat the oven to 180°C/350°F/ Gas 4. Grease and flour the fluted dome-shaped tin or pudding basin. Spoon in the cake mixture and smooth the surface. Bake in the centre of the oven for 35–40 minutes or until a skewer inserted into the centre of the cake comes out clean.

2 ▲ Leave the cake in the tin for about 5 minutes, then turn out on to a wire rack and leave to cool completely.

3 Place about 3 tbsp of the glacé icing in a small bowl. Stir a few drops of yellow food colouring into the larger quantity of icing and colour the small quantity black. Place the cake on the cake board, dome side up, and pour over the yellow icing, allowing it to run, unevenly, down the sides. Fill the piping bag with the black icing. Seal the bag and snip the end, making a small hole for the nozzle.

4 ▲ Starting on the top of the cake, in the centre, drizzle the black icing round the cake in a spiral, keeping the line as continuous and as evenly spaced as possible. Use the wooden skewer to draw through the icing, downwards from the centre at the top of the cake, to make a web effect. Wipe away the excess icing with a damp cloth, then allow the icing to set at room temperature.

5 To make the spiders, place the chocolate and cream in a small, heavy-based saucepan and heat gently, stirring frequently, until the chocolate melts. Transfer the mixture to a small mixing bowl and allow to cool.

6 ▲ When cool, beat the mixture for about 10 minutes or until thick and pale. Stir in the ground almonds, then chill until firm enough to handle. Dust your hands with a little cocoa, then make a ball the size of a large walnut out of the chocolate mixture. Roll each ball in chocolate vermicelli until evenly coated. Repeat this process until all the mixture is used.

7 ▲ To make the spiders' legs, cut the liquorice into 4 cm/1½ inch lengths. Make small cuts into the sides of each spider, then insert the legs. To make the spiders' eyes, pull off a piece of sugarpaste icing about the size of a hazelnut and colour it with black food colouring. Use the white icing to make tiny balls and the black icing to make even smaller ones. Use a little water to stick the eyes in place. Arrange the spiders on and around the cake.

Daisy Cow

*A really fun cake to make for a child who
loves animals or the countryside.*

INGREDIENTS
Serves 10–12
1½ x quantity Quick-Mix Sponge
Cake mix
9 tbsp apricot jam, warmed
and sieved
1.67 kg/3 lb 12 oz/5 x quantity
Sugarpaste Icing
black, brown, blue, yellow and red
food colourings

MATERIALS AND EQUIPMENT
2 x deep 18 cm/7 inch round
cake tins
25 x 33 cm/10 x 13 inch cake board
4 cm/1½ inch and 2.5 cm/1 inch
plain round pastry cutters
6 cm/2½ inch fluted round
pastry cutter
wooden cocktail stick
25 cm/10 inch florist's wire covered
in florist's tape

STORING
*The finished cake can be kept in a
cool, dry place for up to three days.*

1 Preheat the oven to 180°C/350°F/
Gas 4. Grease the tins, line the bases
with greaseproof paper and grease the
paper. Divide the cake mixture equally
between the two tins and smooth the
surfaces. Bake in the centre of the oven
for 30–35 minutes or until a skewer
inserted into the centre of each cake
comes out clean. Turn out on to wire
racks, peel off the lining paper and leave
to cool completely.

2 ▲ Using a sharp, pointed knife, cut
a crescent-shaped piece from the
side of one cake, then cut it in half to
make the cow's ears.

3 ▲ This is how the cake should be
assembled. On the work surface,
brush the cake with apricot jam and
push the two rounds together to make
the face.

4 Colour 950 g/2 lb 2 oz of the
sugarpaste icing with black food
colouring. Cut off 500 g/1 lb 2 oz and
set aside, wrapped in clear film. Roll
out the remainder on a work surface
dusted with icing sugar into a rectangle
about 5 mm/¼ inch thick. Roll out two-
thirds of the white icing, then cut into
rounds using plain round cutters. Place
some of the rounds of white icing in a
random pattern on the rolled-out black
icing and roll again lightly with the
rolling pin to flatten them into the
surface. Cover the cow's face with the
black and white icing, trimming it
neatly around the bottom edge. Brush
the cake board evenly with apricot jam.
Roll out 275 g/10 oz of the reserved
black icing into an oblong large enough
to cover the cake board.

5 Arrange the circles of white icing on
top of the black icing and roll lightly
into the surface. Lay over the cake board
and trim the edges. Set aside 50 g/2 oz of
the black icing, break off two marble-
size pieces and set aside from the rest for
the cow's eyes. Roll out the icing that is
left and use to cover the ear shapes.

6 Carefully lift the cow's head on to
the cake board, set aside 90 g/3½
oz of the white icing then roll out the
rest thinly. Cut out a pear shape for the
cow's nose. Brush the back with a little
water and stick on to the cake. Roll two
small pieces of white icing into walnut-
size balls, then flatten with a rolling pin
and reserve for the eyes.

7 To make the cow's eyes, colour
40 g/1½ oz sugarpaste icing brown,
then cut out two rounds with the
4 cm/1½ inch round pastry cutter.
Colour 25 g/1 oz icing blue, then cut
out two rounds with the 2.5 cm/1 inch
round cutter. Assemble the cow's eyes
from the brown and blue rounds and
the reserved white and black icings.
Stick them in place with a little water.

8 Divide the reserved 50 g/2 oz of the
black sugarpaste icing in half, and
roll out one half thinly into a rectangle
of about 15 × 10 cm/6 × 4 inches. Cut
along the icing at intervals, leaving a
1 cm /½ inch border along the top, to
create the fringe. Position between the
ears. Divide the remaining sugarpaste
icing in half and use for the nose.

9 ▲ Colour 25 g/1 oz of the remaining
icing bright yellow and the rest red.
Roll two-thirds of the red icing into a
sausage shape, to make a mouth. To
make the flower, roll out the remaining
red icing and cut out a 6 cm/2½ inch
round, using the fluted cutter.

10 Roll the edge of the red icing using a
cocktail stick to make it frilly (see
Teddy Bear Christening Cake, step 7).
Roll the yellow icing into a ball to finish
off the flower. Push the florist's wire
through the cake. Remove before serving.

Monsters on the Moon

A great cake for little monsters!
This cake is best eaten on the day of making.

INGREDIENTS
Serves 12–15
1 quantity Quick-Mix Sponge
Cake mix
115 g/4 oz/¹3 quantity
Sugarpaste Icing
edible silver glitter powder
(optional)

For the Icing
375 g/12 oz/1¾ cups plus 2 tbsp
caster sugar
2 size 3 egg whites
4 tbsp water

MATERIALS AND EQUIPMENT
ovenproof wok
various sizes of plain round cutters
30 cm/12 inch round cake board
several small monster toys

1 ▲ Preheat the oven to 180°C/350°F/ Gas 4. Grease the wok, line the base with greaseproof paper and grease the paper. Spoon in the cake mixture and smooth the surface. Bake in the centre of the oven for 35–40 minutes or until a skewer inserted into the centre of the cake comes out clean. Leave the cake in the wok for about 5 minutes, then turn out on to a wire rack, peel off the lining paper and leave to cool completely.

2 ▲ With the cake dome side up, use the round cutters to cut out craters. Press in a cutter about 2.5 cm/1 inch deep, then remove and use a knife to cut out the cake to make a crater.

3 ▲ Pull off small pieces of the sugarpaste icing and press them into uneven strips which can be moulded around the edges of the craters. Make one of the craters especially deep by adding an extra-wide sugarpaste strip to make the edges higher.

4 Place the cake on the cake board. To make the icing, place all the ingredients in a heatproof bowl, then sit the bowl over a saucepan of simmering water. Beat until thick and peaky. Spoon the icing over the cake, swirling it into the craters and peaking it unevenly. Sprinkle over the silver glitter powder, if using, then position the monsters on the cake.

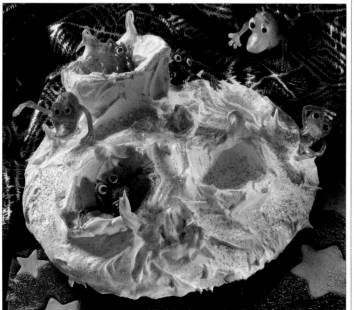

Tip

To cover the cake board, roll out 450 g/1 lb of black sugarpaste icing. Trim the edges. Using various sizes of star-shaped cutters, stamp out stars from the black icing. Roll out 285 g/8 oz of yellow marzipan thinly and use the star-shaped cutters to stamp out replacement stars. Dust with a little extra silver powder.

*I*ce-Cream Cornets

Individual cakes make a change for a party, the idea being that each guest has one to themselves. You could even put a candle in the special person's one.

INGREDIENTS
Makes 9
1 quantity Quick-Mix Sponge Cake mix
9 ice-cream cornets
1 quantity Butter Icing
red, green and brown food colourings
selection of coloured vermicelli, wafers, chocolate sticks, etc.

MATERIALS AND EQUIPMENT
9 fairy cake paper cases
bun tin

STORING
The finished cake can be kept in a cool, dry place for up to a day.

*T*ip

To have 3 sets of 3 ice cream cakes placed on the table, you will need 3 egg boxes, which hold 12 eggs each. Place a ball of marzipan in 3 evenly spaced holes in the up-turned egg box. Cover the box in foil, then pierce the foil and make a small hole with your finger where the marzipan balls are. Insert the iced ice cream cornets, pressing them in gently, so they stand securely.

1 Preheat the oven to 180°C/350°F/ Gas 4. Place the paper cases in the bun tin, then spoon in the cake mixture until they are all at least half full. Bake in the centre of the oven for about 20 minutes or until the cakes have risen and are golden. Transfer the cakes to a wire rack to cool completely. Remove the cases.

2 ▲ Gently press a fairy cake into a cornet, taking care not to damage the cornet. If the bases of the cakes are a little large to insert into the cornets, trim them down with a small, sharp knife. The cakes should feel quite secure once inserted into the cornets.

3 Divide the butter icing into three small bowls and colour one portion pale red, one portion green and one portion brown.

4 ▲ Using a small palette knife, spread each cake with some of one of the icings. Place in the ice-cream stand (see Tip). Continue coating the cornets, making sure the icing isn't too smooth so it looks like ice cream.

5 ▲ To insert a wafer or chocolate stick into an ice cream, use a small, sharp knife to make a hole or incision through the icing and into the cake, then insert the wafer or stick. Add the finishing touches by sprinkling over some coloured vermicelli.

*M*agic Carpet Cake

The Master of the Lamp can also be made out of coloured sugarpaste icing, instead of marzipan, if you prefer.

INGREDIENTS
Serves 8–10
1 quantity Quick-Mix Sponge
Cake mix
675 g/1½ lb/2 x quantity
Sugarpaste Icing
*blue, brown, red, orange, yellow,
purple and black food colourings*
115 g/4 oz/4 squares milk or plain
chocolate, melted
350 g/12 oz white marzipan
*small sweet or diamond-shaped
cake decoration*
small brightly coloured feather

MATERIALS AND EQUIPMENT
23 x 15 cm/6 x 9 inch cake tin
33 cm/13 inch round cake board
2.5 cm/1 inch and 6 cm/2½ inch
round fluted pastry cutters
small piece of yellow crepe paper

STORING
The finished cake can be kept in a cool, dry place for up to three days.

1 Preheat the oven to 180°C/350°F/ Gas 4. Grease the cake tin, line the base and sides with greaseproof paper and grease the paper. Spoon in the cake mixture and smooth the surface. Bake in the centre of the oven for 30–35 minutes or until a skewer inserted into the centre of the cake comes out clean. Turn out on to a wire rack, peel off the lining paper and leave to cool completely.

2 Colour 275 g/10 oz sugarpaste icing with blue food colouring. Remove a piece about the size of a walnut and set aside, wrapped in clear film. Roll out the rest of the blue icing thinly on a surface dusted with icing sugar into a round about the same size as the cake board.

3 ▲ Roll out about 150 g/5 oz of white icing and cut out rounds using the pastry cutters. Arrange these on the blue icing to resemble clouds, then roll lightly into the icing. Brush the cake board lightly with water and cover with the blue and white icing, smoothing it with your hands to exclude air bubbles. Leave the icing draped over the edge of the board, if liked, or trim level with the edge of the board.

4 ▲ Colour 175 g/6 oz sugarpaste icing thinly into an oblong large enough to cover the top and sides of the cake generously. Trim the edges. Knead the trimmings into a ball and set aside, wrapped in clear film. Brush the cake with melted chocolate, then place on the cake board. Drape the brown icing over the top of the cake, being careful not to flatten it at the sides too much.

5 Divide 75 g/3 oz sugarpaste icing into two equal pieces. Colour one piece red and the other orange. Then unwrap the reserved pieces of blue and brown icing.

6 Divide each of the four colours into three or four smaller pieces, then knead them together to make a marbled ball of icing. Roll it out into a rectangle slightly larger than the top of the cake. Trim the edges, then lay over the brown icing and stick into place with water.

7 ▲ Colour 75 g/3 oz marzipan yellow, then roll most of it into a long, thin sausage shape. Press it around the edge of the carpet to make a trim. Decorate with small balls of yellow marzipan. Snip pieces of yellow crepe paper with scissors to make tassels. Push into the small balls of icing.

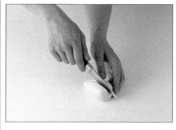

8 ▲ To make the figure, roll about 75 g/3 oz of white marzipan into a pear shape, then cut in half to make two legs. Bend the legs into a sitting position. Colour 65 g/2½ oz marzipan dark brown and shape into a head, body and arms. Make the eyes and mouth from tiny pieces of coloured icing or marzipan and press on to the face. Press the head and body on to the legs. Colour 25 g/1 oz of marzipan purple and use it to make the jacket. Press the arms on to the figure.

9 Colour small pieces of marzipan black and deep red or purple and use to make hair and a hat respectively. Colour the remaining marzipan bright orange. Roll a tiny piece into a ball and press on to the hat. Decorate with a tiny diamond-shaped sweet or cake decoration and coloured feather. Use the rest of the orange marzipan to make slippers and a lamp. Position the figure and the lamp on the carpet.

Crazy Caterpillar

A no-bake cake made from sponge cake crumbs, home-made or bought. You can double the quantity for an extra-large party, but remember the cake is rich and heavy in texture so you only serve a small amount. One ball per person is more than enough!

INGREDIENTS
Serves 11
1 quantity Truffle Cake mix
675 g/1½ lb yellow marzipan
green, brown and orange
food colourings
selection of coloured liquorice
sticks, or sweets, for the feet
green-coloured desiccated coconut
(see Puppies in Love, step 4),
for the grass
small flowers, to decorate (optional)

MATERIALS AND EQUIPMENT
40 x 20 cm/16 x 8 inch cake
board (optional)
small round fluted cutter
round fluted aspic cutter

STORING
The finished cake can be kept in
a cool, dry place for up to four days.

1 ▲ Using slightly damp hands, roll the truffle cake mixture into balls about the size of a large walnut. Place them on a baking sheet as you make them, then cover with clear film and set to one side.

2 ▲ Divide the marzipan into three equal portions, then colour one portion green, one portion brown and the other portion orange. Remove a small amount of orange and green marzipan, to make the face features, and set aside, covered with clear film.

3 ▲ Roll each colour of marzipan into a sausage shape about 45 cm/18 inches long on a work surface lightly dusted with icing sugar. Make sure the sausage shape is even all the way along; if it breaks, compress the marzipan into a ball and start again.

4 ▲ Place the three long sausages side-by-side on the work surface. Starting at one end, hold them together firmly and start to turn them in a twisting motion — do not squeeze. Place the twist back on the work surface, then use a rolling pin to push and roll the twist gently until it is flat and the colours merge. It should be about 50 cm/20 inches long.

5 Lay the truffle balls all along the length of the marzipan strip, then wrap the marzipan evenly around the balls, sealing the join by pinching the marzipan together. (An extra pair of hands is useful for this stage.) Turn the caterpillar over so the join is underneath, tucking in and cutting off any excess marzipan from the ends. Lift the caterpillar on to the cake board, if using, otherwise position it on the table, curving it slightly.

6 Roll out the reserved orange and green marzipan thinly and use the fluted cutters to stamp out rounds for the eyes. Use a little water to stick the smaller green rounds on the orange rounds, then stick them on to one end of the caterpillar to make the face. Roll a tiny piece of orange marzipan into a little sausage, shape and stick it on to make the mouth. Cut the liquorice sticks into small pieces and position them along either side, to make the feet. Scatter the green-coloured coconut all around. Add a few flowers, if you like.

Dinosaur Cake

For a dino-crazy kid, this cake is just the ticket.
Put it on a cake board or build a little scene using bits
and pieces from around the house and garden.

INGREDIENTS
Serves 8–10
1 quantity Quick-Mix Sponge
Cake mix
½ quantity Butter Icing
1 quantity Truffle Cake mix
900 g/2 lb/2⅔ x quantity
Sugarpaste Icing
pink, yellow, green and black
food colourings
4 tbsp apricot jam, warmed
and sieved

MATERIALS AND EQUIPMENT
900 g/2 lb heart-shaped tin
5 x 25 cm/2 x 10 inch piece of card
small block of wood, for raising
the cake

STORING
The finished cake can be kept in a
cool, dry place for up to two days.

1 Preheat the oven to 180°C/350°F/
Gas 4. Grease the heart-shaped tin,
line the base with greaseproof paper
and grease the paper. Spoon in the cake
mixture and smooth the surface.
Bake in the centre of the oven for
35–40 minutes or until a skewer
inserted into the centre of the cake
comes out clean. Turn out on to a wire
rack, peel off the lining paper and leave
to cool completely.

2 ▲ Cut the heart-shaped cake in half
vertically, then sandwich the halves
together with the butter icing so they
form a half heart shape. Place the cake
in the centre of the strip of card,
positioned on the long, straight side.
Stand the cake on the small block of
wood to raise it up slightly.

3 ▲ Divide the truffle mixture in half.
Shape one portion into the tail,
making it thicker and flattened at one
end and more pointed at the other.
This will fit on the pointed end of the
cake. Mould the other half of the truffle
cake mix into the head shape, starting
with a ball and then flattening one side,
so the diameter matches the width of
the head end of the cake. Mould the
other end of the head into a pointed
shape for the nose.

4 Place the head and tail in
position at either end of the cake,
moulding the truffle cake mix on to
the cake a little. Cut off about 500 g/
1¼ lb of the sugarpaste icing and
colour it pink. Lightly dust the work
surface with icing sugar and roll out
the icing to a long, thin, rectangular
shape. Brush the cake evenly with jam
and cover the dinosaur with the icing in
one piece from head to toe. Smooth
down the sides and edges with your
hands, then trim.

5 ▲ To make the dinosaur's legs,
cut off about 115 g/4 oz of the
remaining sugarpaste icing and colour it
yellow. Remove about 25 g/1 oz and set
aside, wrapped in clear film. Use the
remainder to roll out 10 evenly sized
balls, each about the size of a small
walnut. Squeeze together two balls for
each of the back legs and three for each
of the front ones. Indent the toes with a
fork, then using a little water stick the
legs on the dinosaur.

6 ▲ Use the reserved yellow
sugarpaste icing to make one small
and three large horns, then stick these in
place with a little water. Cut off about
75 g/3 oz of the remaining icing and
colour it green. Divide it into about 11
evenly sized pieces and shape each into a
cone. Stick these on to the dinosaur with
a little water. Divide the remaining icing
in half and colour one portion black.
Use the white and black icings to make
the mouth, eyes and eyebrows for the
dinosaur. Stick on with a little water.

Personal Stereo

This loud cake in noisy colours will be a smash hit!
The cake board is optional.

INGREDIENTS
Serves 4–6
1 quantity chocolate-flavour Quick-
Mix Sponge Cake mix
¼ quantity chocolate-flavour
Butter Icing
4 tbsp apricot jam, warmed
and sieved
350 g/12 oz/1 quantity
Sugarpaste Icing
orange, green, purple and black
food colourings
3 sweets, for the buttons
2 liquorice sweets, for the
cassette holes
2 long liquorice bootlaces
2 liquorice wheels

EQUIPMENT AND MATERIALS
20 x 13 cm/8 x 5 inch shallow
cake tin
edible black ink pen

STORING
The finished cake can be kept in a
cool, dry place for up to two days.

1 Preheat the oven to 180°C/350°F/
Gas 4. Grease the cake tin, line the
base and sides with greaseproof paper
and grease the paper. Spoon in the cake
mixture and smooth the surface. Bake
in the centre of the oven for 35–40
minutes or until a skewer inserted into
the centre of the cake comes out clean.
Turn out on to a wire rack, peel off
the lining paper and leave to cool
completely. Trim the top of the cake
to make it perfectly flat, then cut
horizontally in half.

2 ▲ Spread the chocolate butter icing
over one half, then top with the
other half. Brush the cake evenly with
the apricot jam. Colour about 250 g/
9 oz of the sugarpaste icing orange.
Lightly dust the work surface with icing
sugar and roll out the icing until it is
large enough to cover the cake. Smooth
and ease it over the sides and edges.
Trim the edges.

3 ▲ Colour about 50 g/2 oz of the
remaining sugarpaste icing green.
Colour all but a small ball of the
remaining icing purple, then colour the
small ball black. Roll out the green and
purple icings thinly. Cut the green icing
into a rectangle about 1 cm/½ inch
smaller than the top surface of the cake.
Stick it in place with a little water. Cut
the purple icing into a 2.5 x 10 cm/1 x
4 inch strip and stick in place on top of
the green rectangle with a little water.

4 Press the sweets for the buttons into
one side of the cake through the
orange icing, then position the liquorice
sweets for the cassette holes, sticking
them in place with a little water. Use
the edible ink pen to draw tiny lines
around the sweets.

5 Cut a few short pieces off the
bootlace liquorice and stick on the
personal stereo with a little water. Stick
the reserved piece of black icing in place
at the side of the cake with a little
water.

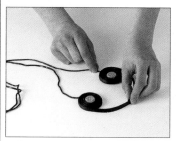

6 ▲ To make the headphones, unravel
a little of each of the liquorice
wheels and place in position on the
table or board, if you are using.
Overlap the unravelled ends of the
liquorice wheels, sticking them together
with a little water. Use a pin or thin
metal skewer to make a small hole in
the bottoms of the liquorice wheels,
then press a liquorice bootlaces into
each one. Brush three-quarters of the
liquorice bootlace with a little water
and stick them together with your
fingers, removing the excess water.
Press the joined end into the black icing
on the cake.

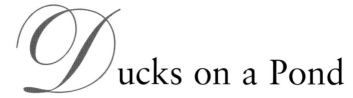

Ducks on a Pond

*A real treat at a children's party. A scrumptious combination of
coconut cake, jelly and cream.*

INGREDIENTS
Serves 8–10
*1 quantity Quick-Mix Sponge
Cake mix*
*575 ml/1 pint/2½ cups double cream
green, yellow and red food
colourings*
*225 g/8 oz/4 cups desiccated
coconut*
*1 x 135 g/4½ oz packet of green
jelly, made up to the manufacturer's
instructions*
*200 g/7 oz/½ quantity
Sugarpaste Icing
a few tiny sweets
75 g/3 oz marzipan
5 pink marshmallows*

MATERIALS AND EQUIPMENT
*18 cm/7 inch flan tin
23 cm/9 inch round cake board
duck-shaped cutter
cocktail sticks
garlic press*

STORING
*The finished cake can be kept in the
refrigerator for up to three days.*

1 Preheat the oven to 180°C/350°F/
Gas 4. Grease the flan tin, line the
base with greaseproof paper and grease
the paper. Spoon the cake mixture
into the prepared tin and smooth the
surface. Bake in the centre of the oven
for 35–40 minutes or until firm to the
touch. Leave the cake in the tin for
about 3 minutes, then turn out on to a
wire rack, peel off the lining paper and
leave to cool completely.

2 ▲ Add a few drops of green food
colouring to the double cream, and
beat until it holds soft peaks. Place the
cake on the cake board and spread the
cream evenly over the cake.

3 ▲ To make the grassy bank, place
the coconut in a bowl and add a few
drops of green food colouring diluted
with a dash of water. Stir until the
coconut is speckled green and white.

4 ▲ Cut up the set jelly into 1 cm/
½ inch pieces. Carefully place the
jelly pieces in the centre of the cake.

5 To make the ducks, take 75 g/3 oz
of the sugarpaste icing and colour it
yellow. Roll out on a work surface
lightly dusted with icing sugar until
about 5 mm/¼ inch thick.

6 ▲ Using a duck-shaped cutter,
stamp out the ducks, then skewer
the bottom of each one with a cocktail
stick. Lay the ducks on a baking sheet
and leave them in a warm, dry place
to harden.

7 Use the tiny sweets, or sugarpaste
icing, for the ducks' eyes, securing
with a drop of water. Take off a small
piece of marzipan, about the size of a
hazelnut, then colour the remainder
green and shape into a frog, using a
small, sharp knife to open the mouth
and make the feet. Colour the reserved
piece of marzipan red, shape into the
frog's tongue and secure in position
with a little water. Use sweets or blue
and white sugarpaste icing for the eyes.
Place the frog on the cake board.

8 To make the grass, colour the
remaining sugarpaste icing green
and push through a garlic press, cutting
it off with a small, sharp knife. Place
the grass around the pond. To make the
flowers, flatten the marshmallows with
a rolling pin, then snip the edges with
scissors to make the petals. Place the
flowers around the pond and put a
coloured sweet in the centre of each.
The wooden cocktail sticks must be
removed from the ducks before serving.

*D*umper Truck

Any large, round biscuits will work well for the wheels, and all sorts of coloured sweets can go in the truck.

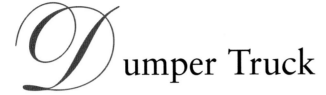

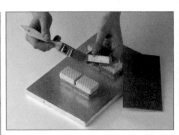

INGREDIENTS
Serves 8–10
1½ x quantity Quick-Mix Sponge
Cake mix
6 tbsp apricot jam, warmed
and sieved
900 g/2 lb/2⅔ x quantity
Sugarpaste Icing
yellow, red and blue food colouring
icing sugar, to dredge
sandwich wafer biscuits
4 coconut swirl biscuits
115 g/4 oz coloured sweets
5 cm/2 inch piece blue
liquorice stick
demerara sugar, for the sand

MATERIALS AND EQUIPMENT
900 g/2 lb loaf tin
30 x 18 cm/12 x 7 inch cake board
18 x 7.5 cm/7 x 3 inch piece of cake
card, brushed with apricot jam
small crescent-shaped cutter

STORING
The cake can be completed up to
three days in advance and kept in
a cool, dry place.

1 Preheat the oven to 180°C/350°F/
Gas 4. Grease the tin, line the base
and sides with greaseproof paper and
grease the paper. Spoon the cake
mixture into the tin and smooth the
surface. Bake in the centre of the oven
for 40–45 minutes or until a skewer
inserted into the centre of the cake
comes out clean. Turn out on to a wire
rack, peel off the lining paper and leave
to cool completely.

2 Using a large, sharp knife, cut off
the top of the cake to make a flat
surface. Then cut off one-third of the
cake to make the cabin of the truck.

3 ▲ Take the larger piece of cake,
and, with the cut side up, cut a
hollow in the centre, leaving a 1 cm/½
inch border. Brush the hollowed cake
evenly with apricot jam.

4 ▲ Colour 350 g/12 oz of the
sugarpaste icing yellow and remove
a piece about the size of a walnut. Set
aside, wrapped in clear film. Roll out
the remainder on a work surface lightly
dusted with icing sugar until about
5mm/¼ inch thick. Use to cover the
hollowed out piece of cake, carefully
pressing it into the hollow. Trim the
bottom edges and set aside.

5 Colour 350 g/12 oz of the
sugarpaste icing red. Cut off one-
third of this and set aside, wrapped in
clear film. Roll out the rest on a work
surface until about 5mm/¼ inch thick.
Use to cover the remaining piece of
cake and trim the edges.

6 Take the reserved red icing, break
off a piece the size of a walnut and
wrap in clear film. Roll out the rest and
use to cover the cake card.

7 ▲ Brush the wafers with a little
apricot jam and stick them together
in two equal piles. Place the piles on the
cake board, about 7.5 cm/3 inches
apart. Place the red-covered cake card
on top of the wafers. Place a little of the
remaining white sugarpaste icing about
halfway along the covered card in order
to tip the dumper part of the truck
slightly. Place the dumper on top, with
the cabin in front. Stand the coconut
biscuits in position for the wheels.

8 ▲ Roll out the reserved piece of
yellow sugarpaste icing to make a
5 x 2.5 cm/2 x 1 inch rectangle. Colour
the remaining white sugarpaste icing
with blue food colouring and roll out
thinly. Use the crescent-shaped cutter to
stamp out the eyes. Make simple ones,
or overlay with white crescent shapes
for detail.

9 Roll out the reserved red sugarpaste
icing thinly and stamp out a mouth
shape with an appropriate cutter. Use a
little water to stick the yellow panel on
to the front of the truck, then stick on
the features in the same way.

10 To finish, fill the dumper part of
the truck with brightly coloured
sweets and push a piece of coloured
liquorice into the top of the cabin.
Scatter the sugar around the base of the
dumper truck to resemble sand.

Train Cake

This quick-and-easy train cake is made from a shaped tin, so all you need to do is decorate it!

INGREDIENTS
Serves 8–10
1½ x quantity Quick-Mix Sponge
Cake mix
yellow food colouring
2 x quantity Butter Icing
red liquorice bootlaces
6–8 tbsp coloured vermicelli
4 liquorice wheels

MATERIALS AND EQUIPMENT
train-shaped cake tin
25 x 38 cm/10 x 15 inch cake board
2 fabric piping bags
small round and small star nozzles
pink and white cotton wool balls

STORING
The decorated cake should be made
and served on the same day.

Tip
When applying butter icing to a
cake, it is a good idea to have a
small bowl of very hot water at the
ready to dip your palette knife into.
This will ensure you get a really
smooth finish on the cake.

1 Preheat the oven to 180°C/350°F/
Gas 4. Grease and flour the cake tin
and stand firmly on a greased baking
sheet. Grease some strips of foil and
press along the edges of the cake tin
to prevent the cake mixture escaping.
Spoon the cake mixture into the
prepared tin and smooth the surface.
Bake in the centre of the oven for 40–
45 minutes or until a skewer inserted
into the centre of the cake comes out
clean. Leave the cake to cool in the tin.

2 ▲ Slice off the top surface of the
cake to make it perfectly flat. Run a
knife around the edges of the cake to
release it from the tin, then turn out the
cake and place on the cake board.

3 ▲ Add a few drops of yellow food
colouring to the butter icing and
beat well until evenly blended.

4 ▲ Using a palette knife, cover the
cake smoothly with about half the
butter icing.

5 ▲ Fit a piping bag with a round
nozzle and fill with about one-
quarter of the remaining butter icing.
Pipe a straight border around the edges
of the cake. Repeat the process to make
a double-edged border.

6 ▲ Position the red liquorice
bootlaces around the edge of the
cake, on top of the piped border. Snip
the bootlaces with scissors as you bend
them around the curves on the train.

7 Fit a piping bag with a small star
nozzle and fill with the remaining
butter icing. Pipe small stars evenly over
the top of the cake. Add extra details to
the train with the liquorice, or by
piping, if you like. Use a palette knife to
press on the coloured vermicelli all
around the sides of the cake.

8 Pull a few balls of cotton wool apart
for the steam and stick in position
with a little butter icing. Press the
liquorice wheels in place.

Telephone Cake

A great idea for a first or second birthday, as the telephone is an endless source of amusement for many toddlers.

INGREDIENTS
Serves 8–10
1 quantity chocolate-flavour Quick-Mix Sponge Cake mix
6 tbsp apricot jam, warmed and sieved
550 g/1¼ lb/1⅔ x quantity Sugarpaste Icing
1 quantity Butter Icing
red, blue, yellow and green food colourings
black liquorice ribbon

MATERIALS AND EQUIPMENT
18 cm/7 inch square cake tin
20 cm/8 inch square cake board
3 greaseproof paper piping bags
small round cutter

STORING
The iced cake can be kept in a cool, dry place for up to three days.

1 Preheat the oven to 180°C/350°F/ Gas 4. Grease the tin, line with greaseproof paper and grease the paper. Spoon the mixture into the tin and smooth the surface. Bake in the centre of the oven for 35–40 minutes or until firm. Turn out and leave to cool.

2 ▲ Cut off a 4 cm/1½ inch strip for the receiver. Cut the main body of the telephone in half. Cut about one-quarter off the top half of the main body of the telephone for the receiver rest.

3 ▲ Brush the centre of the main cake with apricot jam and reposition the top of the cake, leaving space to replace the receiver rest.

4 ▲ To shape the receiver rest, cut a 1 cm/½ inch cross out of the centre of this portion, then cut away the four end corners. Brush the base with apricot jam and position on the cake.

5 ▲ Brush the top surface of the cake evenly with apricot jam. On a work surface lightly dusted with icing sugar, roll out 350 g/12 oz of the sugarpaste icing to a 30 cm/12 inch square and use to cover the telephone cake. Place the cake on the cake board.

6 ▲ Divide the butter icing into three separate bowls, colouring one red, one blue and one yellow. Fill the piping bags with the coloured butter icings and snip the end off each one to make a small hole. Pipe spots in all three colours evenly over the cake.

7 Colour 175 g/6 oz of the remaining sugarpaste icing green. Cut off about 25 g/1 oz and set aside, wrapped in clear film. Brush the receiver piece of cake with a little apricot jam, then roll out the larger piece of green sugarpaste icing and use to cover the receiver. Position the receiver on the cake.

8 Take a small piece of the remaining green sugarpaste icing and roll it into a ball. Stick it on to the side of the receiver with a little water.

9 Roll out the remaining green sugarpaste icing and cut out a flower pot shape, measuring approximately 7.5 cm/3 inches across the top. Place on the front of the telephone, sticking it down with a little water. For the dial, colour the remaining sugarpaste icing red and roll out to a 7.5 cm/3 inch round, or stamp it out using a cutter. Use a tiny round cutter to stamp out the finger holes, then position the dial on the cake. Use any remaining butter cream to pipe in the numbers.

10 To make the telephone cord, twist the piece of liquorice around a pencil until tightly coiled and leave it for about 10 minutes. Carefully remove the pencil, and press one end of the liquorice into the ball of green sugarpaste icing on the receiver and the other end into the back of the cake.

*P*uppies in Love

*Out of one Swiss roll come two gorgeous puppy dogs.
This cake looks extremely impressive, without
being too difficult to prepare.*

INGREDIENTS
Serves 8–10
*1 quantity chocolate-flavour Swiss
Roll mix
¼ quantity chocolate-flavour
Butter Icing
115 g/4 oz yellow marzipan
green, brown, pink and red food
colourings
75 g/3 oz/1½ cups desiccated
coconut
450 g/1 lb/1⅓ x quantity
Sugarpaste Icing
4 tbsp apricot jam, warmed and sieved*

MATERIALS AND EQUIPMENT
*33 x 23 cm/13 x 9 inch Swiss roll tin
25 cm/10 inch square cake board
small round cutter
10 cm/4 inch piece of thin ribbon*

STORING
*The finished cake can be kept in a
cool, dry place for up to two days.*

1 Preheat the oven to 180°C/350°F/
Gas 4. Grease the Swiss roll tin, line
with greaseproof paper and grease the
paper. Spoon in the cake mixture and
smooth the surface. Bake in the centre
of the oven for about 12 minutes or
until springy when touched in the
centre. Leave to cool in the tin, on a
wire rack, covered with a clean, just-
damp cloth. Then invert the cake on to
a sheet of greaseproof paper, dredged
with icing sugar.

2 Trim the edges of the cake, then
spread with the chocolate butter
icing, reserving a tiny amount. Roll up
the Swiss roll, using the greaseproof
paper as a guide, then cut in half
widthways.

3 ▲ To make the faces, cut the
marzipan in half and roll each portion
into a ball, then into a squat cone shape.
Use a little of the reserved butter icing to
stick the faces on to the bodies.

4 Place a few drops of green food
colouring in a bowl with the
desiccated coconut. Add a few drops of
water and stir until the coconut is
flecked with green and white. Scatter it
over the cake board then position the
two puppies a little apart on the board.

5 Cut off about 25 g/1 oz of the
sugarpaste icing and set aside,
wrapped in clear film. Colour half the
remaining icing brown and half pink.
Cut off about 50 g/2 oz from each
colour and wrap in clear film.

6 ▲ Lightly dust the work surface
with icing sugar and roll out the
larger portions of brown and pink
icings into 11 × 35 cm/4½ × 14 inch
rectangles. Cut in half widthways and
trim the edges. Cover all four sections
with clear film and set aside.

7 ▲ Roll out the reserved pieces of
brown and white icings, then use
the small round cutter to stamp out
several shapes. Gather up the icing
trimmings and set aside, wrapped in
clear film. Stick the white rounds on to
one of the brown rectangles, then the
brown rounds on to one of the pink
rectangles, using a little water. Use a
rolling pin to press them in slightly.

8 Use a sharp knife to slash all four
icing rectangles along the two short
edges. Brush the body of each puppy
with jam, then lay the brown icing
without spots over one body, and the
pink icing without spots over the other.
Place a little water on the back of each,
then put the brown spotty icing over
the brown dog and the pink spotty
icing over the pink dog.

9 ▲ Roll half of the reserved icings in
your hands to make little tails. Stick
them in place with a little reserved
butter icing. Make a little fringe from
the brown icing for the brown puppy,
and tie a few strands of pink icing
together with the ribbon to make a
fringe for the pink puppy. Stick them in
place with a little water.

10 Use the remaining pieces of
sugarpaste icing to make the
facial features for each puppy, choosing
your own expressions, then stick them
in place with some water. The little
heart-shaped food bowl is an optional
extra, or you can make a small bone, if
you prefer.

$\mathcal{L}$ion Cake

For an animal lover or a celebration cake for a Leo, this cake is quick and surprisingly easy to make.

5 ▲ Grate the remaining marzipan on to a sheet of greaseproof paper. Use a palette knife to lift the grated marzipan carefully on to the cake, evenly covering the sides and top up to the edges of the face panel.

INGREDIENTS
Serves 10–15
1½ x quantity Quick-Mix Sponge
Cake mix
1 quantity orange-flavour
Butter Icing
orange and red food colourings
675 g/1½ lb yellow marzipan
50 g/2 oz/⅙ quantity
Sugarpaste Icing
red or orange liquorice bootlaces
long and round marshmallows

MATERIALS AND EQUIPMENT
25 x 30 cm/10 x 12 inch roasting tin
30 cm/12 inch square cake board
cheese grater
small heart-shaped cutter

STORING
The finished cake can be kept in a cool, dry place for up to four days.

1 Preheat the oven to 180°C/350°F/ Gas 4. Grease the roasting tin, line the base and sides with greaseproof paper and grease the paper. Spoon the cake mixture into the prepared tin and smooth the surface. Bake in the centre of the oven for 45–50 minutes, or until a skewer inserted into the centre of the cake comes out clean. Leave the cake in the tin for about 5 minutes, then turn out on to a wire rack, peel off the lining paper and leave to cool completely.

2 ▲ Place the cake, base side up, on the work surface. Use a small, sharp knife to cut around the edge of the cake in an uneven scallop design. You may need to do this several times in order to cut through to the bottom. Discard the excess cake from the edges. Turn the cake over and trim the top so that it sits squarely.

3 ▲ Place the cake on the cake board. Mix the orange-flavour butter icing in a bowl together with the orange food colouring. Spoon the butter icing on top of the cake and spread evenly over the surface and down the sides, using a small palette knife.

4 On a work surface lightly dusted with icing sugar, roll out about 115 g/4 oz of marzipan to a 15 cm/ 6 inch square. Place the marzipan square in the centre of the cake, gently pressing down to secure.

6 ▲ Colour the sugarpaste icing red, then roll out on a work surface lightly dusted with icing sugar. Use the heart-shaped cutter to stamp out the lion's nose and position on the cake, securing it with a little water. Take a little of the excess sugarpaste icing and use your fingers to roll out two thin, short strands for the mouth. Position on the cake, securing with water.

7 Cut the liquorice sticks into graduated lengths, and place on the cake for the whiskers. For the eyes, flatten two round marshmallows and place on the cake, securing with water.

8 ▲ To make the eyebrows, cut the long marshmallows into 5 cm/2 in lengths, and snip along one side. Place them on the cake, securing with water.

Jack-in-the-Box Cake

An impressive, colourful cake which will delight a small party of young children. This cake does require a little extra time and patience, so be sure to start the cake well in advance and not on the morning of the party!

INGREDIENTS
Serves 6–8
1 quantity chocolate-flavour Quick-Mix Sponge Cake Mix
6 tbsp apricot jam, warmed and sieved
1 kg/2¼ lb/3 x quantity Sugarpaste Icing
purple, yellow, orange and green food colourings
1 large round doughnut
1 small round doughnut
2 marshmallow sweets, for the eyes
2 coloured sweets, for the buttons

MATERIALS AND EQUIPMENT
deep 10 cm/4 inch square cake tin
18 cm/7 inch cake board
9 cm/3½ inch square piece of stiff card
3 cocktail sticks
garlic press
ice-cream cornet
balloon
small star cutter
butterfly cutter
wooden skewer

STORING
The finished cake can be kept in a cool, dry place for up to four days.

1 Preheat the oven to 180°C/350°F/ Gas 4. Grease the cake tin, line the base and sides with greaseproof paper and grease the paper. Spoon the cake mixture into the prepared tin and smooth the surface. Bake in the centre of the oven for 35–40 minutes, or until a skewer inserted into the centre of the cake comes out clean. Leave the cake in the tin for about 5 minutes, then turn out on to a wire rack, peel off the lining paper and leave to cool completely.

2 ▲ Place the cake on the work surface and cut a 2.5 cm/1 inch slice off the top for the lid. Use a small, sharp knife to hollow out the centre of the box section of cake, leaving a 1 cm/½ inch border. Spread a little apricot jam in the centre of the cake board and some on the square piece of card. Place the bottom section of cake on the cake board and position the lid on the card. Brush the box and lid with apricot jam.

3 ▲ Pull off a walnut-sized piece of sugarpaste icing, wrap in clear film and set aside. Then take about half of the remaining sugarpaste icing and marble in the purple food colouring. Cut off about one-quarter of the marbled icing and roll out on a surface lightly dusted with icing sugar to about a 15 cm/6 inch square. Use to cover the lid section of the cake, wrapping the icing around the card. Set aside, card side down. Reserve the trimmings.

4 Roll out the remaining marbled icing and use to cover the box section of cake, lightly pressing the icing into the hollow. Reserve the trimmings.

5 Colour about half of the remaining sugarpaste icing yellow and pull off two pieces, each the size of a cherry. Wrap these in clear film and set aside. Cut a thin slice off the side of the large doughnut for the body to give it a flat base. Lay it down on the work surface and place the small doughnut above it for the head. Brush the head and body with jam. Roll out the large portion of yellow sugarpaste icing until about 5mm/¼ inch thick and use to cover the head and body of the clown. Wrap the icing around the back and pinch it together to seal.

6 ▲ Pierce a cocktail stick into the base of the body, leaving about half of it exposed. Place the body in position on the box section of the cake, pressing the exposed cocktail stick into the cake for extra stability.

7 ▲ Cut off about half of the remaining sugarpaste icing and colour it orange. Push about one-quarter of this through a garlic press on to a sheet of greaseproof paper for the hair. Stick it on to the clown's head with a little water. Use the remaining orange icing to make one hand, the nose, mouth and a few spots for the bow tie. Allow the hand to dry out on a baking sheet, but cover the other features with clear film and set aside.

8 ▲ Colour the remaining sugarpaste icing green. To make the hat, cut off about 15 g/½ oz of the green icing and roll out into a thin strip. Brush the pointed end of the ice-cream cornet with a little apricot jam, then roll the strip of green sugarpaste icing around it, starting at the pointed end and working downwards. Use scissors to cut off the excess cornet. Stick the hat in position on the clown's head with a little water. Reserve any trimmings.

9 Use the reserved piece of yellow sugarpaste icing to make two small ovals for the arms. Thread each one on to a cocktail stick and carefully press the hand on to one of them. Press the cocktail sticks into the body of the clown. Tie a slightly blown up balloon on to the arm without the hand.

10 Roll out the remaining piece of white sugarpaste icing and stamp out two small stars with the star cutter. Use a little water to stick them in place for the eyes. Stick the marshmallow sweets on top.

11 Position the orange nose and mouth, sticking them in place with a little water. Roll out the remaining green icing to about 5mm/ ¼ inch thick and stamp out a butterfly and six small stars with the cutters. Stick the reserved red spots on to the butterfly bow tie, using a little water, then place the bow tie on the clown in the same way. Place the green stars around the edges of the cake board. Stick the two coloured sweets in place for the clown's buttons, using a little more water.

12 To position the lid, carefully sit it, card side out, on the back edge of the box section of the cake. Use the wooden skewer and the reserved icing trimmings to support the lid and hold it in place. This stage is best completed when the cake is in position on the table and unlikely to be moved again.

Peepo Rabbits

*An easy cake to make for a chocoholic who loves rabbits.
All the fun is in the decorating.*

INGREDIENTS
Serves 6–8
For the Toadstools
2 size 3 egg whites
25 g/1 oz/2 tbsp caster sugar

For the Cake
1 quantity Swiss Roll cake mix
1 quantity chocolate-flavour
Butter Icing
150 g/5 oz/2½ cups desiccated
coconut
25 g/1 oz/3 tbsp cocoa powder, plus
a little extra for dusting
225 g/8 oz/⅔ quantity
Sugarpaste Icing
pink, yellow, green and brown
food colourings

MATERIALS AND EQUIPMENT
*piping bag fitted with a small
round nozzle
23 x 33 cm/9 x 13 inch Swiss
roll tin
23 cm/9 inch square cake board
small rabbit cutter
small butterfly cutter
1 cocktail stick
small leaf cutter*

STORING
*The finished cake can be kept in the
refrigerator for up to two days.*

1 Preheat the oven to 135°C/275°F/
Gas 1. To make the meringue
toadstools, place a sheet of baking
parchment on a baking sheet. Place the
egg whites in a clean, dry mixing bowl
and whisk until they hold soft peaks.
Whisk in half of the sugar, then add the
rest. Whisk until the mixture holds stiff
peaks. Fill the piping bag with the
meringue mixture and pipe several
small rounds and several 2.5 cm/1 inch
stalks. Bake for about 1 hour, or until
dry. Leave to cool completely.

2 ▲ To assemble the toadstools,
gently press a stalk into a small
meringue round. Set aside. Increase the
oven temperature to 180°C/350°F/Gas 4.

3 Grease the tin, line the base and
sides with greaseproof paper and
grease the paper. Spoon the cake
mixture into the tin and smooth the
surface. Bake in the centre of the oven
for about 12 minutes, or until firm to
the touch. Leave the cake in the tin,
covered, to cool completely.

4 Lay a sheet of greaseproof paper on
the work surface and sprinkle with
icing sugar. Tip the cake on to the
greaseproof paper and remove the lining
paper. Spread with about one-third of
the butter icing and roll up. Cut off one-
third of the roll and stand the larger
section on the cake board, sticking it in
place with a little butter icing.

5 ▲ Position the smaller log next to
the larger one, then cover both in
the remaining butter icing. Peak and
swirl the icing quite unevenly to make it
look like bark.

6 Place the coconut in a bowl and sift
in the cocoa powder. Stir well until
evenly blended. Spoon the coconut all
around the cake.

7 ▲ Take half of the sugarpaste icing
and divide into two portions.
Colour one portion pink. Roll out each
piece on a work surface lightly dusted
with icing sugar until about 5 mm/
¼ inch thick. Stamp out two rabbits in
each colour. Use the pink and white
trimmings to make tiny balls for the
eyes, securing them in place with a little
water. Place the rabbits on a baking
sheet and leave until dried out.

8 Cut off about one-quarter of the
remaining sugarpaste icing and
colour it yellow. Roll out until about
5 mm/¼ inch thick and stamp out a
butterfly. Use the cocktail stick to
indent the centre of the butterfly gently
and fold it a little. Press half of the
cocktail stick through the base of the
butterfly. Place the butterfly on the
baking sheet with the rabbits, resting
one wing on the edge of the baking
sheet so that it dries in that position.

9 Cut off one-third of the remaining
sugarpaste icing and colour it green.
Roll it out thinly, then cut it into strips
using scissors and snip the strips into
pointed sections to make the grass.
Position the pieces of grass randomly
in the coconut around the cake.

10 Colour the remaining icing
brown and roll out thinly. Cut
out several leaf shapes, and then use
a small, sharp knife to make the leaf
indentations. Gently twist and bend the
leaves a little, then place them in the
coconut. Reserve the trimmings.

11 To assemble the rabbits, use a
little of the reserved brown icing
to stick them securely in place around
the cake. Press the butterfly's cocktail
stick into the back of the cake. Finally,
position the meringue toadstools and
dust them with a little cocoa powder.

Nurse's Set

This is a simple cake to make. Any toy medical equipment is suitable to use, but make sure it doesn't get confused with the edible bits!

INGREDIENTS
Serves 12–15
1½ x quantity chocolate-flavour Quick-Mix Sponge Cake mix
8 tbsp apricot jam, warmed and sieved
675 g/1½ lb/2 x quantity Sugarpaste Icing
pink and red food colourings

MATERIALS AND EQUIPMENT
35 x 20 cm/14 x 8 inch roasting tin
25 cm/10 inch square cake board
selection of toy medical equipment

STORING
The finished cake can be kept in a cool, dry place for up to two days.

1 Preheat the oven to 180°C/350°F/ Gas 4. Grease the roasting tin, line the base and sides with greaseproof paper and grease the paper. Spoon in the cake mixture and smooth the surface. Bake in the centre of the oven for 45–50 minutes or until a skewer inserted into the centre of the cake comes out clean. Leave the cake in the tin for about 5 minutes, then turn out on to a wire rack, peel off the lining paper and leave to cool completely.

2 ▲ Place the cake, dome side down, and cut in half widthways.

3 ▲ Turn one half of the cake dome side up, then use a small, sharp knife to indent a border about 1 cm/½ inch in from the edge and about the same measurement deep, around the three uncut edges. Cut out the centre in strips, keeping the edges neat. Brush the tops and sides of both halves of the cake with the apricot jam.

4 Cut off about 150 g/5 oz of the sugarpaste icing and colour it deep pink. Cut off about 15 g/½ oz from this and shape into a small handle for the box. Carefully wrap in clear film and set aside. Lightly dust the work surface with icing sugar and roll out the remaining pink icing and use to cover the cake board. Trim the edges. Cut off about 15 g/½ oz from the remaining white icing and colour it red. Cover with clear film and set aside. Colour the remaining icing light pink and divide into two portions, one slightly bigger than the other.

5 Roll out the slightly bigger portion of light pink icing and use to cover the base of the nurse's box, gently easing it into the hollow and along the edges. Trim the edges, then position the covered cake on the cake board.

6 ▲ Roll out the other portion of light pink icing and use to cover the lid of the box, using your hands to ease it over the edges. Trim the edges. Place on top of the other cake, back a little and slightly turned to an angle.

7 ▲ Stick the handle on to the bottom section of the box, using a little water. Roll out the red icing and cut out a small cross. Use a little water to stick the cross on the lid of the box. Carefully insert a few toy items into the box, allowing them to hang over the edges a little. Arrange any other items of toy medical equipment around the board and cake when it is positioned on the table.

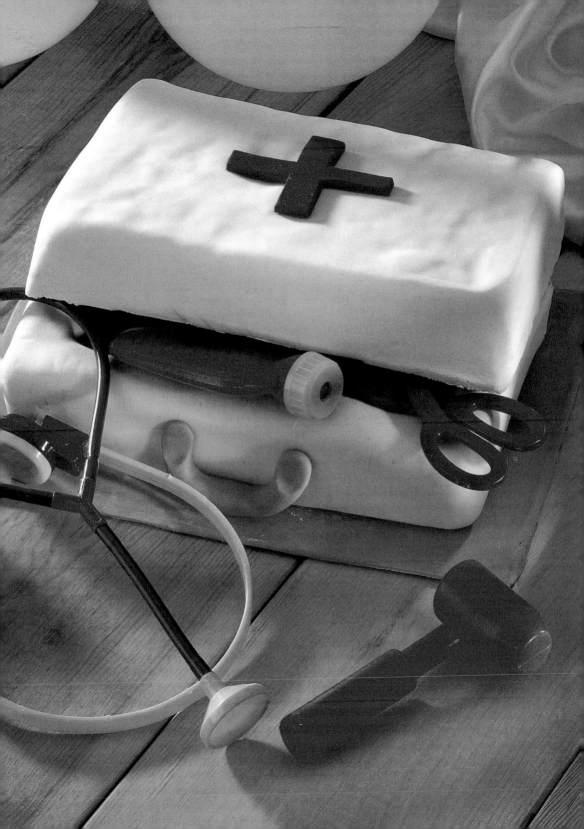

H ot Dog Cake

*Make a meal of a cake! This hot dog tastes nothing
like the real thing – it is much more delicious and
looks very attractive when cut into slices.*

INGREDIENTS
Serves 6–8
1 quantity Swiss Roll mix
icing sugar, to dredge
½ quantity coffee-flavour
Butter Icing
⅓ quantity Truffle Cake Mix
6 tbsp apricot jam, warmed
and sieved
450 g/1 lb/1⅓ x quantity
Sugarpaste Icing
brown and red food colouring
1–2 tbsp toasted sesame seeds
¼ quantity Glacé Icing

MATERIALS AND EQUIPMENT
*23 x 33 cm/9 x 13 inch Swiss
roll tin
2 small greaseproof paper
piping bags*

STORING
*The decorated cake should be made
and served on the same day.*

1 Preheat the oven to 180°C/350°F/
Gas 4. Grease the tin, line the base
and sides with greaseproof paper and
grease the paper. Spoon the cake
mixture into the tin and smooth the
surface. Bake in the centre of the oven
for about 12 minutes or until springy
to the touch. Cover and leave to cool.

2 Turn the cake out on to greaseproof
paper dusted with icing sugar and
remove the lining paper. Spread over
the butter icing, then roll the cake up
using the greaseproof paper.

3 ▲ Shape the truffle cake mix into a
sausage about 23 cm/9 inches long.

4 Place the Swiss roll on the work
surface and slice along the middle
lengthways, almost through to the
bottom. Ease the two halves apart to
resemble a partially opened bun.

5 Colour the sugarpaste icing brown,
then cut off about 50 g/2 oz and set
aside, wrapped in clear film. Roll out
the rest on a work surface lightly dusted
with icing sugar until about 5mm/¼
inch thick and use to cover the bun.
Ease the icing into the centre and down
the sides of the cake.

6 ▲ Dilute a few drops of brown food
colouring in a little water and paint
the top of the bun very lightly to give a
toasted effect. Dab on a little colour,
then rub it around gently with a finger
until blended in. Carefully place the
truffle cake sausage in position.

7 ▲ Divide the glacé icing between
two small bowls. Colour one half
brown and the other red. Fill the piping
bags with the icings and snip off the
ends with scissors. Pipe red icing along
the sausage for the ketchup, then
overlay with brown icing for the
mustard. Sprinkle the sesame seeds over
the bun.

8 Roll out the reserved brown
sugarpaste icing and cut thin strips
to resemble onion rings. Place on the cake
so that the joins lie under the sausage.
Carefully place the cake on a napkin
and serving plate, with a knife and fork.

Hallowe'en Coffin

A simple, spooky cake for the centrepiece of a Hallowe'en party.

INGREDIENTS
Serves 4–6
1 quantity Quick-Mix Sponge
Cake mix
5 tbsp apricot jam, warmed
and sieved
350 g/12 oz/1 quantity
Sugarpaste Icing
black food colouring
75 g/3 oz yellow marzipan
¼ quantity Butter Icing
golden caster sugar, for dusting

MATERIALS AND EQUIPMENT
900 g/2 lb loaf tin
23 cm/9 inch square piece of
thick card
small fluted oval cutter
small plastic skeleton and other
Hallowe'en toys
piping bag with a small star nozzle

STORING
The finished cake can be made up
to two days in advance kept in a
cool, dry place.

1 Preheat the oven to 180°C/350°F/
Gas 4. Grease the tin, line the base
and sides with greaseproof paper and
grease the paper. Spoon the mixture
into the tin and smooth the surface.
Bake in the centre of the oven for 35–
40 minutes, or until a skewer inserted
into the cake comes out clean. Leave the
cake in the tin for 5 minutes, then turn
out on to a rack, peel off the lining
paper and leave to cool.

2 To shape the cake, use a large,
sharp knife to slice off the risen
surface to make it completely flat. Turn
the cake upside-down and score the
shape of the coffin in the cake. Cut off
the two top corners at an angle, then
cut diagonally down from the corners
to the base of the coffin.

3 ▲ To make the lid of the coffin, slice
about 1 cm/½ inch off the top of the
cake. To make a base to reinforce the
coffin and lid, place both pieces of cake
on the card and draw around them with
a pencil. Remove the cakes and cut out
the shapes on the card. Brush the cakes
with apricot jam.

4 Use a small, sharp knife to hollow
out the base of the coffin, leaving
about a 1 cm/½ inch border. Place the
coffin and lid on the cards. Brush the
cakes with apricot jam.

5 Colour the sugarpaste icing black,
then cut off about one-third and set
aside, wrapped in clear film. Roll out
the larger portion of sugarpaste icing on
a work surface lightly dusted with icing
sugar and use to cover the base of the
coffin, easing it into the hollow and
down the sides. Trim the edges. Roll out
the remaining black icing and use to
cover the lid. Trim the edges.

6 ▲ To make the coffin handles, pull
off six small pieces of the marzipan
and shape into sausages with rounded
ends. To make the plaque on the lid, roll
out the kneaded trimmings of marzipan
thinly and stamp out a fluted oval with
the cutter. Stick the handles and plaque
in position with a little butter icing.

7 Lay the skeleton in the coffin.
Colour the remaining butter icing
black and use to pipe a small star border
around the coffin and down the sides.
Sprinkle with sifted caster sugar and
decorate with the Hallowe'en toys.

Mermaid Cake

Pretty, elegant and chocolatey! Every little girl's dream.

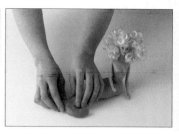

INGREDIENTS
Serves 6–8
1 quantity chocolate-flavour Quick-
Mix Sponge Cake mix
450 g/1 lb plain chocolate
25 g/1 oz/3 cups unflavoured popcorn
450 g/1 lb/1⅓ x quantity
Sugarpaste Icing
lilac and pink food colouring
3 tbsp apricot jam, warmed
and sieved
1 egg white, lightly beaten
demerara sugar

MATERIALS AND EQUIPMENT
900 g/2 lb loaf tin
30 x 15 cm/12 x 6 inch cake board
doll, similar in dimensions to a
'Barbie' or 'Sindy' doll
small crescent-shaped cutter
small fluted round cutter
15 cm/6 inch piece of thin
lilac ribbon

STORING
The finished cake can be made up
to three days in advance and kept
in a cool, dry place.

Tip

For an even more chocolatey version
of this cake, cut the sponge into
three horizontally and use 1 quantity
chocolate-flavour Butter Icing to
spread between the layers. Re-
assemble the cake and then cover
with chocolate popcorn.

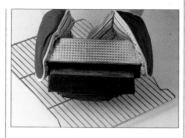

1 ▲ Preheat the oven to 180°C/350°F/
Gas 4. Grease the tin, line the base
and sides with greaseproof paper and
grease the paper. Spoon the cake
mixture into the prepared tin and
smooth the surface. Bake in the centre
of the oven for 35–40 minutes, or until
a skewer inserted into the centre of the
cake comes out clean. Leave the cake in
the tin for about 5 minutes, then turn
out on to a wire rack, peel off the lining
paper and leave to cool.

2 ▲ Turn the cake dome side up and
place on the cake board. Melt the
chocolate in a bowl placed over hot
water. Add the popcorn and stir until
evenly coated. Spoon the popcorn
around the sides of the cake and on the
cake board. Spread any remaining
melted chocolate over the top of the
cake until evenly covered. Set aside at
room temperature.

3 Cut off about one-quarter of the
sugarpaste icing. Colour the larger
piece lilac and the smaller piece pink.
Cut off about one-third of the lilac
icing, wrap this and the pink icing
separately in clear film and set aside.

4 ▲ On a work surface lightly dusted
with icing sugar, roll out the larger
portion of lilac sugarpaste icing to an
oblong shape wide enough to wrap
around the doll's legs and about 5 cm/
2 inches longer. Brush the doll from the
waist down with the apricot jam, then
wrap her in the rolled out sugarpaste
icing, lightly pinching and squeezing it
around her legs to make it stick.
Working downwards towards her feet,
pinch the end of the tail to form a fin
shape, curling the ends slightly.

5 ▲ Position the mermaid on the
cake, moving her slightly until she
feels secure and then pressing down
firmly. Roll out the reserved lilac and
pink sugarpaste icing and use the
crescent-shaped cutter to stamp out the
scales. Cover the scales and the reserved
trimmings with clear film to prevent
them drying out. Starting at the fin end
of the tail, brush the scales with a tiny
amount of egg white and stick on to the
tail, overlapping all the time, until the
tail is completely covered.

6 Re-roll the reserved icing trimmings
and use the small fluted cutter to
stamp out a shell-shaped bra top for the
mermaid. Make indentations on the top
with the back of a knife, then stick in
place with a little extra apricot jam. Use
the ribbon to tie up the mermaid's hair.

7 Position the cake on the serving
table or large board, then scatter the
demerara sugar around the base of the
cake for the sand and add a few real
shells, if you like. Remove the doll
before serving the cake.

Helicopter Cake

Perfect for a party of boys or girls who are partial to helicopters. The cake involves a little creative use of non-edible items which must be removed before eating.

INGREDIENTS
Serves 6–8
1 quantity Quick-Mix Sponge
Cake mix
2 fan wafers
6–8 tbsp apricot jam, warmed
and sieved
450 g/12 oz/1 quantity
Sugarpaste Icing
red, blue and black food colourings
small round sweet
¼ quantity Butter Icing
2 sweets, for the headlights
2 x 15 cm/6 inch pieces of
flat liquorice
4 x 2.5 cm/1 inch pieces of
liquorice sticks
50 g/2 oz/1 cup toasted
desiccated coconut

MATERIALS AND EQUIPMENT
900 g/2 lb loaf tin
small round cutter
2 wooden skewers
wood glue
small wooden block, to
raise helicopter
18 cm/7 inch square cake board
13 cm/5 inch piece of white ribbon
piping bag fitted with a small
plain nozzle

STORING
The finished cake can be kept in a
cool, dry place for up to two days.

1 Preheat the oven to 180°C/350°F/
Gas 4. Grease the tin, line with
greaseproof paper and grease the paper.
Spoon the cake mixture into the tin and
smooth the surface. Bake in the centre
of the oven for 35– 40 minutes, or until
a skewer inserted into the centre of the
cake comes out clean. Turn out on to a
wire rack, peel off the lining paper and
leave to cool.

2 ▲ To shape the cake, stand it flat
side down and use a large, sharp
knife to cut it into the shape of a
teardrop. Trim the sides from top to
bottom so that the top is wider than the
bottom. Turn the cake on its side, and
cut a wedge shape out of the back part.

3 ▲ Invert the cake so the flat side is
uppermost. Use the cutter to stamp
out a hole for the cockpit, indenting
about 2.5 cm/1 inch. Remove the round
piece and reserve.

4 Cut a thin slice from each of the
wafers, reserve one for the tail fin
and discard the other slice. Cut each
wafer in half lengthways. Measure the
long side of one of the wafers and then
cut the wooden skewers double that
length. Glue the skewers together in the
centre to form a cross and set aside.

5 Remove a small piece of sugarpaste
icing. Take another piece of icing
about the size of an egg and colour it
deep blue. Wrap these pieces in clear
film and set aside.

6 Colour the remaining sugarpaste
icing pale blue. Remove an egg-
sized piece, wrap in clear film and set
aside. Brush the cake with apricot jam.
Roll out the pale blue sugarpaste on a
work surface lightly dusted with icing
sugar and use to cover the helicopter.
Position the covered cake on the small
block of wood on the cake board.

7 To make the propeller support,
brush the reserved piece of round
cake cut out for the pilot's cockpit with
apricot jam. Roll out the reserved pale
blue sugarpaste icing and cover the
round cake. Reserve the trimmings.
Position the propeller support on the
helicopter, halfway between the cockpit
and the tail, sticking it in place with a
spot of jam. Place the crossed skewers
on top of the propeller support and
secure them in place with a little of the
pale blue icing. Place the wafers over
the skewers, securing them underneath
with more icing. Place the small round
sweet on top.

8 ▲ To make the pilot, shape the dark
blue sugarpaste icing into a small
head and body to fit into the cockpit.
Colour a little of the reserved white
icing red for the nose and mouth and
use white icing for the buttons. Stick the
details in place with a little water.
Shape some of the reserved pale blue
icing into the pilot's hat and place on
his head, securing with a little water if
necessary. Sit the pilot in his seat and tie
the ribbon scarf around his neck.

9 Colour the butter icing black and
fill the piping bag. First pipe in the
pilot's eyes, then pipe the zigzag and
straight borders around the helicopter.
Stick the headlight sweets in position
with a little of the remaining butter
icing and stick the tail fin on in the
same way. To make the landing feet,
smooth out the flat pieces of liquorice
and fold in half lengthways. Position
on the cake board, wedged in with the
liquorice sticks. Scatter the desiccated
coconut around the cake board.

Index

Acknowledgements

The publisher and authors would like to thank Scenics Cakes Boards, Colours Direct (020 8441 3082) and the Cloth Store (01293 560943) for supplying props and materials, Braun and Kenwood for the use of their equipment, Stork Cookery Service for the Rich Fruit Cake chart and Jackie Mason for her help.